BEHIND THE LINES

THE FIGHTING LINE AT HOME.

Whilst our sons and brothers are fighting abroad the Labour Party is also
fighting our enemies at home.

BEHIND
THE LINES

―――――◆―――――

East London Labour 1914-1919

JULIA BUSH

United States distributor
DUFOUR EDITIONS, INC.
Booksellers and Publishers
Chester Springs, PA 19425
215-458-5005

MERLIN PRESS
LONDON

First published in 1984 by
The Merlin Press
3 Manchester Road
LONDON E14

©The Merlin Press 1984

British Library Cataloguing in Publication Data
Bush, Julia
   Behind the Lines
   1. Labour Party—Great Britain—History
   I. Title
   324.24107'09   JN1129.L32

ISBN 0-85036-304-7
ISBN 0-85036-306-3 Pbk

Cover design by Louis Mackay

Typesetting by
Heather Hems
The Malt House
Chilmark
Wilts

Printed by
Whitstable Litho
Millstrood Road
Whitstable
Kent

To Godfrey Hainton

CONTENTS

ILLUSTRATIONS

Cartoons

All cartoons are taken from the *Railway Review*, journal of the National Union of Railwaymen.

Plates

All the plates are by kind permission of the Tower Hamlets Local History Library except for plates (x) and (xv) which are by kind permission of the Local Studies Library, London Borough of Newham.

(i)   Pereira Street, Bethnal Green, 1915

(ii)   Upper North Street, Poplar, 1910

(iii) Inside Poplar Workhouse, c. 1910

(iv) 'Carmen's Strike' in East London, 1911

(v)   The Poplar Battalion of the National Reserve march to their first church parade, 20 October 1912

(vi) Presentation of badge, 20 October 1912

(vii) Army recruiting, August 1914

(viii) 130 St Leonards Street, 23 September 1916

(ix) Silvertown explosion, January 1917

(x)   Silvertown explosion

(xi) Funeral of 15 infants, 1917

(xii) Jews of all nations suffer attack, 1915

(xiii) Women's Hall and Sylvia Pankhurst, 1914

(xiv) Street Market, 1919

(xv) Will Thorne and Jack Jones, c. 1919

(xvi) George Lansbury, Mayor of Poplar, 1920

The photographs which appear on the front cover are by kind permission of the National Museum of Labour History.

ABBREVIATIONS

AATVW	Amalgamated Association of Tramway and Vehicle Workers
AGM	Annual General Meeting
ASCJ	Amalgamated Society of Carpenters and Joiners
ASE	Amalgamated Society of Engineers
AST	Amalgamated Society of Tailors and Tailoresses
BSP	British Socialist Party
DORA	Defence of the Realm Act
EC	Executive Committee
EE	East Ham Echo
ELA	East London Advertiser
ELFS	East London Federation of Suffragettes
ELO	East London Observer
Federation	National Federation of Discharged and Demobilised Soldiers and Sailors
FJPC	Foreign Jews Protection Committee
FRD	Fabian Research Department
FVC	Food Vigilance Committee
GER	Great Eastern Railway
ILP	Independent Labour Party

LCC	London County Council
LLT	London Ladies Tailors Trade Union
LPU	London and Provincial Union of Licensed Vehicle Workers
LRC	Labour Representation Committee
NAFTA	National Amalgamated Furnishing Trades Association
NFGW	National Federation of General Workers
NFWW	National Federation of Women Workers
NSP	National Socialist Party
NUBSO	National Union of Boot and Shoe Operatives
NUGGL	National Union of Gasworkers and General Labourers
NUGW	National Union of General Workers
NUJ	National Union of Journalists
NUR	National Union of Railwaymen
NUTGW	National Union of Tailors and Garment Workers
RCAI	Royal Commission on Alien Immigration
SDF	Social Democratic Federation
SE	Stratford Express
SNDC	Socialist National Defence Committee
SPGB	Socialist Party of Great Britain
SSS	Socialist Sunday School
TUC	Trades Union Congress
TURC	Trades Union Rights Committee
UGW	United Garment Workers Trade Union
USR	Union of Stepney Ratepayers

WEA	Workers Educational Association
WNC	War Emergency Workers National Committee
WSF	Workers Suffrage Federation (from 1917, Workers Socialist Federation)

ACKNOWLEDGEMENTS

I would like to thank the many people who have helped me to produce this book. Dr J.A. Ramsden of Queen Mary College, University of London, supervised my doctoral research. Mr W.J. Fishman of Queen Mary College read sections of my thesis and kindly shared with me his immense knowledge of the Jewish community in East London. The staff of all the libraries where I have worked gave me invaluable assistance, especially at Tower Hamlets Local History Library, West Ham Central Library, the London School of Economics and Political Science, the British Newspaper Library, the Guildhall Library, the Imperial War Museum, the Marx Memorial Library, the Modern Records Centre, University of Warwick, the National Museum of Labour History, and the International Institute of Social History, Amsterdam. Organisations fully occupied with their own important, non-academic responsibilities have generously allowed me facilities for my research, including the Labour Party, the Trades Union Congress, the Jewish Welfare Board, the Jews Temporary Shelter and the Jewish Day Centre in Beaumont Square, Stepney Green. I have visited the headquarters of the National Union of Railwaymen, the Amalgamated Union of Engineering Workers, the General and Municipal Workers Union, the National Union of Public Employees and the National Union of Tailor and Garment Workers, and gratefully recall happy hours exploring union records in basements and attics as well as neatly ranged on library shelves. These acknowledgements would be very incomplete if I did not also express my gratitude to the many East Londoners who have talked to me about the area and its politics, past and present. I have quoted briefly from tape-recorded interviews; there were many less formal conversations on street corners and doorsteps and at political meetings.

Mrs Ceri Chapman and Mrs Pat Bromley have typed my manuscript with conscientious efficiency. The staff at Merlin Press have been unfailingly helpful from then onwards. Lastly, my thanks are due to my family, especially to my mother and to my husband.

INTRODUCTION

Definitions of East London tend to be subjective. For Jews it is the square mile of Stepney which they made their own; at the other end of the scale, it would be hard to convince a West Ham docker that he is any less of an East Londoner than his Poplar neighbour. The sheer size and diversity of the conurbation lying east of the City focuses the local loyalties of its inhabitants on a smaller area within the whole. However aspects of economic life drew East London together in the First World War period. Small-scale workshop trades occupied both natives and Jewish immigrants in the northern boroughs of Bethnal Green, Shoreditch and south Hackney, as well as in central Stepney and to a lesser extent in north Poplar. Trades dependent directly or indirectly on the docks linked the riverside boroughs of Stepney and Poplar with West and East Ham and south Barking. The varied politics of the area, like its economy, spilled over man-made boundaries. There seems to be as much danger of under-estimating as of over-estimating the size of East London. A line must be drawn, if arbitrarily. For the purposes of this study, it encompasses the six boroughs of Shoreditch, Bethnal Green, Stepney, Poplar, West Ham and East Ham.

Few parts of the country can match East London's claim to be a Labour Party stronghold. In the 1919 local elections Labour won majorities on every borough council, apart from East Ham. By 1922 most East London constituencies were safe Labour seats, and have remained so ever since. During the 1970s the party enjoyed a complete monopoly of local council, GLC and parliamentary seats in the newly-created borough of Tower Hamlets. Labour's historical roots go deep. Local heroes such as Will Thorne, George Lansbury and Clem Attlee are affectionately remembered by an older generation,

xvii

whilst the mythology of the 1889 dock strike, the imprisonment of Poplar council, the battle of Cable Street, the Blitz,
even the campaign for the release of the Pentonville dockers
in 1972, has spread its influence far beyond East London. As
recently as 1979 one of East London's outstanding historians
wrote of the apparently 'changeless course' of local politics:
'It is now parochially ingrained, as holy writ, that, whatever
its shortcomings, it was Labour who helped succour the
East End poor in an uncaring society.'[1]

Yet one may doubt the importance of history for younger
voters in an area where changes are far more striking than
continuity. The population has more than halved since the
1920s; old industries decay to the point of extinction; the
urban landscape has been transformed beyond recognition;
and Jewish immigrants have been replaced by newcomers
from more distant shores. Adherence to earlier political
traditions requires a more tangible explanation than collective memory. Does it lie, instead, in the link between social
class and political loyalty? The link was strongly forged
early in the twentieth century, as this book demonstrates.
Its enduring strength has been repeatedly illustrated by the
researches of electoral sociologists.[2] Few would deny that,
for all its outward change, most of East London remains
distinctively working class. Does this important historical
continuity explain the Labour Party's pre-eminence? Does it
guarantee Labour's future? The much-publicised launch of
the Social Democratic Party from within the heart of the
Labour Party's East London territory was a conscious
challenge to the past.

The arrival of the SDP, and the Labour Party crisis of
which it is a symptom, has provoked an outbreak of intro-
spection and crystal ball-gazing amongst Labour's supporters
and opponents alike. It has also encouraged a long overdue
reappraisal of political and institutional aspects of twentieth
century labour history. New approaches to the social and
economic history of labour have contributed importantly to
such a reappraisal by reminding us of the dangers of
compartmentalising political history into a narrow parliamentary study. Though the detailed re-writing of labour's
recent political history is still in its early stages, it is already

clear that huge, unexplored areas of extra-parliamentary politics will yield evidence which, apart from its intrinsic interest, sheds important new light on some traditional puzzles. How did the Labour Party break into the existing two-party system? The present study is addressed to this central question. The answers supplied here relate to East London in the period 1914–19, but undoubtedly have a wider relevance. Its extent can perhaps only be truly tested by similar local studies elsewhere.

The First World War produced an official party truce which has deprived political historians of the election fodder on which they traditionally depend. Perhaps for this reason, there are even fewer studies than usual of the extra-parliamentary politics of this period. Supposition rather than evidence fuels the assertions of historians who nevertheless invoke war-time and post-war politics to support their theories. During the past decade a fierce debate has been fought over the 'inevitability' of Liberalism's decline and of Labour's post-war success.[3] How were these two developments linked, and to what extent did the war itself create that link? Peter Clarke, in *Lancashire and the New Liberalism,* strongly criticised the view 'that a disinterested observer could have seen before 1914 that Liberalism was played out and that only with its displacement by the Labour Party would class find its proper expression in politics'.[4] The proponents of a viable 'new Liberalism' seem recently to have retreated from the electoral fray to the impregnable heights of intellectual history (from whence its ideological superiority to anything which the Labour Party had to offer cannot easily be disproved).[5] But the odd side-swipe at events, which so cruelly undermined a splendid theory, suggests that their attitude to the war is similar to that of an earlier historian of Liberalism: it was the 'rampant omnibus. . . which mounted the pavement' and was 'mainly responsible' for the party's subsequent demise.[6] Research has revealed every detail of Liberalism's war-time and post-war agonies at Westminster, but disappointingly little direct evidence of how these events and other (surely at least equally politically influential) aspects of the war affected the views of Liberal voters. Thus critics of the 'rampant omnibus' theory can justifiably claim

xix

that 'the "war" argument has never been satisfactorily demonstrated'.[7]

On the other hand, neither has it been disproved. Even among historians who generally subscribe to Henry Pelling's view that long-term social and economic changes gave Labour its electoral chance (rather than the cataclysmic impact of war on the rival Liberal Party), there is little agreement about the war's political importance. Ross McKibbin, the most trenchant of Clarke's critics, carries his attack on 'the war argument' to extremes, less on the basis of his knowledge of war-time Liberal or Labour politics than on the basis of an analysis (conducted with H.C.G. Matthew and J.K. Kay) of the 1918 Representation of the People Act and its consequences: 'We wish to suggest that changes in the structure of British politics are at least as significant as chronological developments: in other words, that the changes in the franchise are at least as significant as the effects of the First World War.'[8] The juxtaposition is a curious one. Still more curious than this attempt to divorce parliamentary reform from its war-time context is McKibbin's view that the 'war argument' necessarily assumes that 'mass political behaviour is largely conditioned by the actions of a number of political elites—by events at Westminster'.[9] Any possible attempt to show that war affected political attitudes beyond Westminster is apparently dismissed as too 'hard to show'.[10] Though McKibbin and his colleagues skilfully demonstrate the extent to which Labour benefited from the new franchise, and the likelihood that they would have done so sooner (to the detriment of Liberalism) had more workers possessed the vote, their arguments are open to obvious criticism. The extent of new working class enfranchisement is over-stated (as Clarke has pointed out).[11] More importantly, speculation (even highly informed) about how workers *might* have voted in 1914 is of less historical interest than the reasons why they *did* vote for Labour in the post-war years. If the failings of Liberalism, both before and during the war, do not offer sufficient explanation, then other reasons must be sought. Continuities with pre-war politics were indeed important (and are demonstrated throughout this book). But continuity and change are not mutually exclusive; neither needs to be

over-emphasised at the other's expense. Only detailed
evidence of the ways in which war-time politics involved
both party activists and potential voters can provide a suitable basis for analysing the war's political impact and its
contribution to the Labour Party's rise to power. We need to
know about 'during' as well as about 'before' and 'after'.
Both the major modern studies of London labour end in
1914.[12] Both provide a broadly socio-economic explanation
(in line with Pelling's 'inevitabilism') for the Labour Party's
relative lack of electoral success by this date, and for its
contrasting post-war achievements. Gareth Stedman-Jones'
research into the casual poor (a very large proportion of
whom were to be found in East London) leads him to an
especially gloomy view of the pre-war political prospect: 'the
most striking characteristic. . . was neither their adherence to
the left, nor yet their adherence to the right, but rather their
rootless volatility'.[13] Paul Thompson's more detailed political
researches suggest that Labour's outlook was in fact much
brighter than election results suggest. But, like Stedman-Jones,
he passes silently over the First World War to list long-term
structural changes (the consolidation of working class
districts, industrial expansion, falling birthrates, higher
income, better education) as the principal reason for the
eventual fulfilment of pre-war potential.[14] Such changes
certainly did help the Labour Party to consolidate its base
in London. But the dates of Labour's post-war victories do
not really back up an explanation weighted so heavily towards
long-term factors. The rise in Labour voting was immediate;
it was a striking feature even of the 1918 'coupon' election.
This suggests once again that the political developments of
the war years have been unjustly neglected.

Social and economic changes which occurred during and as
a result of the war of course deserve detailed attention. The
impact of the war economy on trade unionism was vitally
important for the Labour Party. Developments already
under way like the erosion of wage differentials between
skilled and unskilled workers, and the general devaluation of
craft skills through the introduction of machine tool
technology, were accelerated by the war and helped to
create a more homogeneous post-war working class. How-

ever few historians would maintain that any fundamental transformation of society was apparent in 1918-19. Its only too obvious absence was a prime reason for Labour voting. What had occurred was a major change in the level of popular expectations. Social inequality had been spot-lighted. So too had the power of government to take ruthless and effective action in chosen directions. Most important of all, a new political leadership for working people had acquired the conviction, experience, funds and organisation which it needed to challenge the existing parties. Without such a leadership, Labour's victories would not have been possible— let alone 'inevitable'—however great the disarray of the Liberals, and the opportunities offered by the wider franchise.

This book investigates the making of the local Labour Parties in East London. It is contended that their growing strength at the end of the war was as much a cause as a result of the 1918 national Labour Party reorganisation. Local parties could not be handed down from above, nor did they smoothly evolve. They had to be built by small groups of determined socialists and trade unionists who learned to sink major political differences over the war itself, Sovietism, and the status of the Jewish community, in the interests of independent political representation for workers. Agreed policy often went little further than that. In 1918-19 the London Labour Party eagerly plied party activists with policy documents, election programmes and opportunities for educative discussion, but at local level the diffuse rhetoric of class (pragmatically related to known East London circumstances) was sufficient to bring out Labour majorities. War had created both more determined propagandists and more receptive audiences than East London had ever seen before. This change (like so much else in the history of the Labour Party) cannot be explained by analysing and comparing election results, or even franchise levels, nor by reference to events at Westminster. The election campaigns reveal more than the results, and local political activities between election campaigns reveal more than either. Evidence about such activities is not always easy to find, especially for a period now almost beyond the reach of oral research. But without seeking out what remains of this evidence we cannot adequately explain the successful launch of the Labour Party into British politics.

NOTES

1. Fishman, W.J., *The Streets of East London* (1979), 129.
2. Research on this subject is conveniently summarised in Forester, T., *The Labour Party and the Working Class* (1976).
3. See Brown, K., *Essays in Anti-Labour History* (1974), including essays by Douglas, R., Morgan, K.O. and Wrigley, C.; Clarke, P., *Lancashire and the New Liberalism* (1971), Cook, C., *A Short History of the Liberal Party 1900-1976* (1976), Emy, H., *Liberals, Radicals and Social Politics 1892-1914* (1973), Marwick, A., *The Deluge* (1965), McKibbin, R., *The Evolution of the Labour Party 1910-24* (1974), Pelling, H., *Popular Politics and Society in Late Victorian Britain* (1968), Thompson, P., *Socialists, Liberals and Labour* (1967) and *The Edwardians* (1975), Wilson, T., *The Downfall of the Liberal Party 1914-35* (1968), Wrigley, C., *David Lloyd George and the British Labour Movement* (Brighton, 1976) and 'The First World War and its aftermath: changes in the Battersea Labour Movement 1914-19' (duplicated article, 1977).
4. Clarke, P., op. cit., vii.
5. See Bentley, M., *The Liberal Mind 1914-39* (1977), Clarke, P., *Liberals and Social Democrats* (1978), Freeden, M., *The New Liberalism* (1978).
6. Wilson, T., op. cit., 20-21.
7. Matthews, H.C.G., McKibbin, R.I., Kay, J.A., 'The franchise factor in the rise of the Labour Party': *English Historical Review*, CCCLXI (October 1976), 723.
8. Ibid.
9. Matthews, H.C.G., et al., op. cit., 736.
10. Ibid.
11. Clarke, P., Review of McKibbin, R., op. cit., *English Historical Review*, CCCLVIII (January 1976), 158.
12. Stedman Jones, G., *Outcast London* (1971) and Thompson, P., *Socialists Liberals and Labour* (1967).
13. Stedman Jones, G., op. cit., 343.
14. Thompson, P., op. cit., 287-289.

CHAPTER 1

EAST LONDON IN 1914

By 1914, East London was one of the largest and most overcrowded working class areas in Britain. A hundred and fifty years earlier, maps showed riverside hamlets and inland villages set amid orchards, fields and marshes. But as the Port of London developed to cater for the massive expansion in British trade and empire the region was transformed. It emerged at the end of the nineteenth century as a vast, unplanned, urban sprawl, housing over a million inhabitants.

Intrepid visitors, who explored the unknown East in increasing numbers after the publication of Andrew Mearn's *The Bitter Cry of Outcast London* in 1883, were impressed by its apparently universal poverty. 'People, shops, houses, conveyances—all together are stamped with the unmistakable seal of the working class', wrote Walter Besant in 1903. Like other philanthropists, he lamented the absence of most of the benefits of civilisation in East London; no city in the world could match 'the unparalleled magnitude of its meanness and its monotony'.[1] Charles Booth more objectively demonstrated the absence of the middle classes in his massive sociological study begun seventeen years earlier. Over nine-tenths of the population of Shoreditch, Bethnal Green, Stepney, Poplar and Hackney were workers, and more than a third of these lived below an ungenerous 'poverty line'.[2] As Percy Alden, warden of an East End settlement, remarked in 1904, the exodus of the well-to-do had occurred within living memory. 'There is far more uniformity now than there ever was, and unfortunately the average is lower rather than higher.'[3]

It seems paradoxical that such an area should have produced, between 1900 and 1914, a mere couple of Labour Members of Parliament. Indeed, until 1906 it returned a

1

majority of Conservatives. This is in remarkable contrast to the political face of East London since the First World War.[4] Yet explanations for Labour's pre-war weakness are not difficult to find. Though the vast majority of the population were workers, this did not automatically produce any large measure of political consensus. One reason is simply that a great many workers had no vote, and were therefore deprived of the most obvious means of political self-expression, as well as of political motivation. But the most fundamental reason lies in the fact that the superficial appearance of social uniformity was deeply misleading. Elsewhere in Britain social institutions such as chapels, friendly societies, clubs, co-operatives, and above all trade unions, provided a local focus for working class loyalty, and direct or indirect assistance towards its political expression through the Labour Party. In East London such institutions had to struggle for survival. Among its other defects, Besant accused the area of having a history which was 'mostly a blank'.[5] However East London's history in the nineteenth century goes a long way towards explaining its disunity in 1914. This century witnessed not merely an expansion in numbers, but the emergence of an extraordinarily piecemeal and varied employment structure.

The river was the backbone of East London's economy. River traffic and dock development grew side by side after the completion of the London and West India Docks in 1805, providing thousands of jobs in associated trades as well as in the docks, wharfs and warehouses. Mechanisation was slow to replace manpower because cheap dock labour was readily available, and adaptable to the demands of a fast 'turn-round'. In 1914 dockers were the largest group of workers in West Ham and Poplar, and the second largest in East Ham and Stepney.[6] But they were by no means a united body. Less than half those employed by the Port of London Authority (PLA) were 'perms' (i.e. paid a regular weekly wage, even in slack times). The rest competed for a fluctuating supply of casual work, made scarcer at the up-stream docks by the migration of business to the new deep water Royal and Tilbury docks. Henry Mayhew wrote his famous description of the 'call-on' in 1861:

Presently you know, by the stream pouring through the gates and rush towards particular spots, that the 'calling foremen' have made their appearance. Then begins the scuffling and scrambling forth of countless hands high in the air, to catch the eye of him whose voice may give them work. As the foreman calls from a book of names, some men jump up on the backs of others, so as to lift themselves high above the rest, and attract the notice of him who hires them. All are shouting. . . it is a sight to sadden the most callous, to see thousands of men struggling for only one day's hire; the scuffle being made the fiercer by the knowledge that hundreds out of the number there assembled must be left to idle the day out in want.[7]

Colonel R.B. Oram, who began work in the Port of London in 1912, remarks that, 'Conditions as late as the 1930s had not, to my recollection, substantially altered.'[8] Uncertainty, fierce competition, and poverty for the under-employed, were endemic in a system which suited the employers because of its flexibility.

The variety of different port employers was a further divisive factor. Though the PLA took control of all quay work and discharging at the upriver docks in 1908, stevedoring contractors retained control of much shipwork and various shipowners (who employed contractors) were in control of discharge at the Royal and Tilbury docks. The gradual expansion in the number of 'perms' and preference men employed by the PLA may be interpreted as an attempt to mitigate the evils of casualism. On the other hand, it also created new splits in the labour force. It was hoped that the more fortunate dockers would think twice before putting their privileges in jeopardy by joining strikes. The lesson was driven home after the failure of the 1912 strike, when the Authority refused to reinstate any of its 'perms', they could be reinstated only as casuals in their former departments.[9] An old dockland joke wryly illustrates the point:

Lady to hairdresser: Which style do you recommend?
Hairdresser to lady: Oh a PLA perm, madam. It will never come out.

Even among dockers lucky enough to be working regularly, there were endless rivalries and divisions of status. Riverside wharves competed against the enclosed docks. Stevedores were the highest-paid ship workers, but all ship workers considered themselves superior to shore workers who merely carried cargo back and forth on the quay. Many shore workers were specialists in one type of cargo or another, and rated themselves above general labourers who were prepared to turn their strength to whatever was required.[10]

It is not surprising that a workforce so unstable, and so divided against itself, proved very difficult to unionise. Ben Tillett, who founded the main dockers' union in 1887, labelled the Port of London 'the great unmanageable'.[11] But although it proved impossible to build a strong, stable union in the years before 1914, the great strikes of 1889 and 1911 showed the tremendous power of dockers briefly united in action. Both strikes broke out suddenly and were the cause, rather than the result, of big increases in union membership. With the help of socialist propagandists, the 1889 strike became a memorable crusade. Yet the strike's gains were swiftly eroded, and by 1911 less than half London's dockers were organised. At the beginning of his *History of the London Transport Workers' Strike, 1911,* Tillett describes an apparently hopeless situation in which the majority seemed indifferent and the better-paid dockers selfish. However, to the surprise of union leaders, a poor wages award provoked a second mass strike which was joined not only by other transport workers but by thousands from the East End's lowest-paid industries. Again, victory was short-lived. The old divisions and sectionalism, combined with rising unemployment, defeated the 1912 strike. A decline in union membership in the years before the war was the inevitable result.[12]

Because of the irregularity of most dockers' earnings, their wives often worked to supplement the family income. More women were employed in Shoreditch, Bethnal Green and Stepney than in the docklands of Poplar, West and East Ham, however. Female labour and Jewish immigrants were the mainstay of the notorious sweated industries centred on the inner East London boroughs. The most important of these were tailoring, furniture making, and boot and shoe making. 'Sweating' was not a very exact description of such trades. Amongst Victorian social reformers it became a term of abuse used generally against bad employers.[13] Yet these trades did have many features in common. Small-scale firms, aiming at fast and cheap production, competed ruthlessly in a fluctuating market. The only way in which employers could keep themselves in business, let alone accumulate profits, was by working hard themselves and exploiting every available source of cheap labour. Production processes were subdivided to such an extent that very little skill or training was required, and much work could be farmed out to home workers at even lower rates than those paid in the workshops. For different reasons, the workers in the sweated industries were even more poor, divided and uncertain of their future than those in the docks.

Tailoring was already the largest source of sweating in Booth's time, and continued to expand in the following decades. The industry was overwhelmingly concentrated in the Jewish quarters of Stepney. But the investigations of the 1903 Royal Commission on Alien Immigration found little to justify current accusations of 'alien job-stealing'. The trade in cheap, ready-made clothing was satisfying a new and rapidly growing demand, rather than displacing native labour. Adaptability to the whims of fashion and a low fixed investment were the keys to success, so workshops employing less than a dozen people and only the most basic machinery remained typical of East London. It was often possible for a hard-working, penniless 'greener' to rise from the ranks of sweated labour to those of the sweaters. In his 1911 diary, Joseph Leftwich describes how he and an unemployed friend contemplated hiring a Singer sewing machine, making their own cutting table, and setting up in business on a capital of £3.[14] The seasonal nature of the trade increased the temptation to overwork at every opportunity, since loss of the coveted employer's status was equally easy. The intense pressure on both workers and employers at busy times was increased by the effects of sub-divided labour and piecework wages, described by Mick Mindel:

The type of system in small workshops was that a machiner had his own little set with him. He had his second machiner and his plain machiner, and piece-rate was divided proportionately. It was the

5

same with pressers, and therefore the attitude of the piece-worker was that he wanted as good a team as he possibly could. The management was in the hands of the workers—*they* forced them. This is one of the features about these workshops which doesn't emerge in books, the natural pressure of worker on worker, to maintain the continuity and flow of production because his earnings are related to it.[15]

Such a situation presented almost insuperable obstacles to trade unionism. Some of the most hostile evidence to the 1903 Commission came from British trade union leaders who had tried to organise Jewish workers in tailoring and other sweated trades, and failed.[16] Separate Jewish unions did exist, but they were small and unstable. In 1912 the powerful anarchist leader Rudolf Rocker helped briefly to unite 13,000 workers behind a West End tailoring strike, and important concessions were made on wages and conditions.[17] However, the strong union needed to enforce the strike settlement terms failed to emerge. By 1914 the old pattern of sporadic militancy had reasserted itself. There were at least nine separate clothing unions in the area, containing together scarcely one tenth of the industry's workforce.[18]

The furniture trade was also expanding in East London at the beginning of the twentieth century, principally in Bethnal Green and Shoreditch. The quality of the products varied enormously but, as with tailoring, poor quality work tended to gravitate eastwards, where it could be undertaken cheaply by unskilled labour. Though many new carpentry machines had been invented by 1914, they were not to be found in East London workshops. Small masters bought their timber ready-sawn from the mills then assembled it by fast, slipshod means. Jewish penetration into the industry was less extensive than in tailoring; many branches even of cheap work (such as polishing and upholstering) remained largely in the hands of English workers. Most cheap furniture found its way to the wholesalers clustered in the Curtain Road area, but it was not unusual for a man to hawk his wares on the pavement, or even from door to door. Robert Shube remembers loading the outcome of his week's labours onto a barrow and touting it round the neighbouring retailers on Saturday afternoons.

> They used to put the pressure on you, make you knock the price down. If they wanted one, they'd give you a cheque and the governor used to cash it at the Green Gate public house, and I used to get five bob as an apprentice. If you didn't sell the suite, his wife had a bit of jewellery and we used to go and pawn it. That was regular. And the Monday, you'd sell the suite, and he'd redeem it.[19]

This hand-to-mouth existence was again hardly conducive to trade unionism. A few small Jewish unions were beginning to form themselves into Yiddish-speaking branches of the main English unions, but membership remained low except in the larger mills and packing case factories, like Venesta's at Silvertown.[20] The strongest woodwork union was that of the coopers, whose work remained highly skilled and closed to recent immigrants.[21]

Unlike clothing and furniture, the footwear industry in East London was in decline by 1914. Midlands factories equipped with the latest machinery were forcing small workshops out of business, displacing natives and aliens alike and depressing the wages of the remaining hand workers.[22] Joseph Letfwich recalls his father, 'a shoemaker who loved making shoes and was rather proud of his craftsmanship', receiving only occasional orders and turning instead to shoe-repairing.[23] Mrs Kaye's father found a little home work painting the soles of boots (to waterproof them). 'He'd get up Wednesday morning and didn't go to sleep until Friday night, to earn a living. . . Come the end of the week, time they'd paid the rent and paid the grocery bill, there was nothing left.'[24] A successful East London strike in 1890 swelled the members of the National Union of Boot and Shoe Operatives, bringing in several hundred Jewish members, but the worsening conditions in the trade soon undermined this progress.[25]

Thousands of East Londoners were employed in smaller trades which shared the main characteristics of the clothing, furniture and footwear industries. Overcrowded workshops, low wages, long hours, the substitution of cheap, adaptable labour for machinery, and a greater or lesser degree of sub-contracting and homework, were to be found in box-making, brush-making, umbrella-making, cap-making, millinery, artificial flower making, basket-weaving, stick-making and the fur trade. Sweating was not invented by Jews, though anti-semitism and the large proportion of Jewish workers in the sweated trades encouraged this belief. The absence of effective government or trade union controls perpetuated it in 1914, especially in the inner East London boroughs which lacked alternative employment.

One alternative which did exist in these boroughs, and was taken up vigorously by both Jews and gentiles, was street trading. There were over two thousand costermongers, hawkers and street-sellers in Stepney alone. Elderly inhabitants have vivid childhood memories of the muffin man, lavender and watercress sellers, chair-menders, clock-menders, driftwood sellers, scissor grinders and many others who came knocking at the door.[26] Street performers, described in all their colourful variety by Henry Mayhew fifty years earlier, were as numerous as ever. But the main business of buying and selling took place at the street markets where working class wives did their daily shopping. Stalls were open from eight o'clock in the morning till ten o'clock at night, or even twelve o'clock on Saturdays. Shoppers looked for cheapness rather than quality, and stall-holders had to cut their profits to the bone in order to stave off competition from their neighbours. Working in close proximity, they soon discovered that another method of preserving some profit was to form a union, initially to bargain with the local authorities over street licence fees. The divisions which weakened other East London unions were not absent from the Costermongers' Unions either. In 1903 the Hoxton Union accused Jewish traders of unfair practices and refused to admit them. The Whitechapel and Spitalfields Union, on the other hand, contained both Jewish and gentile members, and was the largest in the area.[27]

The fact that in many trades sweating continued to be a profitable (though precarious) method of production was an important reason for the slow development of alternative, factory employment in the inner boroughs. Lack of space for large-scale building was another. But by the 1880s factory production was already becoming general in certain East London industries, and newer industries were growing up, based on more extensive use of machinery, especially in the less crowded boroughs of Poplar, West Ham and East Ham. The tobacco industry was exceptional, in that the licensing requirements of the Inland Revenue confined most manufacture to fairly large, well-capitalised factories. Booth's survey found cigar and cigarette makers better-paid and better-organised than other workers in Stepney and Bethnal Green, where the majority lived.[28] Women were generally employed on inferior work, but their opportunities expanded with the growing fashion for cigarette smoking. Factory production of food and drink also grew rapidly at the turn of the century. East London had long been the home of such old-established breweries as Truman, Hanbury and Buxton in Brick Lane, Mann, Crossman and Paulin in the Mile End Road, Charrington's nearby, and Taylor Walker's Barley Mow Brewery in Limehouse. By 1914 women were employed even here, on bottling work, as well as in the newer mineral water and soft drinks factories in West Ham. Flour mills, margarine factories, jam, sweets and sugar factories, sprang up along the Silvertown river-front and round the Victoria and Albert Docks, bringing large-scale employment to East London under such familiar names as Henry Tate, Abram Lyle, Keiller and Sons, and Loder and Nucolene.

Working conditions in the factories, several of which employed a labour force of over a thousand, were inevitably a marked contrast to those in small workshops. Walter Besant painted quite a glowing picture of life in a jam factory in 1903.[29] A factory girl had pocket money to spend on cheap finery, and time in the evenings and at weekends to enjoy herself. She liked the company of her fellow-workers, and groups of girls often formed boot clubs or hat clubs, or departed together for a few weeks' hopping in Kent during the summer. They could also band together for more serious purposes, as the famous Bryant and May match girls' strike had shown in 1888. But although factories undoubtedly did offer workers more opportunities to make a collective effort to improve their lot, the reality of factory life was less rosy than Besant suggested. Wages remained low because employers could afford to pick and choose their workers. They did not hesitate to sack large numbers when trade declined, which was a regular occurrence in such seasonal industries as jam-making. Hours were often long, especially for male workers. A history of the Lyle sugar refinery tells of a regular sixty-seven hour week, with no paid holidays in 1914. Men employed on certain processes might find themselves working even longer, since 'if a man's mate did not relieve him he just had to carry on and do a "thirty-sixer". . . I don't remember anyone complaining about these awful hours; everyone accepted them as a matter of course'. There was no canteen, and the lavatories consisted of 'a long trough of running water and a bar on which the men sat in a row'.[30] The National Federation of Women Workers discovered equally bad conditions for many female employees, when it began to unionise East London food factories after the 1911 strikes. In April 1914 over nine hundred women signed up from Morton's pickle factories in Cubitt Town and Millwall.[31]

The strongest unions in the area were those which could rely on the strength of national as well as purely local organisation. Unions like the Amalgamated Society of Engineers, the Boilermakers, and the National Union of Railwaymen, were to be found in the exclusively male heavy industries of East London. Ship-building, once a staple industry, had declined to the point at which the last two big firms closed down in the decade before the war. But ship-repairing was still important, and former shipyard workers found employment elsewhere in heavy engineering in Poplar and West Ham. Constructional and electrical engineering were both expanding. Machine tools and precision instruments were also manufactured. Skilled engineers were required in all the large factories using modern machinery, whether they produced metal goods or not. For example, the giant Silvertown Rubber Company boasted in a 1920 publicity booklet that 'nearly the whole of the machinery used in the Works had been made in the factory itself'. The Stratford works of the Great Eastern Railway was the largest single employer in East London, with over 6,000 workers.

West Ham's industrial development benefited from the advantages of space (the GER works covered 75 acres), a long river front, deep water docks, and a borough council which viewed more leniently than the London County Council such 'nuisances' as smoke, smells and factory waste. In the 1900s West Ham council was enthusiastically advertising for new industrial users of its cheap electricity. As large-scale employers, a flourishing chemical industry began to overtake the established engineering and food industries. The task of unionising chemical workers fell mainly into the hands of the National Union of Gasworkers and General Labourers, founded at the nearby Becton gasworks in 1889. The Gasworkers Union spread its influence nationwide, but retained a special status in East London, largely owing to the personal reputations and propaganda work of Will Thorne and Jack Jones. Despite much seasonal unemployment, gas workers throughout the area were strongly unionised; no other general union had comparable success in organising unskilled workers.[32]

Some West Ham industries spilled over into neighbouring East Ham, but in general factory development was on a smaller scale in this borough. Though Becton and the Royal Albert Dock were situated in East Ham, the bulk of their workforce was drawn from Canning Town and Plaistow, to which the railway linked them. Much of the southern part of the borough was unsuitable for building, though drainage was in progress. In the north the ever-expanding grid of streets lined with neat, terraced houses provided employment for several thousand building workers. It also provided homes for a slightly better-off class of worker than was characteristic elsewhere in East London. Many commuted to inner East London or to the City to work. Some were skilled manual workers, such as printers; even larger numbers belonged to the 'black-coated proletariat'[33] of teachers, clerks and shop assistants who were also unusually numerous in West Ham's more salubrious regions of Upton and Forest Gate.

It is clear that most of East London remained unfavourable territory for the growth of permanent, well-organised trade unions in 1914. In the sweated industries small workshops and home work physically divided the labour force. Casualism at the docks exacerbated rivalries and status divisions amongst what was potentially one of the strongest

11

sections of workers. Even in the bigger factories of Poplar and West Ham, unionisation was hampered by the large variety of different employers and industries, and by the competition for uncertain employment. Poverty by itself was an obstacle to organisation, while lack of organisation bred continued poverty. After successful strikes and in periods of relative prosperity union membership soared, only to fall away again equally rapidly when more normal conditions reasserted themselves. But trade unionism was already politically important, for all its limits and weaknesses. It is no coincidence that Poplar and West Ham, the only East London areas to send Labour men to Parliament before the First World War, had a higher proportion of trade unionists among their inhabitants than any other parts of East London. In most East London boroughs the trades council (consisting of union delegates) and the Labour Representation Committee were almost indistinguishable. Socialists realised that, by organising themselves industrially, workers were making a positive step towards political organisation. For this reason, on the morrow of George Lansbury's 1910 election victory the secretary of Poplar Labour Representation Committee appealed to the 'Workers of Bow and Bromley' to 'join one or other of the organisations in the borough': he went on to list the details of local trade unions, alongside the meeting times and places of the Independent Labour Party, the Church Socialist League, the Social Democratic Party, and Poplar Labour League. Unorganised workers were urged to seek further trade union information from the LRC headquarters in Campbell Road.[34]

The numerical strength or weakness of the unions is not the only indicator of the level of class-conscious activity among East Londoners. The mass strikes of 1889–90 and 1911–12 also helped to forge class attitudes, despite the transience of membership gains. On these never-to-be forgotten occasions the barriers between different trades and different unions were demolished, and unionists united with non-unionists against their employers. For socialists who had laboured over the years in East London, the strikes were an astonishing and inspiring experience. As Lansbury wrote in the *Bow and Bromley Worker:* 'The glory of this movement amongst the sweated and the destitute, from the pickle-workers on the one hand and the men in the transport trade on the other, is this fact, that they all stood solidly together, realising as never before their class solidarity as workers. . . here, in dear old London, the despair of all social reformers, we have proved our real worth, demonstrated our solidarity, and won all-round increases in wages.'[35] There was an uneasy feeling in many quarters that the pre-war 'industrial unrest' had political overtones. Anxious politicians, academics and journalists investigated the spread of American and French syndicalist ideas in Britain, though the basic economic causes of the strikes were not hard to discover. Lansbury was over-optimistic in his prediction that 'in future fights for a living wage Labour will never again fight sectionally but solidly, as one united whole'. Yet the strikes undoubtedly made a lasting contribution towards the development of greater confidence and unity in East London.

Unusually full employment formed a necessary back-ground to the 1911 'unrest'. During most of the pre-war decade (especially in 1904–5 and 1908–9) the presence of large numbers of unemployed and under-employed workers was a serious hindrance to industrial organisation. Most un-employed East Londoners could turn to only two sources of help—the Poor Law or charity—since they were not protected by the 1911 National Insurance Act. The *East London Observer* carries many tales of the state of poverty to which unemployment reduced families. On 14 January 1914, 'A poor-looking woman, Elizabeth Rawlings, was charged with stealing 1s. 3d. from a slot meter belonging to the Commercial Gas Company.' In reply to the charge, she explained, 'Me and the two children were starving. We have not had a bit to eat or drink. I am sorry I did it and am willing to pay it back. I will try and borrow the money and pay it back tomorrow.' Even the old age pension was scarcely enough to stave off starvation for those too old to work and with no family to support them. On 22 February 1913 the *East London Observer* reported the inquest on Frances Helen Dodds, aged seventy-one: 'On her seventieth birthday she left the workhouse to claim the old age pension. For the last six months she had occupied one room, for which she paid

1s. 9d. a week rent. Her landlady found her lying dead across her bed. . . her furniture consisted of a bed and two chairs.'

She would, perhaps, have lived longer if she had remained in the workhouse. But no-one wanted to stay there longer than they had to. Lansbury wrote a chilling description of his first visit to Poplar workhouse, in the 1890s:

> Going down the narrow lane, ringing the bell, waiting while an official with a not too pleasant face looked through a grating to see who was there, and hearing his unpleasant voice—of course, he did not know me—made it easy for me to understand why the poor dreaded and hated these places, and made me in a flash realise how all these prison or bastille sort of surroundings were organised for the purpose of making self-respecting, decent people endure any suffering rather than enter. . . everything possible was done to inflict mental and moral degradation.[36]

By 1914 Lansbury and other Labour Poor Law Guardians had done as much as they could locally to humanise conditions in the workhouse, incurring the wrath of Whitehall and political opponents in the process. In both West Ham and Poplar, socialists were acting on his policy of 'decent treatment for the poor, outside the workhouse, and hang the rates!'[37] The number of paupers receiving out relief in these boroughs rose steeply. But in neighbouring Stepney, Whitechapel, St. Georges-in-the-East and Bethnal Green, the Poor Law authorities pursued their more orthodox belief in 'discouraging' pauperism by refusing out relief to all but a handful of applicants.[38]

Philanthropic and charitable activities proliferated in East London from the mid-nineteenth century onwards. Wealthy patrons tried to ease the housing problem by building model dwellings, such as Columbia Square, the Peabody Buildings, and the erections of the Four Per Cent Dwellings Company in Whitechapel. Columbia Market (1869) was intended to promote honest toil, and the People's Palace (1887) a higher level of culture. Academics and clerics established missions and settlements, and tried to help the poor by living amongst them. Dr Barnado cared for destitute children, and William Booth's Salvation Army combined material with spiritual succour. Other charities frowned on the open-handedness of the latter: Poor Law thinking was reflected in the Charity Organisation Society's determination to help none but the 'deserving' poor. Doubtless many East Londoners were grateful for charitable assistance. But all the efforts of philanthropists could not provide a real alternative to the Poor Law. Sometimes the help offered was unsuitable; sometimes it was short-lived, while the need was permanent. It is certainly true that most charities saw their purpose as to alleviate poverty rather than to abolish it. In the *East London Observer* (18 January 1913) a member of the Evans Hurndall Mission reports with self-satisfaction on a Poor Children's Treat: 'The treat has passed, the echo of the children's cheers has died away, the workers have long since dispersed, but the little people cannot soon forget the exceeding brightness of that single blessed ray of social sunshine which briefly illuminated their little lives.'

Socialists, believing that there was an alternative to poverty, tried to organise the unemployed to demand 'the right to work'. The Social Democratic Federation (British Socialist Party from 1911) led this campaign in the decade before the war, centring much of its effort on the East End.[39] Unemployment was one of the main issues in local Labour election manifestos; proposed solutions included (apart from full-blooded socialism) a shorter working day, the establishment of 'labour colonies' in the countryside, and the abolition of child labour. After 1906 the failure of the new Parliamentary Labour Party to force through a Right to Work Bill provoked demonstrations in East London, and even a brief SDF takeover of some unoccupied land in Plaistow. The SDF's work with the unemployed helped to improve its standing in London, but did not make it into a mass movement. Socialists discovered that, though the unemployed were numerous, they were not a strong section of the working class. Demoralised by poverty and uncertainty, they were normally more concerned with where the next meal was coming from than with politics and long-term solutions.

The East London churches had equally little success in recruiting among the very poor. In an effort to attract

15

parishioners to the fold, despairing vicars turned their churches into welfare centres, and some began preaching a socialistic form of Christianity. A few outstanding figures such as Arthur Chandler and William Lax in Poplar won personal respect, and church treats and charities were as much appreciated as any. Yet congregations failed to increase. Mudie-Smith's 1903 survey of *The Religious Life of London* showed that a mere 17 per cent of the population of Shoreditch, Bethnal Green, Poplar and Stepney attended a place of worship, compared with an average of 22 per cent for Inner London and 28 per cent for Outer London.[40] Nonconformist chapels scored slightly higher than Anglican churches, but even here there was a marked absence of 'the working classes proper. . . It is almost a universal rule that as the middle classes move out, congregations decline'. Apathy and carelessness were thought to explain the majority of absences, but there was also evidence of 'a sort of subconscious and unrecognised feeling of antagonism, to the Church as an institution or corporate body, and to the parson as a paid teacher of religion'.[41]

Amongst two groups of East Londoners—the Irish and the Jews—religion did play an important role in 1914. The main influx of Irish had occurred in the mid-nineteenth century. The original immigrants were unskilled labourers who built the docks and railways; many continued to work in the docks or in general labouring, though others moved into street trading, where they competed fiercely with the Jews. Early prejudice against the Irish in East London had died down, but they maintained a degree of separateness, especially in matters of religion. Booth was impressed by the devotion of even the poorest Irish Catholics who managed to find a penny for the Mass collection.[42] The 1903 survey cast doubt on the regularity of Catholics' church attendance, but it was clear that priests exerted an influence in the Irish communities of Wapping and Shadwell which went far beyond mere statistics of formal religious observance. They lived in close personal contact with their parishioners, and were often the first source of advice, comfort or discipline.

Religion was still more closely interwoven into the fabric of the Jewish community. Though the organised anti-semitism of the British Brothers League was in abeyance by 1914, the Jews were widely regarded as unwelcome newcomers in East London, and far more alien than the Irish had ever been. They clung to the language and customs of the East European ghettos from which they had fled. Their persecuted religion was their chief source of identity and support, and provided even the less *froom* with a sense of security amid a life full of difficulties. The *Jewish Year Book* of 1913 lists no less than thirty-five East London Synagogues, the great majority in Whitechapel and Spitalfields. Around these places of worship there developed a network of community services, providing Jewish food, education, entertainment, and even employment. To many English Jews the Whitechapel *stetl,* so vividly depicted in Israel Zangwill's novels, seemed as foreign and inward-looking as it did to the local gentiles. East London Jews perpetuated their separate traditions and beliefs through a formidable apparatus of religious education. Though only about a quarter of the children went to Jewish voluntary schools, by 1903 sixteen local state schools were 'practically Jewish', observing Jewish holidays and giving lessons in Judaism.[43] Nightly sesssions at the back-street *chederim,* where Hebrew was taught, supplemented these efforts. The Talmud Torah in Brick Lane had over eight hundred pupils, while the one in Great Garden Street guaranteed 'a minimum of nine hours instruction a week in Hebrew and religion'.[44] This experience is recalled with not mixed pleasure by Harry Blacker:

> In ill-lit overcrowded classrooms, short-tempered yarmelke-covered rabbis would teach Hebrew, with a book in one hand and a cane in the other. Punishment was dished out liberally. Woe betide the unfortunate who failed to grasp the meaning of a phrase, or did not readily recognise the shape of a letter. Tears and lamentations were threaded through the Sh'ma Yisroel like metallic thread through a Torah vestment. Despite this, we learned to read and write Hebrew.[45]

Such was the enthusiasm for education, among the adults at least, that a specially promising pupil would be rewarded with an extra, free class on Saturday afternoons!

17

The importance of religion certainly helped to cut the Jews off from their neighbours in East London. The self-sufficiency of much Jewish employment was also resented. English workers feared the competition resulting from the ambitious ruthlessness of Jewish employers and from the apparent willingness of Jewish workers to tolerate low wages and bad conditions. The extent of such fears is explained by the nature of Jewish immigration in the late nineteenth century. Instead of a steady inflow which could be gradually absorbed, Russian pogroms provoked sudden waves of immigration which threatened to swamp available housing and jobs. English Jews dreaded such influxes, and (having failed to dissuade the immigrants from coming) set up relief organisations like the Poor Jews Temporary Shelter to appease anti-semitism as well as to assist the destitute.[46] The enquiries of the 1903 Royal Commission coincided with the peak of the British Brothers' League anti-alien campaign: the Aliens Act of 1905 was an inevitable outcome. Within a few years the number of newcomers had declined by two-thirds, and local newspapers had begun to express cautious optimism about the possible future integration of the Jewish community with the surrounding population.[47]

Resentment persisted, however, over such issues as the housing shortage and the high rents in inner East London. Housing problems existed before the main Jewish immigration but were worsened by increased numbers. The Housing Acts of the 1860s and 1870s proved powerless to force landlords to repair or replace jerry-built working class dwellings. Even the stronger Acts of 1890, 1891 and 1903, and the new energy of the London County Council, could not prevent an acute shortage in the early years of the twentieth century. Inspection remained inadequate, and demolitions were no answer when neither the LCC nor the borough councils could finance re-housing on the required scale. By 1914 Stepney had provided a mere 430 new council homes (378 from the LCC and 52 from the borough council).[48] Private philanthropists sometimes merely increased the problem: the utility flats they built were often hygenic but unpopular in design, unrealistically priced, and inadequate in number for the slum-dwellers they had displaced. An alternative to flat-

18

building was the encouragement of movement to the suburbs. The LCC began to erect suburban estates before the war, but for many East Londoners the rents and travelling costs were prohibitive, even if they were willing to leave their old neighbourhoods. The better-off sometimes moved as far as East Ham. Most families seem to have frequently moved house, in search of more space or to escape rent arrears, within the bounds of one or two East London boroughs.

Poor housing probably contributed to the liveliness of street life in 1914. The two-storey workers' cottages which still formed the bulk of accommodation in East London opened directly onto the pavement. This was the children's playground and the meeting place of their elders. Old East Londoners look back nostalgically to the neighbourliness of those days:

Everybody knew everybody's business. Everybody told everybody what they were doing. I don't think there was any secrets anywhere. If anybody was in trouble, they helped each other, and I think they shared things more. People walked in each other's houses just as though it was their own, but knocked at the door. There was no keys. There was a string tied on the latch which was tied to the door knob outside. You just pulled the string and walked in. If anybody was ill there would be someone in the street who could understand the illness, or thought they could.[49]

After sixty years, kind deeds tend to be remembered and the friction of cheek-by-jowl living forgotten. But undoubtedly close contact with neighbours was an important part of a distinctive working class life-style.

Another great meeting place was the street-corner pub. Here the men could escape from over-crowded living rooms in the evenings, and women came in groups to chat, sometimes bringing with them vegetables to prepare for dinner. Opening hours were very long. Some pubs employed a pianist or a singer, or even ran a music hall show in an upstairs room. Music hall proper was one of the most popular entertainments, and performances by the top stars could be enjoyed at low prices in theatres like the Pavilion in Mile End Road and the Queen's in Poplar High Street. By 1914 cinemas were also well-established: the Grand Palace in Robinhood Lane, Poplar, could seat up to a thousand people paying 4d or 7d each.[50] Boxing, football and gambling (often illegal, on street corners) all had their supporters. More serious entertainment was sometimes offered at working men's clubs. However even in Booth's time the club bar was 'the central support—the pole of the tent',[51] and by 1914 there seems to have been a further decline in the clubs' educational role. An exception was the Jewish Working Men's Club in Great Alie Street, where classical concerts were held and in 1911 Joseph Leftwich attended a Yiddish production of Ibsen's *Ghosts*.[52] Rocker's Jubilee Street club offered (besides political meetings) classes in English, history and sociology, dances, plays and concerts, a refreshment room and a library. 'It was a piece of culture', recalls Leftwich. 'Rocker made a lot of that, that his mission was not only to preach anarchism, but to preach culture.'[53] But despite many young Jews' enthusiasm for learning, philanthropists who tried to foist 'enlightened' amusements on East London workers were usually disappointed. As the *East London Observer* commented on 18 July 1914, 'Many such attempts have proved utter failures, largely for the reason that there is a want of real understanding of the character of the people in this part of London. It is useless trying to force people to be good and enlightened.'

The sturdy resistance of the majority of East Londoners to middle class influence is evidence of the gulf which separated their lives from those of inquisitive, or even sympathetic, outsiders. There was a strong awareness of class differences. This suggests that, despite the divisions and rivalries of the workplace, common poverty, common tastes and close-packed living had produced some degree of working class solidarity. It was more consciously felt in communities of a few streets than in larger units such as the boroughs, or East London as a whole. But it provided another hopeful prospect for the future of independent Labour politics.

Looking back on twenty years of Labour Party development, Lansbury wrote in 1925: 'Ours has been a class movement, simply because only our class remains in Poplar.'[54] Socialists' efforts to link the class consciousness of East

Londoners with the politics of one party had made only limited progress by 1914. Yet the situation was far more promising for the Labour Party than pre-war election results suggest. The foundations of Labour Party organisation, as well as of Labour voting, were being laid in ways which were not likely to be reflected in immediate electoral gains. This conclusion is strengthened by a study of the 1914 franchise. In 1914 East London boasted some of the lowest percentage electorates in the whole country. Whitechapel, with a mere 6.4 per cent of its population entitled to vote in parliamentary elections, stood at the very bottom of the list. Not one East London borough or constituency had an electoral register which reached the average percentage for the LCC area as a whole. The twelve-month residence qualification and the extra disadvantages suffered by lodger votes helped to limit the electorate in poor urban areas. Newly-formed Labour Representation Committees could seldom afford the expensive legal game of defending disputed claims to the vote against the agents of opposing political parties.[55]

It is in local, rather than parliamentary, election campaigns that the Labour Party's potential can most clearly be seen before the war. Pelling convincingly argues that Government social reforms were sometimes unpopular with the workers they were intended to help, and did not occupy the foreground in the general elections of the 1900s,[56] but East London evidence suggests a rather different attitude at local elections. Board of Guardians elections centred solely on the social question of Poor Law administration. The great majority of voters were workers, and they turned out to vote in consistently higher numbers than in most other parts of London. In Poplar in 1910 and 1913 the proportion of voters was more than twice the LCC average. Clearly there would be a large protest vote in a Union renowned for its 'extravagance', but the fact that six independent socialist candidates held their seats and eight others scored respectable totals, reveals a strong element of local support for Labour policy.[57] At borough council elections, too, social issues such as housing, public transport and unemployment were among the main subjects for debate. In Poplar, where the Labour Party was strong enough to concentrate voters' attention on

21

such issues, polls were once again above average. Even in areas of East London where Labour organisation was weak, and a successful parliamentary election campaign quite out of reach, local election candidates were not uncommon. Fourteen socialists stood in Shoreditch for the 1912 borough elections (four were elected), and four in Stepney (all failed).[58] The slightly larger electorate, the much smaller expense, and the greater importance of social policy in local elections were all encouraging features for the young Labour Parties.

Other politicians in East London were beginning to recognise the importance and the distinct political interests of the working class voter. Candidates opposed to expensive social reforms grouped themselves into Municipal Alliances to protect the rate-payers. Much of their propaganda was directed at tradesmen and small employers, but it was also designed to frighten the better-off worker with the socialist bogey. The *Poplar Alliance Review,* 22 October 1912, contained a cautionary tale, 'The Wisdom of a Worker's Wife', describing how a man with a steady job and a little money was re-converted back from socialist to Alliance politics. The wife points out that his position is different from that of the unmarried dockers who persuaded him to put a socialist card in the window: 'They're the chaps as works for Socialists and tries to git 'em in becos rates don't make no difference to them.' Vigorous doggerel drives home the message:

Where Socialism holds the sway,
Distress abounds and industries decay. . .
The Socialists' motive is plain,
To filch your freedom and your pockets drain. . .
Obey the Socialist behest,
and ruin comes at your request.

In fact, though the main enemy is here clearly identified as the Socialists (or Labour Party), in most East London boroughs the opposition to the Municipal Alliance was a motley array of Liberals, socialists and trade unionists, loosely united on a Progressive social reform platform. In electoral terms the Progressives were very successful in East London from the 1890s onwards; they held a majority of the area's LCC seats until after the war, and a larger number of borough council seats than Labour, except in Poplar and West Ham. But by 1914 there were already signs that this form of compromise politics could not last.[59] Though many workers voted Progressive, few seem to have identified strongly with Progressivism between elections. Social events organised by the local Liberal Associations were decidedly middle class in tone, political meetings were few, and so-called Progressive Clubs in Poplar and East Ham were coming increasingly under Labour Party influence.

The inconsistency and varied pattern of East London's politics in 1914 reflects the disunity of its poor population. It has been suggested that Labour achieved greater success in Poplar and West Ham largely because those areas were more favourable to trade union growth than inner East London. The existence of the socialist societies was also vital. Trade unions alone were unlikely to provide the impetus to independent Labour politics, as the history of the Labour Party nationally demonstrates, though they provided a framework of organisation within which the socialists did their most productive work. In 1914 British Socialist Party branches existed in every East London borough except East Ham (Poplar, Shoreditch, Stepney and West Ham had two branches each). East Ham was the main stronghold of the Independent Labour Party, which also had branches in Bethnal Green, Shoreditch, Stepney, West Ham and Poplar (two branches in each of the latter two boroughs).[60] Whilst there was no separate Fabian organisation in East London, some members of the ILP were also Fabians, and Fabian speakers and Fabian book boxes found their way into the area.

Much has been written about the doctrinal differences between the various socialist groups. But in pre-war East London the most striking feature of socialist propaganda is its unity of purpose. Socialists, whether of the Marxist or of the gradualist variety, were working towards independent working class representation in Parliament and in local bodies. Their propaganda dwelt on improved welfare services rather than a final expropriation of the owners of wealth.

The political outlook of both the ILP and the BSP was basically reformist, rather than revolutionary, and the differences between them were of style and approach rather than policy. East London branches of the BSP warmly welcomed their organisation's re-entry into the Labour Party in 1914: this was one of the few areas where the BSP was the strongest socialist group, and therefore able to pursue a leading role in local Labour Party activity.[61] East London delegates at the 1914 ILP Conference were almost equally enthusiastic.[62] A Bethnal Green delegate pointed out that BSP members had never been as sectarian as their leaders—a true enough comment on the situation locally, since East London Jewish members were already in the vanguard of Hyndman's critics. In Poplar and West Ham SDF members had virtually ignored their group's official withdrawal from the Labour Party in 1901, by continuing to collaborate with the ILP on the local Labour Representation Committees.

It is difficult to demonstrate that the different socialist societies attracted different types of supporters. In East London the BSP (through Will Thorne's influence in the outer boroughs) was more successful among trade unionists than the ILP, which was all too often 'like a missionary organisation revolving around a middle class leader'.[63] Yet very often the group a socialist joined depended on nothing more than coincidence. Bill Brinson of Poplar signed on with the heavily sectarian Socialist Party of Great Britain in 1911, because a workmate 'converted' him. This did not inhibit his courtship of a young lady in the ILP, nor prevent him soon afterwards entering a life-long membership of the Labour Party.[64] A new convert might join the first group he encountered, or none at all. The 'unattached socialist' is a familiar phenomenon in the columns of socialist newspapers, from which he is warmly invited to take part in social events, meetings and demonstrations. Without being a member of a socialist society, a man might be a listener to socialist oratory, a reader of a socialist newspaper, and a potential Labour voter. If he was a secularist he might send his children to the Socialist Sunday Schools, of which there were several in Poplar and West Ham. If he wished to broaden his social life, he might join one of the Clarion Clubs, inspired by

24

Blatchford's popular newspaper. The 1914 *Clarion Year Book* lists the activities of clubs in East Ham, West Ham and Stepney, ranging from cycling, swimming and dancing to classes in literature and public speaking. Lansbury's *Daily Herald* was trying to get up similar readers' clubs in 1914. As Lansbury wrote on 15 April 1914: 'People ask us for a programme. In a sense we have none, for we believe that before programmes can be of use men and women must be stirred to want a new and better order of society.'

Small numbers of socialists pursued this self-appointed task with unflagging energy and optimism in the years before the war. When they attempted to run candidates without organised trade union backing (for example, John Scurr in the Bethnal Green by-elections, 1911 and 1914) they failed dismally. But in the areas where socialists and trade unionists combined forces, the Progressive and Municipal Alliance parties' hold over working class votes was being seriously undermined by 1914. In Poplar and West Ham the strong Labour Representation Committees forged in successive local election campaigns were ready to mount an independent challenge at parliamentary elections too.

The situation was very different in the inner East London boroughs. Stepney had no local trades council, invariably the focus for successful Labour Party work elsewhere in the area. Union weakness was endemic to the sweated industries, and divisions between such groups as the Irish and the Jews caused further problems. Conflicting loyalties and the powerful effects of candidates' charity on poor voters account for the confused state of party politics in Stepney. Though Liberals occupied most of the parliamentary seats and Progressives won the LCC elections until the war, Moderates (mainly Conservative) controlled the borough council. The Progressives tried to strengthen their local base by adopting a few workers as candidates. But even in Stepney there were signs that Liberal absorption of Labour would not continue indefinitely. The Whitechapel Costermongers Union, whose president had been elected as a Progressive borough councillor in 1912, were planning in March 1914 to run an independent union candidate for Parliament at the next opportunity.[65] Stepney's socialist groups were also unusually active and numerous. The ILP and BSP achieved a brief (and highly unofficial!) alliance in 1911-12, during which they produced three numbers of a joint newspaper, the *Stepney Worker*.[66] Jewish participation gave the socialist politics of the area a unique flavour. Political as well as religious refugees fled to the Whitechapel ghetto, which was visited during the pre-war decade by many of the socialists who were later to become the leaders of the Russian revolution. By 1914 Jewish social democrats were outnumbered by the supporters of Rocker's libertarian socialism, his work for trade unionism, and his Yiddish newspaper, *Arbeter Fraint*. Many young Jewish socialists managed to straddle several organisations, including the BSP, which had greater success than any other group in bringing Jewish and English socialists together.

Bethnal Green had a trades council in 1914, and even an LRC of sorts, but it remained a Progressive and Liberal stronghold. Neither local trade unionism nor socialism seems to have made easy progress. Joseph Leftwich's eye-witness account of the 1911 parliamentary by-election reveals that the majority of socialist speakers, organisers, even audiences (and the candidate himself) were imported from neighbouring boroughs: on polling day Scurr received only 131 votes, compared with 2,745 for the Liberal and 2,561 for the Conservative.[67] This failure was partly due to the weakness of local unionism, and partly to the fact that some of the unions were still closely allied to Liberalism. Correspondence between the Bethnal Green Liberal and Radical Club and a local branch of the Corporation Workers Union throws an interesting light on the situation.[68] In January 1909 a borough council by-election was pending: the Club invited the branch to put forward its secretary, J. Bradley, as an approved Liberal candidate, since 'a good result would be the outcome of such a combination'. The following month Bradley was drumming up support from fellow-unionists, on the grounds that he had 'no other interest but Labour to serve, although I would at all times be prepared to support any proposal for the welfare of the residents of the Borough'. The ambiguities of Bethnal Green Progress-ivism made Scurr's socialist candidature hopeless—so much so that in 1914 the national Labour Party refused him official backing, despite the protests of the secretary of the local trades council.[69]

In Shoreditch the trades council and LRC (formed in 1908) seems to have been more successful in undermining Progressivism. The substantial number of Labour candidates in the 1912 council elections has been mentioned. They were opposed by Progressives in every ward where they stood.[70] Lack of money and organisational experience no doubt deterred the LRC from opposing Liberalism in the LCC and parliamentary elections, despite a promising start in independent municipal politics.

The East Ham Labour Representation Committee was formed in association with the local trades council, in 1906. Two years later its secretary wrote to Ramsay MacDonald requesting affiliation to the Labour Party. Membership was 'between 1,000 and 1,500'; its object was 'To unite the forces of Labour in order to secure: (1) the election of direct Labour representatives on all public bodies; and (2) the formation of an independent Labour Group on all local bodies and in the House of Commons.' Representatives of Socialist Societies, Labour Organisations and Co-operatives were to be included in the Committee, as well as trade unionists, but it was insisted that 'All Delegates to the LRC must be Members of a Trade Union, except in cases where they are not eligible to join a Trade Union.'[71] Affiliation to the Labour Party was readily granted, and by 1914 four of the eighteen East Ham councillors were independent Labour men, despite the willingness of local Progressives to put forward working class candidates. East Ham remained part of the large county division of Romford until 1918, which probably explains the LRC's reluctance to attempt a parliamentary contest before the war. It was clearly their eventual aim. Their secretary in 1914, the energetic ILP school teacher J. Pope, was not one willingly to compromise with Progressivism or Liberalism.

George Lansbury's election as Labour MP for Bow and Bromley in December 1910 was the climax of many years' effort by Poplar socialists and trade unionists as well as a tribute to his immense personal popularity. From the 1890s SDF socialists won Bromley trades council over to support

27

for independent Labour representation. Meanwhile Poplar Labour League pursued similar aims in the south of the borough, under the more moderate influence of Will Crooks, who was an LCC member from 1892, and London's first Labour mayor in 1901. The joint work of Crooks and Lansbury on the Board of Guardians helped the League and trades council to come together in Poplar Labour Representation Committee, which also contained delegates from the various socialist societies. In 1914, nine years later, 43 trade unions with a total membership of over 10,000 were affiliated to the LRC.[72] The parliamentary election victory was made possible by tacit Liberal support, though there was no formal alliance. The *Bow and Bromley Worker*, the LRC's election campaign journal, makes it clear what a difficult piece of political tightrope walking was required of Lansbury in 1910. Even in the January election he clearly hoped to win Liberal votes, so that criticism of Liberal politics is interspersed with assurances that Liberal and Labour have much in common. In December, when the Liberal Party withdrew their candidate, criticism became still more muted, and defence of Lansbury's socialist views almost apologetic.[73] Lansbury was rewarded with a handsome victory over a Conservative whose total vote was slightly lower than in the three-cornered January contest.

But Lansbury's personal views remained socialist, rather than Progressive. His resignation in 1912 was due to his impatience with the compromising politics of the Parliamentary Labour Party, not merely to his support for women's suffrage. Sylvia Pankhurst's launching of the East London Federation of Suffragettes from a shop in Bow Road, in 1911, had brought the latter issue forcibly to his attention. The mass strikes of that year, as well as the stifling complacency of the House of Commons, helped convince Lansbury that the time was ripe for a bold political demonstration. He later acknowledged his mistake.[74] The official disapproval of the Labour Party forced most ILP members to withdraw their support in the subsequent by-election. Though the majority of the LRC decided loyally to support Lansbury once again (being disaffiliated from the national Labour Party in consequence), many of them did not share his admiration for the suffragettes. Suspicion of feminism and dislike of middle class 'do-gooders' caused havoc on election day. The Labour Party secretary refused to send lists of voters to suffragettes, waiting with cars to collect them—while the suffragettes refused to hand control of their cars over to the Labour Party![75] Lansbury lost the election by 731 votes. Poplar LRC remained outside the Labour Party until the war, but this was perhaps a less serious drawback than it appeared, since its trade union base was too solidly established to be shaken by headquarters' disapproval. Labour representation on the borough council and Board of Guardians remained strong. Meanwhile Sylvia Pankhurst stayed in Poplar. She became increasingly concerned with social issues, as well as the fight for the vote, and aired local working class grievances in her newspaper, the *Woman's Dreadnought,* from early in 1914. Her meetings, demonstrations, and efforts to force Asquith to hear the views of East London women, aroused considerable local interest and support, and may have indirectly assisted the Labour Party despite the LRC's reservations.

Independent Labour representation had an even longer history in West Ham than in Poplar. The 1890s saw Keir Hardie's election to Parliament and the first borough council Labour majority in the country. Local trade unionists' early refusal to compromise with Liberalism was due to the strength of the SDF. Will Thorne refused to separate his politics from his union activities. The Gasworkers' Union was the first in London to run independent candidates at local elections. Not only was it the largest union in West Ham, but its leaders could be heard extolling socialism every Sunday morning at Becton Road corner. Unlike Lansbury, Thorne refused to be deflected from his early political allegiance by the SDF's swings in policy. ILP branches developed in West Ham, but never supplanted the SDF; representatives of both organisations managed to work amicably alongside each other on the trades council and Labour Representation Committee, which was affiliated to the Labour Party from 1905. Faced with a united, union-based opposition, the West Ham Progressives rapidly faded from the scene. As in Poplar, by 1914 local contests were almost entirely between independent Labour and Municipal Alliance candidates. Though Labour did not regain its control of the council before the war, it came very close to doing so. No more than two seats divided the parties after 1909. Meanwhile Labour Party strength, as well as Thorne's local prestige, was demonstrated by his return to Parliament with huge majorities from 1906 onwards.

In many ways 1906–14 was a discouraging period for the Labour Party nationally. Its Parliamentary Party seemed unable and unwilling to break free from Liberalism. As Ben Tillett wrote disparagingly: 'The House of Commons and the country, which respected and feared the Labour Party, are now fast approaching a condition of contempt towards its parliamentary representatives. The lion has no teeth or claws and is losing his growl too.'[76] But, as Lansbury and others realised, the position of the party could not be gauged simply by the number and activities of its MPs. Ultimately its success depended on harnessing the political forces of the broad labour movement outside Parliament. In East London the Labour Party faced many difficulties. Charles Key of Poplar wrote from bitter experience that, 'The most poverty-stricken districts are by no means the easiest to win for Labour.'[77] Poverty and unemployment weakened a working class already divided by occupation and nationality, and lacking cohesive social institutions. There was a huge working class, but no correspondingly strong labour movement.

Despite these obstacles, local Labour Party organisation was making progress by 1914. The BSP's decision to re-affiliate to the Labour Party in that year eased the way towards the formation of a central London Labour Party. War prevented the new body from testing its strength, but it offered the optimistic prospect of a more united Labour effort. Meanwhile, as we have seen, in several East London boroughs trade unionists and varied groups of socialists were already successfully combining on Labour Representation Committees. Even in the weaker boroughs, like Stepney and Bethnal Green, efforts were being made to emulate the achievements of Poplar and West Ham. The seeds of a promising future had been sown. Under the new conditions of war-time they were to germinate, and in the aftermath of war to flourish and grow.

NOTES

1. Besant, W., *East London* (1903), 9 and 14–15.
2. Booth, C., (ed.) *Life and Labour of the People in London*, First Series, I (1892).
3. Alden, P., 'The Problem of East London', in Mudie-Smith, R., (ed.) *The Religious Life of London* (1904), 23.
4. See Appendix, p. 243.
5. Besant, W., op. cit., 3.
6. East London occupation statistics can be found in the 1911 Census, Volume 10, part 2: East Ham 140–142, West Ham 155–157, Bethnal Green 302–304, Poplar 350–352, Shoreditch 359–361, Stepney 365–367.
7. Mayhew, H., *London Labour and the London Poor*, III (1861), 304.
8. Oram, R.B., *The Dockers Tragedy* (1970), 93–94.
9. Ibid., 59.
10. See Lovell, J., *Stevedores and Dockers* (1969), Chapter 2.
11. Dock, Wharf, Riverside and General Labourers Union, *Annual Report* 1900, 6.
12. Dock, Wharf, Riverside and General Labourers Union, *Annual Report* 1914.
13. Booth, C., (ed.) op. cit., First Series, IV (1893), 328.
14. Leftwich, J., unpublished diary, 23 August 1911.
15. Interview with M. Mindel (Jewish tailor; son of a founder member of the Workers Circle; close associate of union leader Jacob Fine; became chairman of London Ladies Tailors Union in 1931). Compare with Rocker, R., *The London Years* (1956), 167: 'The evil of the sweating system was that it was so contrived that each drove everybody else.'
16. e.g. Royal Commission on Alien Immigration (hereafter R.C.A.I.), II, Cd. 1742 (1903) Parliamentary Papers 1903, IX, paragraphs 420–473, 473–481, 492–494.
17. Fishman, W.J., *East End Jewish Radicals* 1875–1914 (1975), 294–299.
18. Four clothing unions are listed in the *Jewish Year Book* 1914. Leaflets and posters of others are in the archive of the National Union of Tailors and Garment Workers. Membership figures are hard to come by, but can be deduced approximately from the Amalgamated Society of Tailors and Tailoresses *Annual Report* 1914, and the London Ladies Tailors, Machinists and Pressers Trade Union *Annual Report* 1916.
19. Interview with R. Shube (Jewish woodworker, employed in Bethnal Green; life-long member of NAFTA; later union official and General Secretary 1975–6). Compare with R.C.A.I., II, paragraph 494.
20. Amalgamated Society of Carpenters and Joiners, *Monthly Reports* 1914, General Union of Carpenters and Joiners, *Annual Report* 1914, Cabinet Makers *Monthly Reports* 1914, National Amalgamated Furnishing Trades Association, *Annual Report* 1914.
21. See Gilding, R., *The Journeymen Coopers of East London* (1971).
22. R.C.A.I., II, paragraphs 423–424.
23. Interview with J. Leftwich (associate of Rocker pre-1914 and translater of his autobiography; attender at meetings of all the main socialist groups in pre-war period; active in UDC during the war; worked in tailoring; later became a journalist, Yiddish scholar and Zionist).

24. Interview with Mrs Kaye (Jewish tailoress in Stepney; worked at Schneider's during the war).
25. R.C.A.I., II, paragraphs 470–473.
26. Described in interviews. See also Richman, G., *Fly a Flag for Poplar* (1974).
27. R.C.A.I., II, paragraphs 265-268, 717-722.
28. Booth, C., (ed.) op. cit., First Series, IV (1893), 219-220.
29. Besant, W., op. cit., 135-151.
30. Lyle, O., *The Plaistow Story* (1960), 181 and 186.
31. National Federation of Women Workers, *Annual Report* 1915, and *Woman's Dreadnought*, 4 April 1914.
32. National Union of Gasworkers and General Labourers, *Quarterly Report*, December 1913.
33. Webb, S. and B., *History of Trade Unionism* (1920), 503-509.
34. *Bow and Bromley Worker*, 17 December 1910.
35. Ibid., September 1911.
36. Lansbury, G., *My Life* (1928), 135.
37. Ibid., 133.
38. LCC, *London Statistics*, XXV, 1914-15 (1916), 77 and 80-81.
39. See Brown, K.D., *Labour and Unemployment 1900-1914* (1971).
40. Mudie-Smith, R., (ed.) *The Religious Life of London* (1904), 48-69.
41. Ibid., 36, 24 and 28.
42. Booth, C., (ed.), op. cit., Third Series, II (1902), 38.
43. Gartner, L., *The Jewish Immigrant in England 1870-1914* (1960), 228 and R.C.A.I., II, paragraphs 686-690.
44. *Jewish Year Book* 1913, 43.
45. Blacker, H., *Just Like It Was: Memoirs of the Mittel East* (1974), 21-24.
46. The *Annual Reports* of the Poor Jews Temporary Shelter constantly stress the large number of immigrants leaving London for America and South Africa, the youth and vigour of those who remain, and the variety of useful trades for which they are qualified.
47. *East London Advertiser*, 18 July 1914.
48. Munby, D.L., *Industry and Planning in Stepney* (1951), 81.
49. Interview with J. Beningfield (grew up in the Old Ford Road area of Poplar during the war; later Labour councillor and mayor).
50. Richman, G., op. cit., 24-26.
51. Booth, C., (ed.) op. cit., First Series, I (1892), 96.
52. Leftwich, J., op. cit., 8 November 1911.
53. Interview with J. Leftwich.
54. Key, C., *Red Poplar: Six Years of Socialist Rule* (1925), Foreword by G. Lansbury.
55. See Blewett, N., 'The Franchise in the UK. 1885-1918', *Past and Present*, No. 32 (December 1965), 27-56.
56. Pelling, H., *Popular Politics and Society in Late Victorian Britain* (1968), 2-18.
57. *East London Observer*, 12 April 1913.
58. *Hackney Gazette*, 4 November 1912, and *East London Observer*, 9 November 1912. See Appendix, pp. 239-40.
59. This point is fully developed in Thompson, P., *Socialists, Liberals and Labour* (1967) especially 167-189. Information on Progressive and Liberal activities and organisation in the East London press bears out his conclusions.
60. Figures for socialist branches from Thompson, P., op. cit. Appendix D.
61. BSP *Annual Conference Report* 1914, 13.
62. ILP *Annual Conference Report* 1914, 102.

63. Thompson, P., op. cit., 232. East London examples of this tendency were C. Lloyd in Bethnal Green, R.C.K. Ensor in Poplar, and C. Attlee in Limehouse.
64. Interview with Bill Brinson (has lived in Portree Street, Poplar, since 1912; belonged to the Gasworkers Union then to the Workers Union at Siemens cable factory, Woolwich, during the war; later Labour councillor and mayor).
65. *East London Observer*, 14 March 1914.
66. Attlee, C., *As It Happened* (1960), 47. A friend of J. Leftwich was writing for the *Stepney Worker* in July 1911.
67. Leftwich, J., op. cit., 20 July–30 July 1911.
68. Uncatalogued letters at the headquarters of the National Union of Public Employees, dated 22 January and 7 February 1909.
69. *Labour Leader*, 26 February 1914. Further letters on 12 March and 4 April.
70. *Hackney Gazette*, 4 November 1912.
71. Letters from W.J. Sprague to J.R. Macdonald, dated 3 February and 10 February 1908, in the Labour Party archives. LP/AFF/3/124 and 126.
72. *East London Observer*, 30 October 1915. Also BSP *Annual Conference Report* 1914, 13.
73. *Bow and Bromley Worker*, 18 December 1909 and 3 December 1910.
74. Postgate, R., *The Life of George Lansbury* (1951), 129.
75. Pankhurst, E.S., *The Suffragette Movement* (1931), 426.
76. Tillett, B., *Is the Parliamentary Labour Party a Failure?* (1908).
77. Key, C., *Red Poplar: Six Years of Socialist Rule* (1925), 7.

CHAPTER 2

INTO WAR: LABOUR AND LOCAL GOVERNMENT
1914-16

East London rank-and-file Labour Party supporters more than shared the estimates of their importance and potential strength made by Lansbury, Tillett and others disgruntled with the Parliamentary Party's performance. Despite only modest electoral success in most areas, they were supremely confident. The declaration of war on 4 August 1914 dealt a shattering blow to such confidence. For if there was one general policy on which organised labour claimed to agree, it was that workers could and should prevent war. Only seven years earlier the Second International had passed an anti-war resolution with the unanimous support of a British Section containing representatives of the Labour Party and all the main socialist groups. Not only was it their duty 'to do everything to prevent the outbreak of war by whatever means seem to them most effective'. If the unthinkable occurred, and war broke out nevertheless, their further duty would be 'to intercede for its speedy end, and to strive with all their power to make use of the violent economical and political crisis brought about by the war to rouse the people and thereby to hasten the abolition of capitalist class rule'.[1] Probably most of the delegates who voted for this resolution, like the thousands in the labour movement who reiterated its sentiments in the following years, had little conception that they would ever be called upon to transform lip-service to working class internationalism into action. How would they live up to their promises? Before looking at socialist re-actions, let us take a general view of East London in the first days of the war.

August Bank Holiday was traditionally celebrated with great zest by East Londoners. In the week before war was declared the approach of the summer holiday dominates the columns of the local press. Weather prospects were fair. Details of cheap excursions and boarding houses were provided for those who could afford to travel, while for those confined to London there was news of local flower shows, baby shows, and fancy dress parades. Prince Henry of Prussia paid a private visit to the Bryant and May match factory. The Poplar battalion of the National Reserve attended a church parade in Bow. The most burning political question was not the state of Europe, but the state of the local tram services.[2] No wonder many people's reaction to Britain's declaration of war was one of surprise and excitement, rather than of alarm. Cheering crowds filled Stratford Broadway at 1 a.m. on Tuesday morning, after the government's ultimatum to Germany had expired.[3] Here was a fine way to end a Bank Holiday!

Socialists had little conception of what a world war meant, and neither had the man-in-the-street. The main aim seems to have been to get in on the adventure quickly, before it came to its expected early and victorious end. On 8 August the *East London Advertiser* reported that 'Recruiting in the East End has proceeded on an unprecedented scale, and at the Drill Hall in Tredegar Road the authorities have been kept more than busy attesting recruits.' Those who did not enlist found other outlets for their patriotism, such as admiring the new recruits' first fumbling attempts at drill, and cheering contingents of troops already on their way to the docks. At the Stratford Empire, the enterprising manager introduced 'a series of patriotic airs' into the overture, which was 'cheered to the echo'. Amid fervent singing of 'Rule Britannia', pictures of the Allied monarchs appeared on the screen.[4] As the *Advertiser* approvingly noted,

> Patriotism in the East End is everywhere most marked. It is impossible to mistake the tenor of conversation in public places. Even the youngsters have caught the infection and the Union Jack was of a certainty never in greater prominence than it is at the present time. Even at Bow, where for years the Socialists have zealously tried to stifle national sentiment and patriotism by decrying everything British, the unusual sight has been witnessed of bands of boys parading the streets headed by the Union Jack, singing patriotic songs.[5]

But already patriotism had its more sinister side. Hundreds of East London Germans and Austrians queued outside West India Dock Road and Thames Street police stations to register themselves as 'enemy aliens'. In Devons Road, Bow, two German butchers' shops were attacked and looted.[6] A German bakery suffered the same fate in Old Ford Road.[7] Another section of the population who had good cause to fear patriotic mobs were socialists who publicised their continuing opposition to war. 'For insulting the Army, Thomas Edey, labourer and Socialist worker, was pelted with stones and sticks on Tuesday by an angry crowd near the East India Docks.' The unfortunate Edey was hauled up before the magistrates the next day, and told that 'he must not conduct his meetings in a manner that was likely to arouse the hostility of the public'.[8]

How deep-rooted was the patriotism of East Londoners? Only time would tell. Too much importance certainly should not be attached to the flag-waving of the first week of August 1914. Such manifestations proved merely that government propaganda about Britain's 'just cause' and honourable duty to defend 'plucky little Belgium' spread rapidly and success-fully. Newspapers were avidly read. Soon blood-curdling tales of Hun atrocities were being embellished by politicians of every party from the platforms of recruiting meetings. Many East London workers left for war on a wave of emotion and moral fervour: 'It was sort of the thing to be done in those days—you just did it.'[9]

But for others the reasons for joining up were more mundane. In *A Hoxton Childhood,* A.S. Jasper describes his brother-in-law's sudden departure in the first week of the war:

Gerry joining up was a surprise to us in every way. He had always been against the army. No bloody army would get him, he would say. I think his job in the fish shop was the reason. He worked very long hours: 9 o'clock in the morning, home again at 3 o'clock, on again at 5 o'clock and there he was until midnight. Joining the army was an escape for him.[10]

Bill Brinson of Poplar also remembers the rush to the

recruiting offices:

> There's two ways of looking at that. There may have been some who
> were going to chop the Kaiser's head off, and willing to do it, and
> that sort of thing. But there were also a lot of them who wanted a
> good bed and food and clothes. They couldn't have been all that
> willing, or they would never have had to fetch in conscription,
> would they?[11]

In an area like East London, war caused almost immediate
economic distress. This fact, combined with the poverty
before the war, undoubtedly assisted recruiting. The same
newspaper which reported the rush to enlist also reported
that food prices were rising steeply. Seven-year-old Thomas
Beningfield sat on the kerb outside his Ford Street home
'watching the soldiers gathering up all the horses. When the
horses went, the street seemed to die.'[12] Transport was
commandeered by the army not just from grocery retailers
(such as Passingham's, in this case), but from the main
factories and breweries and also from local bus depots. The
result was unemployment on an even larger scale than usual.
At the docks, normal traffic to the continent had been
halted. Few families had any savings to fall back on. Only
skilled unions provided unemployment benefit for their
members. The majority of workers were protected neither by
union membership nor by the government's insurance scheme.

Nationally, as well as locally, Labour leaders rallied from
their first stupefying despair to face up to such problems. On
5 August a permanent War Emergency Workers National
Committee (WNC) was formed to protect workers' interests.
From the first day of its existence, the WNC set vigorously to
work, preparing detailed and cogent proposals for the relief
of distress. In East London, as elsewhere, this body was to
play a vital role in the war-time labour movement. Sometimes
it succeeded in influencing government policy. Even when it
failed, the mere existence of a committee representing most
aspects of organised labour, and initiated by the Labour
Party, was an important symbol of unity. The influence of
the WNC spread far beyond its own committee room. It drew
information from and gave advice to every local Labour

Party, trades council, trade union, co-operative and socialist society. A Committee which began as a relief organisation was to end up as a political power in its own right.[13]

At first glance it seems as though many of the socialist groups went through an opposite transformation in the early days of the war. Relief work was desperately needed; it also provided a clear purpose and something of an escape from the grim realities of political failure. Lansbury had taken the lead in organising the last major anti-war demonstration in Trafalgar Square on 2 August. A week later he admitted that the labour movement was helpless in the face of events: 'The whole situation shows in fearsome wise how little the millions are free: physically, socially, intellectually, mentally, or otherwise. It is a stupendous illustration of slavery, exterior and interior.' This uncharacteristic lament was not the only message which the *Herald* had for its readers, however. From the government it demanded control of food prices and distribution, and adequate maintenance for soldiers' dependents. Trade unionists and socialists were urged to take militant defensive action against distress. Local relief committees must be made into 'citizen organisations', not mere dispensers of charity. Such tasks were not only urgently necessary, they were in line with socialists' long-term political fight for independent labour representation and the abolition of the Poor Law.[14]

The ILP and BSP made a similar, if somewhat slower, adaptation. The former was reluctant to abandon hope that workers' resistance to war could turn back the wheel. The latter was already finding difficulty in reconciling its pro-war and anti-war members. By late August, however, both *Labour Leader* and *Justice* was vociferously demanding government economic controls and labour representation on relief committees. They claimed to share Lansbury's brave hope in the ultimate value of war as a political educator. At this stage such hopes may have been mere whistling in the dark, though in retrospect they seem strangely far-sighted.

In the first weeks of the war rising prices were 'the chief and most important aspect of the situation, so far as poor people are concerned'.[15] Any increase was a disaster for families used to just 'getting by', the more so if the family income had been reduced by unemployment. During the first week of the war food prices rose by an average of 16 per cent. To make matters worse, many of the biggest increases were on cheap items which formed the mainstay of workers' diet, such as sugar, bread, margarine, eggs and fish.[16] The rises meant instant hunger for many East Londoners. Sylvia Pankhurst understood this, after two years of running her East London Federation of Suffragettes as a welfare centre as well as a political group. Mothers who had been used to bringing their babies to 400 Old Ford Road to have them weighed and to receive advice from the lady doctor now began to bring children who were crying for lack of food.

Sylvia took up the challenge with her usual fiery enthusiasm. The *Dreadnought,* based as it was on one poor area, provided more telling propaganda on distress than any of the national socialist weeklies. On 15 August it reproduced a price list from a small shop in Bow:

	New price	*Old price*
White lump sugar	6d	2½d
White moist sugar	6d	2d
Brown moist sugar	4d	1¾d
Condensed milk	5½d	4d
Nestle's milk	7½d	6d
Rice	4d	2d
4 lb. loaf	5½d	5d
Jam	5d	4d

The human impact of rising prices, unemployment, and the sloth of War Office payment procedures was driven home by a weekly hail of 'Typical Cases' from East London:

Mother of ten children. Husband and eldest son and daughter have lost their work through the war. The lodger, who is a confectioner, has also lost her work.

Wife of a Territorial. Has two children and is expecting another. Gets 1s 5d a day from the War Office, pays 6s rent leaving 3s 11d to buy food etc.

Father a labourer gone to war, left no money, nothing received from

War Office. Three children aged 4½, 2½ and 6 months. Mother earned 3s by trouser finishing last week. . .

Mrs B.—five young children, expecting another any day, two children have dinner at school. Husband dock labourer out of work through war. Landlord has given notice to quit. Pawned everything and now starving.[17]

The editor of the *East London Observer* was unimpressed: 'Miss Sylvia Pankhurst, who apparently lives in an atmosphere all her own, really must try to preserve a sense of proportion. Any attempt to get up a scare about food prices is to be severely deprecated. There are no grounds for apprehension.'[18] Such complacent responses soon became familiar. Driven on by an acute sense of the urgency of the situation, which she claimed even fellow-socialists like Lansbury did not quite share, Sylvia strove to accomplish single-handed all the tasks she saw were necessary. By 15 August she had set up her own employment exchange to place women in work. A week later, she opened her first milk distribution centre. Soon she was running four mother and baby clinics, and providing special diets for babies too ill to digest milk. On 5 September, the Old Ford Road headquarters converted itself into a cost-price restaurant, where free meals were provided for the destitute and over 150 people could be accommodated at each sitting.[19] Sylvia had always claimed that the aim of the ELFS was to rouse working women 'to be fighters on their own account'.[20] But despite her wish to avoid the 'stigma of charity',[21] most of the money and organisational ability needed for new ventures was inevitably drawn from outside East London. Local ELFS meetings abruptly ceased between 6 August and 30 November.[22]

There was a clear intention of treating war relief as a political issue, however. The *Dreadnought* continued to demand 'Votes for Women in order that the mothers and sisters of the nation may aid as citizens, in averting the miseries of war.' Working women must be represented on all war-time committees.[23] 'Typical Cases' and descriptions of the plight of 'Victims of War' were intended to stir the government to action as well as to raise money from private

benefactors. Early in September Sylvia led a deputation of
East London women to the Board of Trade, armed with
their family budgets. Mrs Drake, a barmaid, explained that
she was paying 9s 6d for food which had cost her 8s 0¼d
before the war. Mrs Parsons of Canning Town told the
minister that she 'could not afford to pay the present prices,
and that she and her children had had to go short of food'.
She explained how some shop-keepers were taking advantage
of the situation: 'If a customer bought the margarine she
could have sugar at 2½d per pound, but if she bought butter,
she had to pay 3½d for sugar.' Mrs Walker, a docker's wife,
was still more outspoken. Her Sunday joint had doubled in
price, and 'it was useless to talk about a scarcity of flour and
sugar, there were tons and tons of it stacked up in the docks,
"our men go in and see it, so they know".' The minister had
no answer to this, and indeed little comfort of any sort to
offer.[24]

From a different standpoint, the co-operative movement
also helped to focus East Londoners' discontent over rising
prices in the autumn of 1914. The Stratford Co-operative
Society boasted an impressive total of 32,261 members on
the eve of the war.[25] Co-operation, like so many other working class organisations, had found difficulty in establishing a
sound base in the inner East London boroughs, but was
flourishing in West and East Ham, and expanding strongly
outwards into the Essex suburbs, and as far afield as South-
end. Only a small fraction of the membership were concerned
with the broader aims of co-operation, or even directly
involved in the business decisions of the Society, but the outbreak of war gave co-operation an opportunity to demonstrate the difference between its aims and those of private
traders. It was able to set a uniquely practical example by
refusing to raise prices on its own foodstuffs already in
stock. By October this policy had gained the Stratford
Co-op 783 new members.[26] Despite a long-standing distrust
of party politics, the self-help enthusiasts of co-operation
made joint cause with the Labour Party on national and local
committees, and even echoed the socialists' view that war
would politically educate workers:

42

If the war completely breaks down individualism, as it is doing, and establishes State control of national activities, it will not have been in vain. We must see to it that the Government action does not fall back. Since the war began we have had more lessons in the value of the State than might have been provided in half a century in ordinary circumstances.[27]

Although socialists and co-operators wondered at the new power of the state as the British war economy began to move into action, the history of government price controls shows that *laissez-faire* beliefs died hard. By December 1915 food prices were 46 per cent above the August 1914 level, and a year later the overall increase had reached 87 per cent.[28] Only the acute shortages of 1917 and 1918 at last forced the government into imposing the sort of controls which socialists and others in the labour movement had been demanding from the first weeks of the war. This does not mean that the food prices campaign was completely ineffective, however. The WNC made sure that the details of its proposals and of government inaction were widely publicised, together with the facts about prices and profits. A monthly memorandum on the rising cost of living provided invaluable statistical ammunition for every worker seeking a pay rise, and every socialist demanding additional government food controls.

In the files of the WNC some East London orders for supplies of leaflets still survive. In February 1915 a local branch of the Dockers Union ordered 250 pamphlets on 'Wheat and Coal Prices' and 400 copies of the 'Cost of Living' memorandum. The Education Committee of the Stratford Co-op ordered 100 copies of a pamphlet on food prices. Poplar ILP was one of the WNC's best customers, ordering regular batches of cost of living memoranda. In November 1915 they put in an order for 1,000 copies of a leaflet on 'Why Pay More Rent?' This quantity could be supplied for 3s., carriage paid, which was cheap enough to make mass-leafleting possible.[29] The traffic of information and literature on prices was not entirely one way. The WNC welcomed both information and enquiries from local organisations. For example, in August 1914 it circularised every trades council and Labour Party in the country, requesting price lists (and receipts) for stated quantities of common foods. West Ham trades council replied promptly, and also forwarded information from the Poor Law Guardians about increased tenders for supplies to the workhouse.[30] A few months later the secretary of the trades council wrote angrily to the WNC that the government 'must be made to see that working class opinion is not in favour of being bled while shipowners and others are making fortunes'.[31]

Early in 1915 the WNC began to organise delegate conferences throughout Britain to support its demand for stronger government price controls. In East London the revolt against rising prices was spontaneous and general (as the current strike wave demonstrated), but it was given leadership and political direction by the WNC and local socialists. On 13 February the *Herald* reported food price meetings organised by the Poplar LRC and West Ham trades council. Labour representatives on other bodies were using the prices argument to press for wage increases for council employees (West Ham borough council), increases in out-relief payments (Poplar Board of Guardians) and higher old age pensions (Stepney relief committee). At the end of February Sylvia Pankhurst won the support of 'a large attendance' at Canning Town public hall for government price controls and votes for women.[32] At a similar meeting in East Ham town hall the following week, speakers from the BSP linked their denunciation of high prices to an equally vigorous denunciation of high profits, and indeed of the profit system as a whole.[33] A March food prices meeting in Limehouse town hall was jointly called by Limehouse ILP, Stepney BSP, Limehouse Church Socialist League, and Stepney Clarion Fellowship. Referring to the activity of 'profiteers', Jack Jones (a BSP 'patriot') commented that 'If other people took advantage of the country's position the Clyde strikers were acting quite as legitimately in doing the same thing'. Alf Walls (a BSP 'pacifist') urged those present to join the Labour and Socialist movement: 'As soon as things settled down and they could make their voices heard, then was the time they could put up a fight for their own country, instead of fighting in the landowners' and capitalists' country as it was at present.'[34] So long as socialist arguments

44

were linked to the food prices question, they could be sure of a sympathetic and even enthusiastic reception. Meanwhile discontent over prices was spilling over into militant demands for higher wages. On 20 February the *Stratford Express* reported a brief unofficial strike at the Victoria and Albert Docks, which ended in a hasty announcement from the PLA that they would pay 3s a week war bonus to 'perms' and 6d a day to other dockers. The dockers' position was a strong one because the port was by now exceptionally busy. On 13 March the *East London Observer* reported that West Ham council employees and Bryant and May matchworkers had been granted bonuses, and that the dockers and lightermen were making new demands. At the beginning of April, drainage workers in the NUGGL were threatening to strike unless the LCC met their claims.[35] In May, London's trams came to a halt when the LCC refused to consider the men's demand for a 15 per cent wage increase until their existing wage agreement officially expired the following month.[36] The industrial truce made by the TUC in August 1914 seemed to be breaking down. 'Labour shows itself in a worse and worse light,' lamented the editor of the *East London Observer*. 'It is no use ignoring the facts, which are plain enough for anyone to see, neither is it any use pretending that the "patriotism" of Labour is not in jeopardy. Labour is out for blood money—for all that it can get.'[37]

No wonder that socialists felt encouraged. To Lansbury, who had visited strike-bound Clydeside, anything looked possible. From a decline in 'patriotism' to the growth of a powerful socialist anti-war movement seemed only a short step.[38] But neither his optimism nor the *Observer*'s exaggerated alarm proved justified. The government and the employers were not prepared to play the socialists' game: war bonuses successfully averted strikes in many cases, and the cure for industrial unrest was completed by a number of sharp defeats for weaker groups of workers (such as the tram men). Though many workers accepted the socialists' argument that 'no one could expect all the sacrifices to be on the workers' side and all the profits on the other' (as W.C. Anderson expressed it at the Limehouse town hall meeting), very few were prepared deliberately to sabotage the country's

THE "BOTTOM DOG" AND HIS BON(E)US.

"It's all very fine, but now he has got it will he agree to part with it?"

war effort. Ben Tillett warned his members that delays in production would cause the loss of workers' lives, rather than employers', since 96 per cent of soldiers were workers: 'the responsibility is divided equally between those working at home and those serving at the front'.[39] Such warnings carried great weight until the very end of the war. Despite bad feelings about prices and profiteering, and despite the strike wave, a mass anti-war movement was as far off in the summer of 1915 as it had ever been.

The majority of socialists had acknowledged in August 1914 that the present time was unsuitable for direct propaganda on the war question. Instead they had decided to forward their work of political education and organisation through efforts to solve workers' immediate economic problems. The food prices campaign provided one important platform. Equally important, in the early months, was the battle for adequate and effective labour representation on local relief committees. Sylvia Pankhurst's approach to relief work was essentially individualistic. During 1915 her restaurants served 70,000 meals, 1,000 mothers and babies were seen at her clinics, over £1,000 was spent on milk distribution. But even these admirable achievements were a mere drop in the ocean. The Labour Party, trade unions, co-operative societies and socialist groups saw that large-scale and long-term solutions could only come through the organisation and representation of workers themselves. This had been the basis of their pre-war activity. Now the problems of East London poverty were more pressing than ever, but official war-time relief schemes were also providing unexpected new opportunities for labour activists.

Government relief arrangements were in an extraordinary state of confusion at the outbreak of war. Maintenance allowances for the families of men who joined the forces were very slow to come through and quite inadequate. Inability to produce marriage or birth certificates, or ignorance of form-filling procedures, could prolong War Office delays. During the period of waiting, starvation was averted by rigorously means-tested grants from the charitable Soldiers' and Sailors' Families Association. In the *Herald* Lansbury described a typical scene in Poplar during the third week of war: 'Outside the Public Hall, in Bow Road, E., yesterday morning there was a long queue of women. Haggard and worn, and in many cases unfit for the long period of waiting, they were waiting for the miserable doles allocated by the Soldiers' and Sailors' Wives' Fund, for they were the wives and dependents of reservists who had joined the colours.'[40] The case of those families whose wage-earners were out of work because of the war, but who had not enlisted, was still worse. They were forced to fall back on Poor Law relief, and were likely to be refused even this in those Unions which made a point of not granting out relief to the able-bodied unemployed.

Theoretically, the government had accepted from the outset that it was its duty to provide equally for soldiers' dependents and for those unemployed because of the war. But the meaning of this undertaking was confused by the establishment of the Prince of Wales relief fund on 6 August. A fund which depended on voluntary contributions looked very much like a charity. Government instructions for its distribution reinforced this impression. An early memorandum advised that single men eligible for recruitment should be sent to the end of the queue, and that 'So far as practicable, allowances should be made not in money, but by way of food tickets on local shops or stores. These tickets should be given to the women rather than to the men.'[41] Prince of Wales relief was to be distributed through specially constituted local committees, working in conjunction with existing Distress Committees to find work for the unemployed. In an effort to win support for the scheme, the government stressed the importance of labour representation on the committees. The WNC and its affiliated bodies soon demonstrated their determination to make labour representation an effective reality.

A WNC pamphlet of September 1914 entitled *The War Emergency—Suggestions for Labour Members on Local Committees,* spelt out very clearly how this could be achieved.[42] The Poor Law mentality must not be allowed to restrict the committee's activities. It must aim first and foremost to provide work, if necessary through public works, paid at not less than £1 per week. Special schemes for unemployed women should be administered by a local sub-committee including 'a strong representation of women from working class industrial organisations'. Those unable to work, or not provided with work by the committee, were entitled to 'honourable maintenance'. The WNC pointed out that its amount was being left to the discretion of the local committees until the government fixed a general scale. *'We must not let the scale be fixed at anything lower than the cost of maintenance in health.'* Neither must irrelevant conditions be placed on the payment of relief, such as the recipient's 'moral character', or his unwillingness to enlist. Though means-testing was inevitable, there should be no Poor Law-type 'test of destitution'. The WNC condemned the issue of food tickets, recommending instead that money grants should be paid through trade union branches wherever possible, to prevent women having to queue in a humiliating fashion. The ideas in the pamphlet were not new. The 'right to work' and Poor Law abolition had been amongst the stock in trade of socialists for many years. The value of the pamphlet lay in the fact that it showed how existing Labour demands could be applied to the immediate war-time crisis.

In East London the WNC's relief policy was taken up with a will by both pro-war and anti-war socialists. When they encountered opposition they turned back to the WNC for help and advice, so in the WNC files as well as the local press there can be found a record of the political battles within the committees. One of the most important targets was to secure strong labour representation in the first place. Naturally, this was more readily granted in boroughs where Labour had been a powerful political force before the war. In Poplar, the *East London Advertiser* judged that a full fifteen of the sixty committee members were socialists, among them George Lansbury and Sylvia Pankhurst. The *Advertiser's* editor noted with annoyance that the chairman and agent of the local Labour Party had been included, but those of the Liberal and Conservative Parties had not![43] Labour men and women were present as delegates of Poplar Guardians, Poplar borough council, the Distress Committee, the Health Visiting Association, various 'Special Women's Organisations', and six of the main trade unions in Poplar.[44] In West Ham, also,

49

labour representatives had no difficulty in gaining admittance to the local committee. Six trade unionists and seven women were included.[45] Will Thorne had already made it clear to the crowds at Becton Road corner that the patriotism of many West Ham socialists would not prevent them from making a strong political stand on relief questions.[46] In Shoreditch, Stepney, Bethnal Green and East Ham the situation seems to have been less satisfactory, though in every case some nominal degree of labour representation was allowed.

As Sylvia Pankhurst impatiently discovered, committees move more slowly than individuals. By the time the local relief committees held their first meetings, distress caused by unemployment and inadequate allowances had reached serious proportions. The *East London Observer* reported that the first meeting of the Stepney committee found itself besieged by 'some hundreds of ostensible riverside workers and others who profess to have lost their work'.[47] But a special meeting of Stepney borough council in the same week was informed that 'No funds had yet been allocated for distribution, and it was not likely that any would be received for some time to come.'[48] Distribution was equally slow in getting under way in Shoreditch. A first grant of £100 from the Prince of Wales fund was not received until 12 September, and 276 of the 685 people who had registered for relief by 18 September were refused any assistance at all.[49] This was in line with the mayor's expressed intention of exercising 'discrimination' so as to reduce expenditure.[50] It is interesting to note that in West Ham, where there were plenty of labour representatives to urge the workers' case, relief was speeded up considerably. Even before government aid arrived, £57 had been raised locally to keep the families of reservists from the Poor Law. By 22 August £250 had been received from the Prince of Wales Fund and was being distributed to people in urgent need.[51]

Unemployment in East London was very patchy. It was serious, but short-lived, amongst port workers. More prolonged unemployment was suffered in trades supplying luxury items, such as cigars and millinery, and in those relying heavily on exports. Cabinet making and the building industry were also hard hit. For men, the situation was soon

THE ATTITUDE OF SOME OF THE RELIEF COMMITTEES.

"My dear friend! I fully understand the needs of the lower classes. You may safely leave it entirely to me."

eased by enlistment, but this was of no help to the many unemployed women until a later stage in the war, when labour shortages forced female substitution. Labour representatives in East London urged the provision of work for both men and women at reasonable rates of pay. But despite substantial government grants (£650 in East Ham, £2,100 to West Ham), public works never employed very large numbers.[52] By the time they got under way, unemployment was already declining fast. Government contracts for army and navy supplies began to pour into East London, and local industries rapidly adjusted to the new situation.

There was still plenty of poverty left for the relief committees to deal with, however. Many applicants were too old or ill or encumbered with small children to undertake war work, and all were forced to contend with inflation. In the early months the level of relief payments was hotly debated on the East London committees, especially those with strong labour representation. The inadequacy of labour representation in Shoreditch is reflected in the borough's wretched 'maximum scale' of discretionary relief—at 4s per adult and 1s 3d per child, the lowest in London.[53] The government's national relief scales came into force at the end of October. The official maximum of 10s for the first adult, 4s 6d for the second, and 1s 6d for each child, was denounced by George Lansbury as 'The Depth of Meanness'.[54] The WNC rejected outright the government's efforts to justify small payments on the grounds that the fund might soon be exhausted. 'The needs of the poor are not to be measured by the sums the rich choose to spare; the relief of suffering caused by the War is a national concern, and has to be met by the nation as a whole out of national resources.'[55] This battle cry was taken up by socialists and trade unionists everywhere. On 4 December West Ham trades council sent a relief scheme for WNC approval which was nearly 50 per cent more generous than the official one. 'I should like the amendment scheme to have been higher,' wrote the secretary, 'but I may not have the chance of getting it through the Committee.'[56] Coupled with the campaign for more generous relief were the demands of the WNC and the socialists for adequate maintenance allowances for soldiers and sailors' families. Eventually the

(i)   Pereira Street, Bethnal Green, 1915

(ii)   Upper North Street, Poplar, 1910. Common poverty, common tastes and close-packed living.

(iii)   Inside Poplar Workhouse, c. 1910. No smiles, but the smartly uniformed
         staff, pictures on the wall, bird cage and solid furniture perhaps reflect the
         efforts of Labour guardians to humanise conditions.

(iv)   'Labour unrest' in East London 1911. The carmen's strike was part of a
        wide-spread movement, during which East Londoners 'stood solidly
        together, realising as never before their class solidarity as workers' (George
        Lansbury).

(v)   Playing at soldiers? The Poplar Batallion of the National Reserve march to their first Church Parade, 20 October 1912. Heading the march are the Mace-bearer, the Mayor and General Gaselee, who later inspected the reservists.

(vi)   After Church, the presentation of badges to reservists by the Mayoress, Mrs Sedgwick.

(vii)   The real thing, August 1914, in the East India Dock Road. 'To Berlin and back free, with a full stomach all the time.'

(viii)   Bomb damage. Inside 130 St Leonards Street after a Zeppelin raid, 23 September 1916.

(ix) & (x) Even greater losses were caused by the Silvertown explosion, January 1917.

(xi) Disasters of war. East London turned out to mourn the fifteen infants killed when a bomb fell on Upper North Street School.

(xii) During the Anti-German Riots. Jews of all nationalities suffered indiscriminate attacks after the sinking of the *Lusitania* (May 1915).

(xiii) The first cost-price restaurant in the Women's Hall, 400 Old Ford Road (September 1914). Sylvia Pankhurst is seated at the second table, third from the left.

(xiv) Street Market in East London.

(xv) Will Thorne and Jack Jones at the Trades Union Congress, 1919.

(xvi) George Lansbury, newly-elected Mayor of Poplar, cutting the first sod on the Chapel House Street estate, Millwall, 13 January 1920

government yielded on both fronts. With some justification, this outcome was hailed as a significant victory for organised labour.

As the war continued, more and more local committees were set up to supervise the growing tangle of war-time legislation. Labour representation was always stipulated, as the government wished to reap at local level the same benefits it was reaping nationally from its truce with the Labour Party and trade union leadership. In 1916 it was the turn of conscription tribunals and of pensions committees. In 1917 came national service committees and food control committees. Even in boroughs where Liberal or Tory politicians had little pre-war experience of an independent Labour Party, the government's appreciation of labour's special importance and expertise in certain matters began to permeate down into local government. Such an important and lasting change in labour's status could not occur without problems, as the history of the borough relief committees demonstrates. For political as well as social reasons, the local hierarchy found it hard to accept the arrival of labour, and of the Labour Party, in the corridors of power. Labour was rarely prepared to be a mere token presence. It persisted in stridently voicing its own point of view, which showed a regrettable tendency to be a socialist one.

The kind of running conflicts which developed over labour representation are well-illustrated by events in East Ham in 1916–17. When the local war pensions committee was set up in 1916, the minimum of one labour member was admitted. The trades council (which was also the local LRC) sent along one of its most vocal members, a militant socialist named Allwright. He was soon setting the committee by the ears with his forthright denunciations of every attempt to reduce pensions. For example when it was proposed to deprive a mother of part of her pension because one child was in a convalescent home, Allwright exploded: 'It is a disgrace to people sitting round here, who have a good table at home themselves, that these people shall not have the lousy 2s a week that the government allows. I am ashamed of you all.'[57] Such unparliamentary behaviour was punished by a private decision to withhold certain information on committee work from Allwright in the future. When he protested he was told, 'Members can obtain any information they want from the Treasurer.' Allwright's response to this smooth reply was one of mingled anger and astonishment: 'You live in a different world from us. I go out at 5 o'clock in the morning and return at 9 o'clock at night. How can I go to the Borough Treasurer for information?' After a lively discussion he won his point and was promised that in future all the names and addresses of pensions applicants would be posted to him.[58]

At a meeting a few months later the mayor actually praised Allwright for 'his enthusiasm in nosing out cases of hardship'. But the editor of the *East Ham Echo* was still reproving:

> When Mr Allwright is present he generally has more to say than all the rest of the members put together. Labour representatives are inclined to be a little too sensitive in discussion, and like the rest of us, they must learn philosophically to take the rough with the smooth in public life. We cannot always get our own way.[59]

No doubt the mayor privately agreed with these strictures. In April 1917 he tried to get round the problem of statutory labour representation on the East Ham national service committee by hand-picking an amenable trade unionist. This attempt to circumvent the local trades council ended disastrously, as a second, elected representative eventually had to be appointed to silence their protests! A similar mayoral tactic failed when the members of East Ham's local food control committee were chosen a few months later.[60] Ironically enough, the same local government hierarchy which so distrusted labour representatives was soon being forced by the severity of food shortages into accepting the bulk of the Labour Party's proposals for food control.

The problems in East Ham were not unusual. To a greater or lesser extent they occurred in all the East London boroughs. Labour representatives, whether 'patriots' or 'pacifists', refused to acquiesce in policies which they felt were against workers' interests, and were seldom silenced by appeals to place 'the national interest' first. On elected local government bodies, as well as on the *ad hoc* war-time committees, Labour members were able to exercise an influence disproportionate to their numbers by their determinedly independent stand. Boroughs with a strong body of Labour councillors, such as Poplar and West Ham, were the first to grant war bonuses to their employees, to extend the provision of school meals, and later to open communal kitchens and implement food rationing schemes.[61] In Poplar Labour councillors even resisted pressure on council employees to join the army. The Poplar Board of Guardians became a forum for general political debate when Labour guardians refused to allow economy measures in March 1916, and supported members of the workhouse staff who objected to 'filling in' for men who took Sundays off to drill with the Volunteer Training Corps.[62] On the LCC Poplar's Labour councillor, Susan Lawrence, spoke up regularly on labour questions such as school meals, housing policy, rents and war bonuses.[63]

Labour representatives were more likely to achieve success and local popularity by their stand on this type of issue than by their efforts to extend opposition to the war itself, at least during the first three years. Socialists were as divided on the war question as they were united in defence of working class living standards. Public intolerance of pacifism remained high, despite the fact that positive enthusiasm for the war had diminished rapidly within a few months. Casualty lists in the newspapers, and the loss of friends and relatives, reinforced the attractions of good economic prospects at home. The East London press began to comment on the fall-off in recruitment in the spring of 1915. An editorial in the *Advertiser,* headed 'Work for every East Ender', concluded an account of full employment and high wages with the ominous comment that 'the general impression is that sooner or later some form of compulsory service will be necessary and adopted'.[64] By the autumn the question of conscription was being debated more and more openly. The government was reluctant to introduce a measure which was deeply unpopular in the labour movement, so there were last-minute efforts to make the voluntary system work. Early in October the Great Assembly Hall in Mile End

Road was the rallying point for 'five columns of happy, cheery troops, each more than 1,000 strong, with 29 military bands, drums beating and banners flying—the London streets have not seen such a rousing sight before'.[65] East London crowds turned out to watch, but the organisers were forced to blame bad weather for the small number of recruits, and the *Advertiser* ventured to report 'a lack of cheering and an absence of enthusiasm'.[66] Even the patriotic labour leaders could no longer bring in recruits as they used to, though Will Thorne tried at the Assembly Hall and Will Crooks at the People's Palace. Despite efforts to pass the blame onto a convenient scapegoat—the 'shirkers' of East London's immigrant community—conscription inexorably approached for Jew and Gentile alike. On 5 January 1916 the first Military Service Bill was introduced into the House of Commons.

Meanwhile the anti-war socialists were winning a good deal more support for their campaign against conscription than they could yet hope to obtain for outright pacifism. The *Herald* records a whole series of East London trades council resolutions against conscription. Shoreditch trades council declared it to be 'contrary to the sentiments and principles of the British people, subversive of the free and democratic character of their institutions; and [it] involves a serious menace to the liberty and freedom of the labour movement.'[67] Poplar trades council took a leading role in organising an all-London anti-conscription conference in December 1915. The socialist societies held their own conferences, and even successful open-air meetings (for example, L.S. Dunstan of Poplar ILP 'made a vigorous denunciation of conscription' to a good audience at the East India Dock gates in November 1915[68]). But socialist collaboration on this theme was not without its difficulties. The ILP, which had taken the initiative in forming the No Conscription Fellowship in November 1914, favoured the broadest possible campaign on moral as much as on political grounds. The anti-war wing of the BSP, on the other hand, was wary of diluting its socialist message with too large a dose of moral pacifism.

In January 1916 the leadership of the Labour Party reluctantly accepted conscription as necessary and inevitable.

Hostility continued in East London, however. Will Thorne was summoned before the West Ham LRC to explain his conduct at the Labour Party Conference. He tried to persuade a tense, angry meeting that Asquith's promises against industrial conscription would be kept, but many West Ham socialists remained unconvinced.[69] The ILP vowed to take up the responsibility abdicated by the Labour Party by leading a campaign for the repeal of the Act. An open-air meeting in Forest Gate, organised jointly by the East Ham branch, the No Conscription Fellowship and the ELFS, attracted a crowd of between four and five hundred. They passed an anti-conscription resolution and 'listened to the speeches for an hour and a half in excellent order and apparently with interest', according to the *East London Observer*, which was scarcely biased in their favour.[70] But as conscription got under way, and the military tribunals began their work, it became increasingly difficult to agitate openly against the Act, or to impede its operation, without incurring prosecution under the Defence of the Realm Acts. In May 1916 Frederick Halfpenny, secretary of the Forest Gate No Conscription Fellowship, was charged at Stratford police court with 'circulating statements likely to cause disaffection and to prejudice recruiting'. He was sentenced to three months imprisonment, or a £50 fine.[71] The conscientious objectors became a persecuted, isolated minority. For the bulk of the labour movement, opposition to conscription could only continue along less direct channels, such as the trade unions' resistance to industrial conscription, and the WNC's campaign for the 'conscription of wealth' to counter-balance the conscription of workers' lives.

The military tribunals themselves provided an opportunity to fight a rearguard action against conscription. *Labour Leader* had been quick to spot their potential as well-publicised platforms for airing pacifist views: 'We believe the machinery of the Tribunals provides us with a supreme opportunity of raising in the public mind the whole moral issue relating to War. It enables us to state our case in the manner never before open to us.'[72] The No Conscription Fellowship urged supporters who were not themselves subject to the Act to 'make a point of being present at the

Tribunals to support applicants'.[73] In the coming months the East London tribunals were to be the scene of rousing speeches against capitalism, as well as against war. But even those socialists who were not themselves conscientious objectors were determined to make full use of the statutory labour representation on the tribunals. It would be the task of labour representatives to see that the tribunals worked fairly, without discrimination against the poor. It would be their task to ensure that conscientious objectors got a hearing, whether their objections were religious or political. If the labour representatives were opposed to the war, they could even use their influence to increase the number of exemptions granted. All these different forms of underground resistance to the Military Service Acts are to be found, if we examine the day-to-day work of the tribunals.

As usual, the first problem was to gain adequate labour representation. Local politicians were more ready to take offence at the political opinions of labour when it came to choosing a military tribunal than when it was merely a matter of relief and pensions committees. In Poplar, for example, the borough council turned down two of the trades council's nominees, Lansbury and Alf Watts of the BSP, because both were well-known pacifists. The trades council protested to the Local Government Board, and circulated an angry resolution to all affiliated union branches, but the decision was not reversed. Instead, four other Labour Party men (Banks, March, Sumner and Adams) were accepted on to the tribunal.[74]

In Bethnal Green, the council included two trade unionists on the tribunal, but apart from the fact of their union membership these men were in no sense 'labour representatives'. Complaints were soon being made, and a long correspondence ensued between the Town Clerk and the local branch of the National Amalgamated Furnishing Trades Association (NAFTA). NAFTA accused the council of making 'no effort to get in touch with any Labour body or branch of the Trade Union movement, in order that they might seek representation on the Tribunal', with the result that 'only members of the Borough Council were appointed on the local Tribunal, and that bona fide Labour representatives of the district were ignored'. The trade unionists refused to be mollified by condescending assurances that 'The Borough Council has for long striven in the interests of the working classes', and that its members had 'intimate knowledge of labour and other conditions affecting the working class'.[75] By 'labour representation' they understood representation of labour's own representative bodies: this was the same point of principle which had separated the trades council and the mayor in East Ham. Bethnal Green trades council's protest went to the Local Government Board, but without effect. Meanwhile a report in the *Herald,* from the trades council president, spelt out clearly the politics of the whole affair. One of the strongest objections to the council's chosen candidates was the fact that 'both ran under the auspices of the Liberal Party at the last election'.[76]

Shoreditch provides another example of the political aspect of tribunal selection. Early in February the borough council drew up plans which completely ignored Local Government Board instructions on labour representation. These were rushed through at the beginning of a council meeting before the two most vocal Labour Party councillors arrived. When they eventually turned up, they refused to accept the *fait accompli* and attempted to nominate four labour representatives to the tribunal. Predictably the attempt failed. Undeterred by this setback, Shoreditch trades council and LRC swiftly organised a public protest meeting in the Whitmore ward of Hoxton, where independent Labour politics were strongest. The following Sunday morning a large meeting (estimated by its supporters at 1,000, and admitted even by its opponents to be 200–300 strong) passed a resolution demanding proper labour representation. Backed by this resolution, Labour councillors reintroduced the subject at the next council meeting, demanding seven labour representatives to counterbalance the seven already chosen, 'in view of the expressed wish of the citizens of Shoreditch'. A resolution to allow some further labour representation was narrowly passed. Probably this shift of ground by the council was due as much to a closer study of the Local Government Board's instructions as to the Hoxton meeting. But the attempt to muzzle the Labour Party (and especially its anti-war wing) was not totally abandoned. Councillors swiftly vetoed the trades council's nomination of local socialists Girling (who 'had said things against the constitution') and Taylor ('a paid agitator'), before accepting a trade unionist with a suitably patriotic reputation.[77]

In Stepney, where labour organisation had always been weak, four trade unionists were included on a much larger tribunal. None was to play a very active role in the tribunal's affairs. The other twenty-one members were businessmen, manufacturers, traders and professionals.[78] At East Ham and West Ham several socialists were among the labour representatives, and no complaints were made by the local trades council, so presumably the situation was considered fairly satisfactory.

It is difficult to prove an exact correlation between the strength of labour representation on the various tribunals, and the treatment of the applicants to those tribunals. One thing which is certain is that there was great inconsistency between different tribunals, and it seems likely that the varying number and nature of labour representatives was at least partly responsible. The Stepney tribunal provided some of the worst examples of prejudiced decision-making. A combination of weak labour representation and unusual local circumstances was responsible. The majority of the applicants were Jews, and numbers were very large. On the day that the membership of the tribunal was announced, the *East London Observer* remarked that Stepney 'has the most difficult task of all the tribunals in London', and at the same time hoped that 'absolute exemptions will be unknown'.[79] Most members of the Stepney tribunal were determined to display what the *Advertiser* called 'a necessary amount of firmness'.[80] Their attitudes, and those of Jewish applicants, will be discussed in greater detail in Chapter 6. Press reports make it clear that exemptions were indeed exceptionally rare. Where an exemption was unavoidable, it was given only on condition that the man agreed to attend the Volunteer Training Corps in his spare time. Applicants protested that they had no spare time—but without success. If an applicant failed to appear before the tribunal at the appointed time, his case was dismissed without further enquiry.[81]

Reports of proceedings at the Poplar tribunal convey quite a different atmosphere. Exemptions and referrals to non-combatant service were far more numerous, sometimes to the annoyance of the Military Representative. Labour members were, of course, a minority in the tribunal (four out of thirteen), so they did not always get their own way. But their presence was constantly felt, as they cross-examined applicants to help them put their cases in the most favourable light. Disputes arose mainly between political opponents on the tribunal, rather than between the tribunal members and the applicants or the public, as occurred at Stepney. The tribunal hearing reported in the *East London Observer* on 11 March 1916 provides several examples of such disputes. The first applicant was the owner of a small sweet shop, who claimed exemption because the business was dependent on him. A Conservative on the tribunal pointed out that 'there would be no business at all if we did not win the war'. But the Labour councillors, Banks and March, warmly supported the applicant, on the grounds that 'There should be no distinction between a small man in business and a large one', and that 'People who were making munitions etc. at home wanted something to eat, and people like the applicant supplied it. We were not going to live on potatoes.' A decision on this case was deferred to a future meeting. The next applicant was a conscientious objector who claimed that he had held such views for six years. It was suggested that he should be made to repeat his statement on oath, but this aroused strong protests from Banks against 'the assumption being made that every young man coming there was a liar'. The suggestion was dropped, and non-combatant service granted. Another applicant produced his dependent sister as a witness. Her husband was in the army and she claimed to be unable to live on her allowance—which provided Banks with a good opening for a short speech in favour of more generous allowances. Alderman Bussey enquired indignantly 'if they were there to deal with tribunal matters or to accommodate sectional interests', and suggested Banks should retire from the tribunal if he persisted in 'advocating something which seems to support a witness in a direction which is outside our duty'.

It is interesting to compare the treatment of socialist conscientious objectors by the different East London tribunals. At every tribunal it seems to have been more difficult to sustain an objection on socialist grounds than one based on business or family responsibilities, or even on religious faith. Most socialists came before the tribunal with a prepared statement of their political beliefs, but in many cases they were not allowed to deliver it. Anti-socialists were anxious to prevent the tribunals being used to spread socialist arguments against the war, and a speech against capitalist war-mongering was liable to be cut short. For example, by the mayor of East Ham: 'The capitalist system has nothing to do with your conscience, it is a matter of political economy. Personally I don't think this kind of claim was ever contemplated by the Act.'[82] A socialist school teacher was briskly told by the mayor of Stepney to stop 'indulging in socialist clap-trap'; what he needed was 'military discipline' (appeal refused).[83] At Bethnal Green, a socialist speech was interrupted by 'a member remarking that it was a case of cold feet. The appeal was dismissed'.[84] At Poplar and West Ham most political statements were listened to, and the applicant might be asked to produce a membership card from a socialist organisation. But here, too, the majority of socialist appeals seem to have been voted down.

There were exceptions. Amongst these are to be found such well-known local socialists as Joe Vaughan, president of Bethnal Green trades council. He declared uncompromisingly that he was a member of the BSP, an international socialist, and believed that 'all wars were in the interests of the profit-mongers'. The Bethnal Green tribunal, which had turned a deaf ear to many identical pleas, granted him 'non-combatant service' without a murmur.[85] This suggests that, although the majorities on the tribunals did not wish to be lenient with socialists, they were reluctant to antagonise local labour leaders who might organise working class resistance to conscription and other aspects of the war effort. There may also have been a temptation to remove political opponents from the scene, however. In September 1917 Edgar Lansbury was refused exemption by Poplar tribunal. He lodged a successful appeal, on the grounds that the local tribunal did not adequately consider his evidence:

> I am an active member of the Poplar Borough Council and an active
> worker in the Socialist and Political Labour Movement of Poplar and
> East London. This brings me into conflict with my colleagues on the
> Borough Council. The Tribunal was composed of a majority of my
> opponents, whom I consider to be not the best qualified people to
> consider my application.[86]

The East London trades councils often discussed tribunal affairs. Report-back sessions, such as those organised by East Ham trades council, amounted to a check that the labour representatives were doing their duty in defending working class interests. Other members of the East Ham tribunal objected to James Pope's conception of his duty. When he insisted that he needed to be present at every meeting they protested: 'Surely he had not come there with the idea that he represented Labour and Labour alone? Had not the State some consideration for his services, and the war for his judgement?. . . the introduction of Party was not savoury.'[87] Here was the old argument, levelled against so many Labour committee members in the past, that in war-time the national interest superseded mere politics. The East Ham trades council made clear their disagreement by deciding, soon after, that Pope's tribunal activities needed a little extra outside political backing. They set up 'a small sub-committee with a view of submitting cases to the Labour Party'. Three weeks later the sub-committee had prepared a detailed report (with Pope's help) on the defects of the East Ham tribunal, they forwarded it to the Local Government Board and to the local Member of Parliament, as well as to the Labour Party.[88]

West Ham trades council, despite the large number of patriotic socialists in the borough, was equally vigilant over the conduct of its labour representatives on the military tribunal. In July 1916 a delegation from the London Council Against Conscription attended a trades council meeting to complain that Labour members of the South Essex appeal tribunal were unsympathetic to conscientious objectors and that their conduct was too much 'like that of other members'. The complaint was treated with great seriousness. The labour representatives replied to the allegations during a long discussion. Then a resolution was passed which, whilst carefully avoiding open criticism, clearly defined their duty for the future:

> The council, having heard the deputation and the reply thereto, without expressing regret at the action of the Tribunal, consider much can be done in the future if comrades put up a fight for conscientious objectors, either religious or political, and see that the members of the Trade Union movement generally obtain fair, just and honourable treatment.[89]

Once again, the main emphasis is certainly not on the national interest!

During the first half of the war much of the activity of Labour Party supporters was only indirectly political. The Second International, and its British members, had pledged themselves to 'intercede for its speedy end'. But the realities of war-time public opinion made this an impractical aim in the early years. Instead East London socialists and trade unionists rechannelled their efforts into the relief of economic distress caused by the war and into the active defence of working class interests through existing local government bodies and the new network of local committees. Very considerable indirect political gains could be made through such activities. In an unspectacular but effective fashion, labour activists used war conditions to strengthen their organisation, to broaden their administrative experience, and to educate workers in the value of independent Labour politics. At local level, as well as on the WNC, the organisations of the labour movement were working more closely together than ever before; and this despite the disagreements of 'patriots' and 'pacifists' over the war question itself. Labour representation was sought as eagerly by trade unionists and co-operators as by socialists. Of course not all labour representatives were Labour Party enthusiasts. But joint action on common policies, and the leadership provided by local trades councils and LRCs, were undoubtedly preparing the way for the emergence of stronger East London Labour Parties at the end of the war.

NOTES

1. Joll, J., *The Second International*, 1889–1914 (1955), 139.
2. *East London Observer* (hereafter *ELO*) and *East London Advertiser* (hereafter *ELA*), 4 July–1 August 1914.
3. *East Ham Echo* (hereafter *EE*), 7 August 1914.
4. Ibid.
5. *ELA*, 8 August 1914.
6. Ibid.
7. *ELO*, 8 August 1914.
8. Ibid.
9. Interview with Albert Overland (lived in Bow and managed to get himself accepted into the Navy at the age of fifteen; invalided out four years later; took up Labour politics and later became a Labour councillor and mayor of Poplar).
10. Jasper, A.S., *A Hoxton Childhood* (1969), 55.
11. Interview with Bill Brinson.
12. Interview with Thomas Beningfield.
13. War Emergency Workers National Committee (hereafter WNC) *Report*, August 1914–March 1916, and correspondence files.
14. *Daily Herald*, 10 August 1914.
15. *ELA*, 8 August 1914.
16. WNC *Report*, August 1914–March 1916 and WNC *Minutes*, 10 October 1918.
17. *Women's Dreadnought* (hereafter *Dreadnought*), 22 August and 5 September 1914.
18. *ELO*, 15 August 1914.
19. Sylvia Pankhurst's relief work is described in great detail in *The Home Front* and *Women's Dreadnought*.
20. Pankhurst, E.S., *The Suffragette Movement* (1931), 417.
21. Pankhurst, E.S., *The Home Front* (1932), 43.
22. ELFS Minute Book, 27 May 1913–19 September 1915 (folder Pankhurst 15 at the International Institute for Social History, Amsterdam, hereafter P15). Notes on individuals who contributed funds for relief work are to be found in the front of WSF Finance Committee Minute Book, 31 May–6 November 1919 (P19).
23. *Dreadnought*, 8 August 1914.
24. *Dreadnought*, 5 September 1914.
25. *Co-operative News* (hereafter *Co-op News*), 1 August 1914.
26. *Co-op News*, 31 October 1914.
27. *Co-op News*, 10 October 1914.
28. WNC *Minutes*, 15 April 1918.
29. WNC correspondence, box 33, file 1, items 62, 63, 66, 174, 224 and 415 (hereafter WNC 31/1/62 etc.).
30. WNC 11/1/91 and 10/4/74.
31. WNC 11/1/199.
32. *Stratford Express* (hereafter *SE*), 27 February 1915.
33. *Herald*, 6 March 1915.
34. *ELA*, 20 March 1915.
35. *ELO*, 3 April 1915.
36. *ELO*, 22 May 1915.
37. *ELO*, 3 April 1915.
38. *Herald*, 6 March 1915.

39. *ELA*, 27 March 1915.
40. *Daily Herald*, 22 August 1914.
41. WNC, 25/3/27.
42, WNC, 16/2/47.
43. *ELA*, 29 August 1914.
44. List of Poplar Labour Representative Committee members, with their addresses and organisations they represented (P24).
45. *SE*, 12 August 1914.
46. *SE*, 15 August 1914.
47. *ELO*, 5 September 1914.
48. Ibid.
49. WNC, 28/8/28.
50. *Hackney Gazette*, 12 August 1914.
51. *SE*, 22 August 1914.
52. *EE*, 16 October 1914 and *SE*, 27 March 1915.
53. WNC, 28/8/28.
54. *Herald*, 31/10/14.
55. WNC, 35/1/12.
56. WNC, 28/8/84.
57. *EE*, 4 August 1916.
58. *EE*, 8 September 1916.
59. *EE*, 11 May 1917.
60. *EE*, 27 April, 11 May and 31 August 1917.
61. WNC, 26/2/8 and WNC *Minutes*, 5 July 1917.
62. *ELO*, 11 March and 10 April 1915.
63. LCC reports in *ELO*, e.g. 7 November 1914, 3 April 1915.
64. *ELA*, 6 February 1915.
65. *ELO*, 9 October 1915.
66. *ELA*, 9 October 1915.
67. *Herald*, 19 June 1915.
68. *Labour Leader*, 18 November 1915.
69. *EE*, 12 February 1916.
70. *ELO*, 19 February 1916.
71. *Daily News*, 29 May 1916 (cutting in Walter Southgate collection).
72. *Labour Leader*, 10 February 1916.
73. No Conscription Fellowship leaflet, dated 6 February 1916, in Walter Southgate collection.
74. *Herald*, 26 February 1916.
75. *ELO*, 13 May 1916.
76. *Herald*, 8 April 1916.
77. *Hackney Gazette*, 9 and 16 February, 6 and 13 March 1916.
78. *ELO*, 19 February 1916.
79. Ibid.
80. *ELA*, 1 April 1916.
81. e.g. *ELO*, 18 March, 25 March and 5 August 1916.
82. *EE*, 25 August 1916.
83. *ELO*, 22 April 1916.
84. *ELO*, 18 March 1916.
85. Ibid.
86. Copy of Edgar Lansbury's Notice of Appeal, dated 13 September 1917, and postcard from George Lansbury rejoicing in the outcome, dated 10 January, in the Lansbury Collection, volume 7, item 369 and volume 8, item 3.

87. *EE*, 25 February 1916.
88. *EE*, 7 and 28 April 1916.
89. *SE*, 15 July 1916.

CHAPTER 3

TOWARDS PEACE: LABOUR POLITICS 1916–18

As conscription began to bite, casualties mounted ever higher, and war weariness threatened to sap the patriotism of civilians, the question of war or peace became more and more urgent. For a period in 1916–17 it seemed possible that it would tear apart the East London labour movement. However the pattern of Labour activity in local government established during the early years continued until the end of the war. Successful co-operation in this field helped to paper over political divisions until, by 1918, it was clear that cohesive forces were stronger than those which divided the labour movement and the Labour Party. In the final year of the war patriots and pacifists moved closer together on the war question itself. Many patriots supported the demand for a government commitment to clearly defined war aims, while the majority of pacifists acknowledged the failure of out-and-out peace campaigning by modifying their anti-war views into the demand for early negotiations. The degree of consensus displayed at a national Labour conference on war aims in December 1917 showed that the clash of views was no longer extreme enough to present an insuperable obstacle to Labour Party reorganisation and reunification during the following year.

However this outcome was not easily predictable. The socialist societies, in particular, had been very severely tested by the war and peace dilemma. Unlike the trade unions or the co-operative movement, their identity was defined by agreement on political ideology. The acuteness of political disagreements, and also the manner in which they were eventually subsumed, can be illustrated from the war-time history of the BSP in East London. The BSP was the largest socialist group in the area. Though its local membership never rose above about three hundred, they included socialists whose influential role in the unions and on the trades councils was crucial to the success of the Labour Party. The majority of these East Londoners were to be found in the anti-war camp. Indeed they provided an important section of the opposition to Hyndman's patriotic leadership which, in 1916, led to a national split in the party. But the BSP's pro-war wing was also strongly represented in East London by Will Thorne and his supporters. If any part of the country was likely to witness destructive internecine warfare among socialist comrades, it would be the borough of West Ham, and the ripples from the conflict there might be expected to spread out into the neighbouring boroughs.

Even before 1914, as we have seen, East London members were critical of Hyndman's policies. When war broke out, the internationalists who had opposed re-armament, like Joe Fineberg and Zelda Kahan of Stepney and E.C. Fairchild of Hackney, became leaders of the anti-war movement within the BSP. The party newspaper, *Justice,* was reluctant to publicise the growing volume of protest and the anti-war socialists were soon forced to begin organising outside the party. The ILP's *Labour Leader* offered a willing outlet for their views: in October 1914 it published resolutions condemning Hyndman's support of the recruiting campaign from four East London branches of the BSP.[1] Soon after, Fineberg was elected to the BSP executive, giving the internationalists a five to four majority. Probably because of the political conflicts arising from this situation, the BSP postponed its annual conference in 1915. But this did not prevent East London branches from forwarding militantly anti-war resolutions for approval by local BSP conferences in other parts of the country. Only the South West Ham branch, where Thorne and Jones were dominant, stood by leadership policies at a London conference in March 1915. Overwhelming support was received for a North West Ham resolution roundly condemning the war as 'the outcome of commercial rivalry between the capitalist classes of the various nations involved', and calling upon the working class 'to concentrate upon the greater war at home, namely, the Class War'.[2]

The worst fears of the Hyndmanites were confirmed when,

in February 1916, the first edition of a new anti-war BSP newspaper appeared, under the editorship of Fairchild. The *Call* was sent to every party branch in an effort to build up support for the pacifist internationalists' stand at the forthcoming national conference. On 6 April it proclaimed 'The paralysing indecision of the past twelve months must be abandoned. . . Peace or War! Internationalism or Imperialism! There is no middle course. There can be no compromise.' So it turned out. A fortnight later Hyndman and his supporters walked from the BSP conference on its first day, to the delight of 'the great body of delegates who stood upon the tables and chairs cheering and singing "The Red Flag".'[3] Jack Jones of South West Ham was among the leavers, who proceeded to set up the National Socialist Advisory Committee (later the National Socialist Party) in a nearby hotel. Among those who stayed to adopt Fairchild's views as official BSP policy were delegates from Bethnal Green, Bow and Bromley, Poplar, Stepney, North West Ham and Hackney. Their resolutions on peace, on the defence of working class rights in war time, and in favour of affiliation to the Labour Party, determined the course of discussion during the remainder of the conference. Though they voted in favour of the Zimmerwald demand for working class action to end the war, they did not expect it to be ended by revolution. Instead they foresaw a period of educative socialist activity inside the Labour Party.

In East London such policies were very much based upon the existing situation. Practical collaboration with other socialist and trade union bodies could be seen to be proceeding successfully over the issues of food prices, allowances, relief and conscription. The main potential threat to such joint activity seemed to be the existence of NSP and BSP branches side by side in some boroughs, since the former openly proclaimed its intention of wiping out the latter by winning its members over to what was now the only 'truly socialist' party in Britain.[4] In fact, conflict between the two groups never escalated to the level which this aim implies. In East London and elsewhere, long-established habits of co-operation and the urgency of immediate practical issues blunted the edge of sectarian politics. In South West Ham the

NSP patriots continued to keep their socialism well to the fore. Despite fierce verbal attacks on the BSP pacifists, the NSP refused to become absorbed into the ultra-patriotic British Workers League, and it was as Labour Party candidates that its West Ham members wished to be elected at the end of the war.

At the same time, despite its uncompromisingly pacifist policies and close relations with the ILP, the BSP in East London soon recovered from the excitement of the 1916 conference and re-learned the hard lesson that the time was not yet ripe for a successful public peace campaign. Until mid-1917, the East London pacifists remained a small, unpopular minority. This was not for want of effort by the various groups which struggled bravely to organise peace meetings. Sometimes pacifist speakers won a hearing, but an ILP member of this period remembers the care taken to select speaking pitches which were clear of potential missiles![5] Meetings held by the BSP in Victoria Park often ended in violence. Bill Brinson recalls one occasion early in 1916, when Lansbury was due to speak:

> We all went in at the St. Mark's gate end, thirty or forty, perhaps fifty people, men and women, and set up a platform (we used to carry it on our backs) in the park, and he began propagating. And before we knew where we were, after a few minutes a crowd rushed in the other gate, a lot of them in uniform as well, and we were all knocked flying. And that was that!

Despite such mishaps, the peace campaign temporarily gathered new impetus at the end of 1916. East Londoners played a leading part in a successful Trafalgar Square food price demonstration in November, at which Fineberg declared that 'really effective action against the exploiters could not be taken until peace had been obtained. The fight against the present exploitation must be a struggle for peace.'[6] Sylvia Pankhurst was devoting more and more of her energies to pacifist propaganda. 'Peace is in the air!' declared the *Dreadnought* jubilantly, when the British government received peace overtures from Germany in December.[7] Her group (now re-named the Workers Suffrage

Federation) decided to hold its most ambitious series of meetings so far. Day after day members of the WSF spoke up for peace, at street corners and in Victoria Park. But even Sylvia could not pretend that their reception was entirely enthusiastic. In Chrisp Street speakers were pelted with market refuse, while in Victoria Park 'the little platform was pushed over and smashed; a park keeper, Mrs Drake and Mrs Cressall were thrown to the ground'.[8] A still greater disappointment was in store three months later, when a carefully planned joint socialist demonstration in East London met with a similar fate. Sylvia comforted herself with the knowledge that only a minority of the very large crowd in Victoria Park had been responsible for the violence. But her impatience and chagrin at her working class friends' failure to defend the WSF show through in a stiff moral lecture carried by the next edition of the *Dreadnought*: 'Do not bite the hand that fed you because its owner is with what may be the minority; do not publicly spurn and revile those who have comforted you, whom you respect and to whom you will turn again in time of anxiety and trouble.'[9]

Peace speakers, whether from the WSF, the BSP, the ILP or even the Socialist Sunday Schools, generally received a rough reception in East London on account of their pacifism, rather than because of any strong public hostility to socialism. Few workers made much distinction at this stage between the demand for peace by negotiation, and the demand for immediate surrender to the Germans—'peace at any price'. There were obvious reasons why the latter demand aroused contempt and hatred. Though the exuberant patriotism of 1914 had died away, the very extent of war losses made many people determined not to give in till something was gained in return. Sylvia Pankhurst records that some of the most frenzied protesters at her peace meetings were bereaved women:

We tried to make them understand that they and theirs are but the catspaws in the great capitalist struggle of which this war is the outcome. . . Some answered, 'We want our sons to have their revenge!' and others cried, 'Our sons are dead; your talk of peace can never bring them back!'[10]

On other occasions, when the war brought death and destruction to East London itself, shock and sorrow were again accompanied by cries for revenge. The government, of course, encouraged such reactions. The worst single disaster was the Silvertown explosion, in January 1917, which killed seventy-four, injured many hundreds, and left several streets as heaps of rubble. The government immediately stepped in with promises of full compensation, and the *Advertiser* reported on 27 January that 'the prompt measures taken to cope with the distress have had an excellent effect on the public mind'. Lloyd George visited the scene, and took tea with the patriotic Labour MP Will Crooks and his wife, 'at their home in Poplar'. After a serious air raid six months later, which killed fifteen infants at North Street School, Crooks led the call for revenge in an emotional outburst in the House of Commons. Another distinguished visitor hastened down to East London—this time the King, who got an enthusiastic reception from crowds which were 'angry, but calm'.[11]

For month after month newspaper editors filled their pages (denuded of hard facts by censorship) with tales of Hun atrocities and of British bravery, and with wordy exhortations to patriotism. The crucial reason why most workers were prepared to fight on was that they believed their position would be more intolerable if they refused to do so. Only a drastic change in conditions on the home front, such as the threat of starvation or decisive and irreversible defeats to British forces in the field, might have altered this belief. Thus the revolutionary defeatism fostered by Russian Bolsheviks during 1917 had little chance of success in Britain. But though few workers were pacifist and even fewer revolutionary, during 1917–18 the economic and military situation worsened to such an extent that many began to doubt the possibility of an outright military victory. In this situation the Russian revolutions exercised an important influence on British labour politics.

The March revolution was almost unanimously welcomed. The government, and Labour patriots like Will Thorne, hoped it would shore up the crumbling Russian war effort, as well as contributing to the progress of democracy. But it is

74

not surprising that the first and most joyous celebrations of the revolution in East London were led by the Russian Jewish population. The great majority were refugees from religious or political persecution. Their reluctance to fight in the cause of their Tsarist persecutors had aroused both local and national hostility, and in the spring of 1917 a Bill was before Parliament which would offer them the choice of enlistment in the British army or deportation. The revolution could scarcely have been more opportune. Immigrant Jews instantly assumed it meant not only an end to racial oppression, but an opportunity for returning socialists to play their part in reconstructing a Russia at peace.

Russian socialist groups organised the East London celebrations; however enthusiasm spread far beyond the politically committed few. On 24 March over seven thousand packed the Great Assembly Hall in Mile End Road, and many others had to be turned away. Telegrams and messages of greeting were received from almost every Jewish trade union and labour organisation. Russian speakers shared the platform with anti-war British socialists such as Robert Williams, secretary of the National Transport Workers' Federation, and Val MacEntee of the BSP.[12] On the following day a routine meeting of the Foreign Jews Protection Committee (a socialist-led organisation formed to defend Jews' right of asylum in Britain) became another mass rally to greet the revolution. Sylvia Pankhurst was among the guest speakers: she ridiculed government hopes that the Russian war effort would now improve, proclaiming that the revolution stood not for war, but 'for the abolition of poverty, of wealth, and of rank, and to make men and women brothers and sisters'.[13] The same joy, and the same hopes, were expressed at a BSP meeting at Chandos Hall on 26 March, and at an enormous demonstration at the Albert Hall the following weekend. Under the banner of the Anglo-Russian Democratic Alliance, speakers from the ILP, the Labour Party and the trade unions came together to embrace the Russian revolutionaries' cause as their own. The *Herald* reported ecstatically:

It marked a turning point in the mood, the spirit, the activities of our country. Over and over again during the speeches one note was struck, and it always met with the most enthusiastic response—the note of *beginning*. Here, one felt, was the first light of morning, the first flush of returning liberty in the black skies of loss and oppression and reaction.[14]

But of what, exactly, was the revolution a 'beginning'? As the weeks passed the euphoria in the socialist movement continued, but clarity did not increase. All the socialist groups, apart from the NSP believed that the revolution had brought peace nearer, not just in Russia but in Britain too. Was it possible after all that British workers, defying appearances and past traditions, would end the war by revolution? In a mood of genuine puzzlement, a national conference of Labour Party, trade union and socialist delegates met at Leeds on 3 June to consider the question. East London was well represented. Sylvia Pankhurst and E.C. Fairchild were among the main speakers. Lansbury was prevented from attending by a sudden serious illness, but a letter from him was read out at the conference and his absence had the fortunate result of producing a number of first-hand accounts of events at Leeds, written to cheer him on his sick-bed. A group of Poplar LRC stalwarts (Joe Banks, C.E. Sumner), Sam March and R. Palmer) scrawled a hurried note as they waited for the return train to London: 'the conference was one of the greatest we have ever attended. Your letter was received with great enthusiasm. . . We thought we would take this opportunity of perhaps being the first to let you (know) how things went.'[15] The enthusiasm of the conference is vividly conveyed by a longer, more thoughtful letter from the BSP veteran, Alf Watts, written from his Bow home on 15 June:

> Thanks very much for giving me the opportunity of going to Leeds. It was great. There was a fine feeling about the whole show, and I felt all on the tingle all day. And then we talked about it all the way home. If it enthused an old crock like me, who is by temperament inclined to look on some of these gatherings with a rather cool and detached air, you may agree it was good. . .
>
> The great thing is for us to get to work, and I hear the Prov. Com. is up and doing. Locally I think we must 'get on with it'—I was not at the last E.C. of the L.R.C., but shall reckon to be at the Deleg.

Meeting, and shall see how we shape for action.[16]

Apart from a small minority of patriots (of whom Ben Tillett was one), almost everyone who attended the Leeds conference seems to have shared Watts's delight and renewed determination. Only later did it become apparent that the delegates left Leeds well-satisfied, precisely because all the emphasis had been on unity, and not on thrashing out the differences between various socialist interpretations of what the revolution meant for British workers. After displaying near-unanimity at Leeds, the socialist groups dispersed to each begin 'shaping for action' in its own particular way. The *Herald* outlined plans for a democratic, socialist 'People's Party', to be based on a programme including the conscription of wealth and the expropriation of selected industries as well as a negotiated peace without annexations or indemnities.[17] The ILP warned against any attempt to supplant the existing Labour Party by the new Russian-style Workmen's and Soldiers' Councils proposed at Leeds.[18] Sylvia Pankhurst, on the other hand, was convinced that Europe could follow the Russian example and 'step directly from Capitalism to Socialism'.[19] Her WSF embarked on ultra-left policies which were later to be condemned by Lenin himself.

The BSP had closer connections with the Russian Social Democrats than any other British Labour organisation. Amid the excitement of Leeds it took a similar line to the WSF, declaring that 'the hour of the Social Revolution is close upon us'.[20] But the revolutionary supporters of John Maclean soon found themselves in a minority. At the 1918 BSP conference the North West Ham branch (which had recently come under Maclean's influence when he addressed socialist classes there) put forward a resolution calling for disaffiliation from the Labour Party.[21] Delegates from the other ten East London branches joined the opposition to this proposal. As Fineberg drily put it, 'Revolutionary socialism was a grand faith to have, but it was not our function to have it for ourselves. Our leaving the Labour Party would not be a split. It would not matter very much to the Labour Party.'[22] The gradualists won the day.

Fortunately for the Labour Party in East London, the BSP decided its first task was to help Labour win elections, whilst at the same time trying to infuse the party with a stronger sense of socialist purpose.

Six months after the Leeds conference, nearly all East London socialists had abandoned the idea of an imminent revolution in this country. Much though British socialists envied and admired Russian achievements, by the end of 1917 they no longer believed in direct imitation. This return to pragmatism was not due simply to a lack of courage, as Sylvia Pankhurst scornfully suggested, but to an understanding by socialists involved in the day-to-day work of the labour movement that the British working class did not share the desperate mood of its Russian counterpart. The great interest shown by British workers in the Russian revolution remained a hopeful sign, however. In the summer of 1917 East London socialists found audiences prepared, as never before, to listen seriously to their peace arguments. The *Call* reported a series of successful BSP meetings in Victoria Park, ending in good collections and 'numerous applications to join the branch'.[23] The *Herald* did particularly well in Stepney; within a few weeks over eighty members had been recruited to a new branch of the Herald League.[24] In September a weekly Marxist education class was established at Water Lane School, Stratford, through the joint efforts of local socialist societies, trades councils and the Plebs League. The subjects chosen for study were Economics, Political Evolution and Industrial History, and by the end of the year there was an average attendance of nearly a hundred.[25]

But the socialists suffered set-backs, too, which helped to bring them down to earth again after the revolutionary rhetoric of Leeds. There was still a lot of anti-pacifist feeling among East London workers. After several months of uninterrupted meetings, the BSP was routed once again in Victoria Park—'a crowd of hooligans, who had assembled in another part of the park and had not heard a word of our comrade's speech, marched straight to the meeting and broke it up'.[26] In November the *Herald* reported that 'the reactionary forces of evil are beginning to operate'—in other words, the Herald League speaking pitch in Stepney was under threat.[27] Poplar council also took a hand in checking the progress of socialist peace propaganda, when it cancelled its letting of Bow Baths to the ILP and Herald League for a series of autumn lectures, after anti-pacifist threats of violence.[28]

The most serious setback in the months after the Leeds Convention was the failure of the Workmen's and Soldiers' Councils. At the end of July local conferences were planned to elect representatives to a national council. In London, as in Newcastle and Swansea, the conference was broken up by an angry patriotic mob. The London conference was to have been held in the Brotherhood Church, Southgate Road; hours before it began, an anonymous leaflet was being distributed in nearby Hoxton pubs which proved BSP allegations that the violence was organised:

MEN OF HOXTON

This afternoon at 3 o'clock
in your midst
A meeting of pro-Germans will be held
assisted by
Delegates from the Committee in Russia which
demoralised and ruined the Russian Army.
These people are organising in the hope of doing
the same dirty work in the British Army.

After giving details of the meeting place, the leaflet concluded by inviting local patriots to 'REMEMBER THE LAST AIR RAID AND ROLL UP!'[29] In different circumstances such an attack would have done little lasting damage to the Workmen's and Soldiers' Councils scheme. The real cause of its failure was disagreement among the socialists themselves over the nature and purpose of the councils. The BSP pronounced their obituary at its 1918 conference, and Sylvia Pankhurst transferred her enthusiasm instead to the shop stewards movement.

One reason for the failure of the Councils was that by late 1917 the national Labour Party leadership was beginning to rouse itself from its subservience to Coalition policies. This made it easier for socialists who no longer believed in revolution to redirect their energies back to work within the party. Pacifist socialists never became a majority in the Labour Party, but as the war ground endlessly on their views were increasingly heeded. The socialist press rejoiced in the changed tone of the August 1917 Labour Party conference.[30] No doubt they exaggerated the extent of a change which they very much desired, but its direction was unmistakable. The ILP hailed the December war aims conference as 'heralding the reunion of the Labour and Socialist forces, not only in our country, but throughout the war-afflicted world'.[31]

In February 1918 the Representation of the People Act opened up great new possibilities for the Labour Party by more than doubling the number of working class votes. It introduced virtual manhood suffrage, and a large measure of female suffrage. Equally important, the task of compiling the new electoral registers was transferred from the political parties to town hall officials, so the poorer and less experienced Labour Party would no longer be at a disadvantage. A comparison of the 1918 electorate with that of 1914 suggests that East London constituencies benefited more than most other areas from these changes. In several constituencies which retained their 1914 boundaries (Bethnal Green North East, Bow and Bromley, and South Poplar) the parliamentary electorate trebled.[32] Boundary changes also offered potential advantages to the Labour Party. The urban area of East Ham was detached from the Romford county division and given two members of its own. Representation of West Ham, the south of which was a Labour stronghold, increased from two to four members. On the other hand, Shoreditch and Stepney, which lost one and two members respectively, had traditionally been areas of comparative Labour weakness.

Labour Party leaders realised that improved organisation and an independent political programme were necessary if the new possibilities were to be fulfilled. As part of the general debate over reconstruction, the policies and structure of the party were being intensively re-examined in the autumn of 1917. The new Labour Party constitution, adopted on 26 February 1918, disappointed some socialists by leaving the voting power of the unions intact, and even increasing their influence on the national executive, but the enhanced role of local Labour Parties offered a promising field for socialist propaganda. Still more encouraging was the inclusion of Clause Four: members of the ILP, BSP and NSP believed this paper commitment to socialism could be transformed into the life-blood of the party.

As the socialists turned enthusiastically to building up local Labour Parties in East London, their task was made easier by the changing political mood within the working class itself. The loss of Russia as an ally, not yet fully compensated for by American intervention, made an outright British victory look less likely even to war supporters. Sooner or later peace negotiations must begin. On the home front, too, conditions suggested that war could not continue indefinitely. Casualties had been so heavy that Britain was running short of manpower. In the factories, excessive overtime and speed-up were reducing workers to exhaustion. By January 1918 the influenza epidemic had begun its devastating progress. Meanwhile the food shortage of 1917–18 was causing considerable hardship in poor areas like East London. Government food regulations at first had the effect of driving supplies off the market altogether, rather than making distribution fairer. Few aspects of the war are remembered more vividly than the rigours of the endless food queues, in which the whole family often served their turn day after day. As usual the wealthy seemed able to provide for themselves, and *Herald* articles on 'How They Starve at the Ritz' fuelled the growing resentment.[33] Local newspapers were as much concerned by the effect of the shortages on morale as by their effects on the physical well-being of the population. 'If the East London people were not patient, long-suffering and law-abiding folk, the Government might ere now have received a severe shock', warned the *Observer* in December 1917.[34] But East Londoners' patience was not unlimited. In the *Dreadnought* Melvina Walker described how women who had queued in vain for potatoes ended up forcing a fried fish shop owner to part with his supplies at 1½d per pound.[35] In August 1917 women were prosecuted when an attempt to force a boycott of high meat prices

FOOD CONTROL.

Dedicated to those who think they can see the humour of it.

ended in a riot at Spitalfields.[36] By January 1918, butchers had to queue at Smithfield from 5 a.m. in order to get any supplies at all, and they returned to their shops to find customers 'simply fighting for it. . . they've been glad to get anything—liver, lights, even bones', as one Aldgate butcher told the *East London Advertiser.*[37] An editorial in the same newspaper commented:

> The unequal distribution of food has brought more discontent and dissatisfaction to the people of East London than anything we have known since the war started. Although less terrifying than the air-raids, the food scarcity has produced an amount of exasperation which German terrorism never did. At the back of it all is the feeling that there is plenty of food in the country but that the apportioning of it has been unequal and unjust.

The socialists and co-operators' demands for an end to profiteering and full state control of the food supply gained more public support than ever before. As early as April 1917, the secretary of East Ham trades council compared the food situation in England with that in Russia: 'After the Russian Revolution the Russian towns were flooded with food, showing that there was plenty to be had, and that it was merely a matter of distribution. There were plenty of potatoes in England, but some people were sticking to them. . . The Government should be compelled to take over the food supply.'[38] The trades council went on to organise a series of public meetings in East Ham's Central Park on the same theme, with the assistance of ILP speakers. Even the establishment of local food control committees to enforce strengthened government regulations on prices and distribution did not appease the socialist critics. As usual efforts were made to secure full and effective labour representation, with greater success in Poplar (where four local traders were forced to withdraw[39]) and in West Ham (where a Labour councillor was made committee chairman[40]) than in the other East London boroughs. But the labour movement decided to maintain its own independent Food Vigilance Committees (FVCs) in several areas. An all-London FVC, presided over by A. Barnes, 'the young and strenuous chairman of the Stratford Co-operative Society', pressed for full implementation of WNC food policies,[41] while the East Ham FVC continued to act as a watch dog alongside the official local committee.[42]

Workers' discontent with the food situation and their militant response worried the government. Its sudden decision to put into practice 'socialist' food control policies which it had been resisting throughout the war can be explained by its fear that discontent and war weariness would spill over into mass resistance to the war itself. The peace movement was certainly gaining substantial support by early 1918. A flood of peace resolutions, from East London union branches as well as trades councils and socialist societies, began to arrive at the offices of the *Herald*. Among them were resolutions from the Plaistow branch of the Dockers Union, from Poplar trades council, from Stratford NUR, from the Bakers Union, and eventually even from the London trades council itself.[43] Lloyd George's declaration of war aims to a conference of trade unionists on 5 January shows that the government recognised that majority trade union support could no longer automatically be relied upon. The shop stewards movement was a growing force throughout the country. Though it was less powerful in East London than in the big armament centres of the North and Scotland, London suffered its share of strikes in the summer of 1918, involving dockers, tram, bus and tube workers, gas workers, West Ham council workers, co-operative employees, clothing workers and, most unexpectedly of all, the Metropolitan police. Industrial militancy posed a most serious threat to the war effort. But, though impatience at the government's slowness in seeking peace may have added to the general exasperation about inflation, over-work and food shortages, and although the *East London Observer* hinted darkly at a pacifist-Bolshevik conspiracy,[44] none of these stoppages was intentionally an anti-war strike. Both the *Dreadnought* and the *Call* lamented the strikers' lack of political motivation. The BSP found some consolation in the fact that, from a purely objective viewpoint, 'the prosecution of the class struggle is irreconcilable with support of an imperialist war'.[45] Indeed the Labour Party as a whole, and not just the anti-war socialists, was willing and able to make full use of the *indirect* political advantages presented by industrial unrest. Labour's decision to announce officially the end of the 'political truce' by July 1918 was undoubtedly influenced by the abundant evidence of a growing mood of discontent and independence in the working class. It was widely recognised that a general election must come soon, and the party wanted to be in the best possible position to convert discontent into Labour votes.

Labour Party re-organisation during the final year of the war was not primarily the outcome of the national leadership's decisions on policy and party structure. It is important to recognise that such decisions reflected, rather than caused, important changes in the labour movement and in working class attitudes at local level. It is no coincidence that the raw material for building strong new constituency Labour Parties lay ready to hand in East London. This was the result of patient local political activity throughout the war, as well as of increasingly receptive public opinion in 1917-18. National reorganisation merely acted as a useful spur to a process which had already spontaneously begun. Herbert Morrison, busy transforming the London Labour Party from the loose affiliation of 1914 into a dynamic tool of post-war electoral success, recognised that his main task was to impart administrative rigour to local Labour organisations which already possessed plenty of political drive. 'We do not remember a time when there was so much enthusiasm of the right sort in the London Labour Movement', he wrote in March 1918. 'If we can only steel ourselves against red herrings and hot-heads, and we can only determine that we will get down to detailed organisation as well as rejoice in the contemplation of great ideals—heaven help the capitalist foe!'[46]

The potential danger of Labour's challenge to the older-established parties provoked comment among its opponents as well as its friends. In a survey of the new political outlook under the Representation of the People Act, the *East London Observer* noted that 'little or nothing has been done by existing political organisations, except the Labour Party, to move in the direction of selecting candidates. . . Labour, which must count for so much, is wide awake and working hard.' All the East End constituencies were among those which the London Labour Party 'regarded as potential Labour seats', and which it intended to subject to 'definite siege'.[47] A month later, when the compilation of the new electoral registers had got under way, there was a note of alarm in the *Observer*'s report that 'The Labour Party, with boldly self-assertive advertisement, is scheming to grab the earth and all that's in it'.[48] Why had Labour's position suddenly become so threatening? The following week the *Observer* suggested that it was because, for Labour, the political truce no longer existed, and perhaps never really had done: 'Clearly, the momentous events of the last three years must profoundly affect the organisation of parties, but there has been painful demonstration in many quarters that so far from being dead, during the war party politics had been very much active, sometimes above, but mostly under the ground.'[49]

In Poplar, Labour politics had certainly never been very far underground. As early as October 1916, Poplar trades council and LRC decided to re-adopt George Lansbury as their parliamentary candidate for Bow and Bromley.[50] When political activity really got moving again late in 1917, they decided also to bury the hatchet (after the 1912 by-election row) and to reaffiliate to the national Labour Party. As Lansbury said at the June 1918 Labour Party conference, 'the Movement just now needed every man and woman to build up what the War had pulled down. He had come back because he felt that in the few more years he had to live he must do everything in his power not to divide, but to unite.'[51] As far as Poplar was concerned, reaffiliation meant that the ILP could now thankfully re-join the LRC, and add its full backing to that of the BSP and the trade unions behind Lansbury's candidature. The Poplar LRC was determined to fight a model election campaign. In the first six months of 1918 it increased its affiliated membership by over 3,000 (to 13,550).[52] In June, an impressive conference at Poplar town hall, attended by 54 delegates from 29 trade union and Labour organisations, selected Councillor Sam March of the National Union of Vehicle Workers as the Labour candidate for South Poplar.[53] A few weeks later the *Herald* was advertising for helpers to distribute a special leaflet in support of the candidates, and to take part in a 'systematic canvass of the whole of the constituency'.[54] But the opposition to Lansbury also began organising early. His outspoken pacifist socialism, in the *Herald* as well as in local affairs, had made him many enemies during the war. In October 1917 they demonstrated their unity against him at a public meeting in the Queen's Theatre, Poplar.[55] The subject of the meeting was 'Fighting the Pacifists in East London', and on the platform were four Municipal Alliance councillors (including the mayor), the Liberal MP for Poplar, Sir Alfred Yeo, and the Unionist parliamentary candidate, Captain Wilfrid Allen. A letter was read from Reginald Blair, the Unionist MP for Bow and Bromley, regretting his inability to attend. Speeches at the meeting reflected the level of the political attacks which Lansbury was to face throughout his election campaign. Pacifists were accused of having wormed their way into a dominant position on local committees, where they were 'paid to carry on their propaganda', and from which they should be ejected as 'pro-German foul traitors'. Pacifists as well as Germans were promised a share in reprisals after the war, when they would be treated as 'pariahs and outcasts'. The meeting was held under the auspices of the Poplar branch of the Discharged Soldiers and Sailors Federation, which seems to have had a majority of violently patriotic members with Tory leanings. They later adopted Captain Allen as their own election candidate. But the political diversity within the Federation (to be discussed further in Chapter 7) is illustrated by the fact that in May 1918 Lansbury and other 'well-known pacifists' were invited to take part in the opening ceremony of Bow Discharged Soldiers Federation club.[56]

In the summer of 1918 support for a negotiated peace was strong in Poplar, and the patriotic Federation branch redoubled its attacks on pacifist socialism. As Captain Green warned one meeting: 'when people were tired˙ they were open to suggestions that at other times they would scorn'.[57] The *East London Advertiser* enthusiastically backed the Federation against the 'loud-voiced East London Socialists' and their 'insidious doctrines'.[58] The Federation certainly did not succeed in turning the bulk of the organised working class against Labour politics. They failed in their attempt to take over the traditional East India Dock Gate speaking pitch from trade union and socialist speakers.[59] But their crude rhetoric aroused a certain response among the many workers who had been hostile to Lansbury's pacifism earlier in the war. The accusation of 'pro-Germanism' was designed to distract attention from the issues of social reconstruction on which Labour wished to fight the election, and Lansbury's defeat after a particularly sustained and vicious campaign of this sort shows that it at least partly succeeded. It is interesting to note that the Federation members and their political allies directed their attacks less against Lansbury's newspaper pronouncements than against the war-time role of socialists in local affairs. For example, in May 1918 they attempted to force the Labour members of the military tribunal to retire because of their pacifist bias.[60] It was obviously recognised that voters took a keen interest in such local issues, and that 'labour representatives' were succeeding only too well in making their political presence felt.

In Stepney, too, the Discharged Soldiers and Sailors Federation tried to organise an anti-pacifist witch-hunt. But it remained ineffective, perhaps because local pacifists had not played such a prominent role in war-time administration as in Poplar. The Federation had also to contend with strong Jewish opposition, for example at a 'half-empty' meeting at the Pavilion theatre in June 1918, where an attack on 'shirkers' was shouted down by Jews in the audience.[61] Meanwhile Jewish socialists and trade unionists were making an important contribution to the newly formed Stepney trades council and Labour Party. Effective combination of Jewish and gentile workers in the borough had proved virtually impossible before the war, in the changed circumstances of 1917–18 it became a reality. The BSP was able to build on its earlier Jewish membership after the Russian revolution, and the Herald League had also built up an enthusiastic following among non-Marxist, anti-war Jews. 'Stepney branch members seem to possess enough energy and evangelism to leaven the whole of the East End inhabitants', wrote the Herald League secretary in November

1917.[62] Soon after, the League branch requested the help of the London trades council to form a local trades council.[63] This attempt was made easier by the growth of Stepney trade unionism during the war, as well as by the growth of socialism and the encouragement of Herbert Morrison. On 1 June the *East London Observer* reported that 'a strong committee of active trade union workers' was elected at the Stepney Central Labour Party's inaugural meeting. Amongst them were delegates from most of the Jewish unions, as well as from such major British unions as the Dockers, the NUR, and the NUGW. A Jewish secretary, Oscar Tobin, was chosen.[64] By 24 August three Labour candidates had already been selected to stand in Whitechapel and St. George's, Limehouse and Mile End.[65] Dr. Ambrose (candidate for Whitechapel) was a member of the ILP, and Walter Devenay (candidate for Mile End) was also sympathetic to Lansbury's pacifist socialism.

At the beginning of October 1918, though the war still continued and no election had been announced, the Labour Party in Tower Hamlets was prepared for action. Poplar and Stepney trades councils held a joint conference in the Great Assembly Hall, to present their five local Labour candidates to the public. The *Advertiser* reported that the enormous hall was 'fairly well filled', and that 'many of the trade unions attended in procession preceded by their banners'. Dr Ambrose told the audience: 'Thanks to the war the Labour Party had come to the fore and had now an opportunity of seeing that no longer should the lives of the workers be mortgaged by secret treaties.' Lansbury was still more outspoken: 'In the Labour programme they had their minimum demands put forward, but he was a maximum man. Although he was a Labour candidate he was a convinced, out and out Socialist, a pro-Boer and a Pacifist.'[66] The warm applause which greeted this statement demonstrated the extent of change in the opinions of organised workers during the past year, and to Lansbury must have seemed a reward for the patient 'underground' socialist activity of the war years. Despite the unpopularity of his pacifism, he had been able to retain the confidence and support of the East London labour movement.

A few weeks later the *East London Observer* surveyed the political scene once again. Tories and Liberals were sunk in apathy and confusion, undecided on election policies and even, in Mile End and Whitechapel, undecided on their candidates. 'At present the only clear-cut issue is the Labour party's organised effort to capture the five seats of Poplar, Bow and Bromley, Mile End, Limehouse and Whitechapel. There are no coalition manoeuvres about them. These five candidates stand simply and solely for the "interests" of Labour and nothing else.'[67] Shoreditch had also decided on a Labour candidate, and even Bethnal Green, for so long a stronghold of Progressivism, was considering choosing a candidate, after the trades council's recent decision to affiliate to the national Labour Party.[68]

In East and West Ham, too, political organisation and campaigning by the Labour Party were in full swing before the 'truce' officially ended, and long before an election was declared. The candidature of the national leader of the Labour Party, Arthur Henderson, in East Ham South gave an added interest to local politics. He was accepted by East Ham trades council as a candidate in February 1918, and his defeat in December was certainly not due to political inactivity in the intervening months. Despite his national commitments, Henderson made many major speeches on Labour Party policy in East Ham. He was, of course, relying on the press to carry his message to a wider audience, but his habit of addressing newspaper reporters and the world outside, rather than the East Ham electors, probably cost him votes. It certainly annoyed the East Ham trades council, who would have preferred a local man. When Henderson attended a mass meeting at East Ham town hall, for the purpose of gracefully accepting the candidature, he found himself confronted by trades council hecklers. One tried to move an alternative resolution in favour of a local candidate, whilst another shouted 'We are not going to be bossed by you or anybody else!'[69] Matters were smoothed over when Henderson appointed a local Labour councillor as his election agent,[70] but there may well have been lingering resentment.

In East Ham North efforts were also being made to construct a Labour Party and choose a candidate. A public meeting was called for this purpose at the beginning of July.[71] E.K. Hine was elected as secretary, and he began to recruit members on an individual basis, in accord with the new Labour Party constitution. But this was not to the liking of the East Ham trades council, who sharply informed Mr Hine that only the trades council itself was entitled to establish a new North East Ham Labour Party. As one trades council member put it: 'The quicker we knock these people in the eye and tell them they are not wanted, the better it will be.'[72] Objections to Hine were partly political (he was a keen patriot, and later came under the influence of the National Party), but there was once again a strong element of local and personal jealousy. The trades council persisted in its obstruction, with the result that in December East Ham North ended up with two rival Labour Parties and no Labour candidate.

West Ham Labour Party also had its problems. Will Thorne's and Jack Jones's brand of socialism continued to be very popular with local workers, but after the Bolshevik revolution their attacks on pacifism became so extreme that many members of the BSP and ILP could no longer support them. A split began to develop on the trades council and among the Labour councillors. When Thorne returned from his visit to Russia in May 1917, he was accused by trades council members of having gone there 'on behalf of the government, not on behalf of the workers', and reminded that, 'Men could not represent the robbers and the robbed at the same time.'[73] Despite NSP opposition, the majority voted to send two West Ham delegates to the Leeds Convention. Thorne responded belligerently to criticism from his favourite Becton Road platform, but this did not prevent West Ham LRC from voting against his readoption as a parliamentary candidate at a selection meeting in January 1918.[74] It was an astonishing victory for the pacifists, given Thorne's long and conscientious service as a Labour MP, and his immense local prestige. George Lansbury was moved to plead for him in the *Herald:*

> If, as we hope and believe, the war is drawing to a close, it is high time for men and women who hold progressive and Socialist views to come together prepared to fight the industrial and social evils here at

home. It will suit the capitalists and the landlords to divide us into warring sections, and by so doing prevent Labour coming into its own. We trust the West Ham example will not be followed on either side and that our comrades in the East End will call another meeting, and by unanimous choice once more select Will Thorne to be the standard-bearer for Labour in the Plaistow division of that borough.[75]

But Thorne had no need for such olive branches. He believed himself to be 'a socialist still', and knew that most West Ham workers believed it too. Relying on his popularity and the financial backing of his union and the NSP, he declared the following weekend at Becton Road that he 'intended fighting the Plaistow division against all comers', and won a resounding vote of confidence from 'a larger number than has been seen at the corner for years'.[76] The defeat at the selection meeting was blamed on BSP and ILP manipulation of the vote. The Socialist societies had certainly done their best to sway trade union voting, as the minutes of the North West Ham BSP branch reveal, and as Ben Gardner of the ILP admitted to the Becton Road crowd a fortnight later.[77] Few leading members of the West Ham trades council were not aligned with one or other of the socialist groups. Thorne himself had worked for thirty years to create a politicised trades council, so there was a certain irony in his attempts to justify his defeat on these grounds.

The national Labour Party agreed with Lansbury that the West Ham quarrel should be patched up as quickly as possible. They persuaded the trades council not to run a candidate against Thorne at Plaistow. But a problem still remained, as Jones, who had resigned his own trades council nomination to show his support for Thorne, was determined to stand for Labour in Silvertown. D.J. Davis had been assigned to Silvertown by the trades council, which refused to withdraw once again. So at the forthcoming election Davis and Jones would be in the unhappy situation of competing for the Labour vote. Inevitably this situation and the Plaistow dispute generated a certain amount of heat. In February the eight NSP Labour councillors announced that they could no longer work in the same group as the other eight Labour members of West Ham council (supporters of the BSP and ILP).[78] It was beginning to look as though, in West Ham at least, the split between pro-war and anti-war socialists might become permanent. Yet were matters really as serious as they seemed? The NSP councillors assured the *East Ham Echo* that 'they in no way intend to relax their efforts in support of Socialist and Labour principles'.[79] So long as they lived up to this promise a re-unification seemed inevitable, when the immediate problem of the war had ended. The *Stratford Express* summed up the situation:

> Roughly, we suppose Alderman Thorne and his associates may be taken to represent the thought of practical politicians, and Alderman Davis and his group the idealists of the Socialist Group, but their views and aims may be taken to be, with regard to local and general politics apart from the war, very much what they were, and practically identical.[80]

Despite opposing views on the war, by the autumn of 1918 the Labour Party in East London was undoubtedly in a stronger position than ever before. Both Labour supporters and their opponents believed the party would make big gains at the next election. Until suddenly, on 11 November, the Armistice was announced. Britain had won a more complete victory than most people believed possible at the beginning of the year. In East London, as elsewhere, they rejoiced at the news. But the first excitement was followed by a mood of numbness and exhaustion. The war effort was over, and the cost must be counted. For the many East Londoners employed on war work, relief at the end of the war was coupled with uncertainty about the future. Influenza was once again taking its toll. In the week of the Armistice 2,458 people died in London—more than double the previous week's total.[81]

Within a few days of the declaration of peace, Lloyd George announced that a general election would be held on 14 December. He had decided to take advantage of the situation to confirm his government in power. Exhilarated though they were by peace and by the European revolutions, socialists realised at once that he was likely to succeed.

There were many reasons why a snap election threatened to undo much of the Labour Party's careful preparation. The other parties' lack of preparation could be effectively overcome by use of the Coalition 'coupon' (an official letter expressing government backing for a candidate), and by the simple appeal of victory. The Labour Party's call for peace by negotiation, which had attracted so much support a few months earlier, now appeared to have been mistaken. Military conquest had proved possible, after all. The suddenness of the victory produced a wave of emotion, combining gratitude and vengefulness, neither of which was likely to benefit Labour's cause. On a practical level, the early date of the election made a low poll almost a certainty. Post-war social and economic reconstruction would eventually arouse tremendous political debate, but this could not happen within four weeks of the Armistice. Before people could think and act politically, they needed time to recover. This was especially true of the new working class voters. Another important group who would be unlikely to vote (even if promises to give them the opportunity to do so were kept) were serving soldiers and sailors. Still more than civilians, they needed time to readjust to the peace-time preoccupations of politics.

So from the outset of the official campaign it seemed inevitable that the results of the 1918 election would be an anti-climax for the Labour Party. But its supporters were determined to put up a good fight, nevertheless. They were conscious that the election was a preparation for the future, as well as a test in the present. All over East London, Labour Party activists held a hectic series of meetings to try and put across their policies in the light of the new situation. When the early election was first announced the *East London Observer* rejoiced in the fact that Labour had been 'outwitted' and that 'so far from Labour sweeping the country at the polls, they will have extreme difficulty in even preserving their present numbers in the House of Commons'.[82] But four weeks later the energy of Labour's local campaign had modified such optimism. The *Observer* now felt that Limehouse was 'doubtful' for the Coalition, and Whitechapel and Poplar possible losses, while in Bow and Bromley there was 'grave danger of a miscarriage' (i.e. a Labour win!).[83] Lansbury certainly seemed to be carrying all before him. The enthusiasm of his supporters extended from vigorous heckling at his Tory opponent's meetings to the smashing of Tory committee room windows.[84] But would the number of socialists equal their enthusiasm? Major Reginald Blair had the strong counter-attraction of being a soldier and a believer in 'making the Germans pay'.[85] At Whitechapel Dr Ambrose spoke to 'very large and enthusiastic' audiences on Labour's programme, which he claimed was 'now being stolen by all parties'.[86] Social reform and reconstruction certainly featured prominently in the election manifestos of all East London candidates, though the punishment of Germany was the most popular theme for speeches. Herbert Morrison urged: 'Labour candidates should not be backward in preaching Socialist economics during the election: their opponents will be ready enough to make a brave show with so-called social reform.' But there was too little time, and too few favourable opportunities, for the Labour Party to demonstrate the difference between social reform and socialism, and to turn the campaign into a contest 'between the people of the world and the wrongful owners of the world'.[87]

The quick election deprived the new Bethnal Green Labour Party of the chance to run candidates. It also left the Shoreditch Labour Party with no chance of resolving the political confusion caused by the decision of the popular Progressive Liberal MP for Haggerston, H.G. Chancellor, to run against the Coalition minister Addison for the single Shoreditch seat. The Shoreditch trades council, which had fought unitedly on so many issues during the war and was to reunite politically immediately after the general election, divided down the middle. W.H. Girling (soon to be Shoreditch's first Labour mayor) led one section off to support Chancellor, while Charles Taylor of the Coal Porters Union led the remainder in support of Alfred Walton, the independent Labour candidate who was also general secretary of Taylor's own union.[88] The Stratford division of West Ham was also left in disarray when the Labour candidate resigned, leaving no time to choose and campaign for a successor. But elsewhere in West and East Ham the election campaign was fought as vigorously by Labour as in Poplar and Stepney.

Ben Gardner went through with a full programme of local meetings at Upton, though the candidature of a well-known pacifist in this new division looked a forlorn hope from the start.[89] Labour's main chance in West Ham obviously lay in the southern Plaistow and Silvertown divisions. Victory in the war was a bonus to patriotic socialists such as Thorne and Jones. But neither man staked his election appeal on the popularity of patriotism alone. Both stressed the socialist nature of their reconstruction proposals, and both directed their propaganda primarily at trade unionists. Thorne's success was guaranteed by the fact the Coalition decided not to stand a candidate against him. In Silvertown, however, a Coalition Unionist was in the field against Jones and it seemed possible that the split Labour vote might result in defeat. The election campaign was less a political than a personal battle between Jones and Davis. By the week before the election it was clear that Jones was winning outright. Not only was he a much more effective public speaker than Davis, but he also forced the trades council candidate on to the defensive by attacking his record during the war.[90] Jones's claim to be 'the official Trade Union candidate' was supported by the fact that he could summon almost the whole force of the NUGW to his aid, from its general secretary to the Silvertown branches which he had done much himself to organise.[91] At his last election meeting Davis virtually conceded to Jones, claiming that 'it was better to lose the fight with clean hands than to win it with dirty hands'.[92]

Meanwhile in East Ham Henderson was suffering from more than usually scurrilous attacks on his lack of patriotism. His opponents—a popular local Independent and a Coalition Liberal backed by the British Workers League—accused him of being not only a pacifist, but a Bolshevik as well. In vain he attempted to counter such attacks with high-minded speeches on the international outlook. His talk of 'International goodwill' conveyed nothing but pro-Germanism in a 'coupon' election campaign. As the *East Ham Echo* commented: 'He says he is not for a "revengeful peace" but for "just retribution". Just what does he mean by that, because in spite of the importance of the Labour programme a great many votes will depend upon it.'[93]

Before Henderson had had a chance to answer the latest collection of slanders (that he was 'a friend of Lenin and Trotsky', and 'a German under an assumed name'[94]), election day arrived. Even the local press, which was solidly behind the Coalition, did not feel that it had been a satisfactory campaign. 'Unreality is stamped on the whole proceeding', complained the *East London Observer,* and urged the government to call soon 'an election in fact and not in name'.[95] 'To be candid there has been a certain amount of indifference on the part of many to an election which is really fraught with grave issues', reported the *East Ham Echo.*[96] The *Stratford Express* also remarked on the 'surprisingly small interest' shown locally.[97] Apathy continued to be the dominant mood even on election day itself. 'Bad weather, little enthusiasm and no excitement is the story which is told about last Saturday's polling in most East End constituencies'.[98] It was, as the *Echo* put it, 'as dull as a friendly football match without goals'.[99] This could only be bad news for the Labour candidates. When the results were declared, forecasts of a low turn-out proved correct. Over the whole country 57.6 per cent voted, and about 25 per cent of soldiers and sailors.[100] Nine of the fourteen East London constituencies failed to reach the London average of 45.5 per cent, in five less than 40 per cent of the electorate voted. For a great many East Londoners, the 1918 general election had been an irrelevant formality.

To most commentators at the time, the one overwhelming feature of the results was the unprecedented scale of the Coalition victory. East London followed the national trend by returning eleven Coalition Members.[101] As *Labour Leader* admitted, Labour Party supporters' first reaction was 'one of disappointment akin to dismay'.[102] Yet consolation was not hard to find. The *Labour Leader* editorial continued. 'Surveying more carefully the testimony of the polls, we now discern that the triumph of the reaction is by no means so great or so unimpeachable as it at first appeared.' In East London the only two successful Labour candidates were the patriots, Thorne and Jones. However it was immensely encouraging to the local Labour Parties to find their candidates in second place in six of the other eight constituencies they contested. Where Labour had not won, it had at least succeeded in turning itself into the main opposition party—and this despite the low poll and the pacifist tag which put so many Labour candidates at a temporary disadvantage. Labour had fought to within overtaking distance of the Liberal and Tory Parties, both of which suffered a steep decline in their proportion of votes compared to pre-war elections. The increased size of the working class electorate and the increased number of Labour candidates were obviously partly responsible for this outcome. But the achievement was of fundamental significance, nevertheless. More had changed in East London politics than merely the rules of the game.

The *East London Observer* greeted the election results with a misplaced sigh of relief: 'There was opportunity for a vast upheaval, for a mighty change, and yet not only has nothing happened, but the old Parliamentary representation of East End divisions for all practical purposes remains the same.' However the editorial was well aware that this apparent stability might not last long. The new House of Commons was 'merely a stop-gap body designed to secure us the full fruits of victory. . . another and quite different appeal to the people must be inevitable in a few months' time.'[103] Socialists also turned their attention towards the future in eager anticipation. George Lansbury wrote:

> Our faith in democracy is not at all shaken. It is perfectly true that a great number of voters went to the poll with nothing clear in their heads except some nonsense about hanging the Kaiser and making the Germans pay. On the other hand, it is equally true that a great number went to the poll with a perfectly clear idea in their heads of social reconstruction, and that when the next election comes—and it must come soon—those who desire social reconstruction, and know how they want it brought about, will be far more numerous than now. Education is a slow process and we are only at the beginning of it. The future is inevitably ours. . . The next election will be our chance.[104]

NOTES

1. *Labour Leader,* 24 September and 1, 8 and 22 October 1914.
2. *Justice,* 4 March 1915.
3. BSP *Annual Conference Report,* 1916, 3.
4. *Justice,* 27 April 1916.
5. Interview with Harold Steele (a life-long pacifist brought up in Poplar; conscientious objector and ILP member during the war).
6. *Call,* 16 November 1916. East London Speakers included representatives of local branches of the ILP, BSP, WSF and Herald League, and of West Ham, Poplar and Bethnal Green trades councils.
7. *Dreadnought,* 30 December 1916.
8. *Dreadnought,* 6 January 1917.
9. *Dreadnought,* 21 April 1917.
10. *Dreadnought,* 6 January 1917.
11. *ELA,* 16 June 1917, and *ELO,* 23 June 1917.
12. *Herald,* 31 March 1917.
13. *ELO,* 31 March 1917.
14. *Herald,* 7 April 1917.
15. Lansbury Collection, volume 7, item 330.
16. Lansbury Collection, volume 7, item 348.
17. *Herald,* 16 June 1917.
18. *Labour Leader,* 7 June 1917.
19. *Dreadnought,* 30 June 1917.
20. *Call,* 14 June 1917.
21. BSP North West Ham Branch Minute Book, 12 August 1917 and 20 January 1918.
22. BSP *Annual Conference Report,* 1918, 29 and 35.
23. *Call,* 23 May 1917.
24. *Herald,* 14 July 1917.
25. *Call,* 11 October 1917 and 3 January 1918, *Herald,* 20 October and 3 November 1917.
26. *Call,* 30 August 1917.
27. *Herald,* 17 November 1917.
28. *ELA,* 15 September 1917.
29. *Call,* 2 August 1917.
30. e.g. *Dreadnought,* 25 August 1917, *Labour Leader,* 16 August 1917.
31. *Labour Leader,* 3 January 1918.
32. *London Statistics,* XXIV, 1913-14, 20-21 and F.W.S. Craing, *British Parliamentary Election Results 1885-1918* (1974), 206-207.
33. *Herald,* 24 November 1917.
34. *ELO,* 22 December 1917.
35. *Dreadnought,* 17 March 1917.
36. *ELA,* 4 August 1917.
37. *ELA,* 11 January 1918.
38. *EE,* 13 April 1917.
39. *ELO,* 1 September 1917.
40. *SE,* 26 January 1918.
41. *Co-op News,* 22 September 1917.
42. *EE,* 18 January 1918.
43. *Herald,* 9 February, 2 and 9 March, 22 June 1918.
44. *ELO,* 18 May, 1 June and 14 September 1918.
45. *Call,* 12 September 1918.

46. *London Labour Party Circular,* March 1918.
47. *ELO,* 26 January 1918.
48. *ELO,* 16 February 1918.
49. *ELO,* 23 February 1918.
50. *Herald,* 14 October 1916.
51. Labour Party *Conference Report,* June 1918, 111.
52. *Herald,* 31 August 1918.
53. *ELO,* 1 June 1918.
54. *Herald,* 7 September 1918.
55. *ELA,* 27 October 1917.
56. *ELA,* 4 May 1918.
57. *ELA,* 15 June 1918.
58. Ibid.
59. Ibid.
60. *ELA,* 25 May 1918.
61. *ELA,* 8 June 1918.
62. *Herald,* 8 September 1917.
63. London Trades Council Minutes, 29 November 1917.
64. *ELO,* 1 June 1918 and Stepney Labour Party *Annual Report* 1919-20.
65. *Herald,* 24 August 1918.
66. *ELA,* 5 October 1918.
67. *ELO,* 9 November 1918.
68. *Herald,* 26 October 1918.
69. *EE,* 8 March 1918.
70. *EE,* 21 June 1918.
71. *EE,* 5 July 1918.
72. Ibid.
73. *SE,* 2 June 1917.
74. *SE,* 12 January 1918.
75. *Herald,* 19 January 1918.
76. *SE,* 16 January 1918.
77. BSP North West Ham Branch Minute Book, 7 and 21 October 1917, 6 January 1918 and *SE* 6 February 1918.
78. *SE,* 6 February 1918.
79. *EE,* 9 February 1918.
80. *SE,* 9 February 1918.
81. *SE,* 9 November 1918.
82. *ELO,* 16 November 1918.
83. *ELO,* 7 and 14 December 1918.
84. *ELA* and *ELO,* 7 December 1918.
85. *ELO,* 14 December 1918.
86. *ELO,* 7 December 1918.
87. *London Labour Chronicle,* December 1918.
88. *Hackney Gazette,* 29 November and 6 December 1918.
89. *SE,* 30 October and 30 November 1918.
90. *SE,* 30 November and 7 December 1918.
91. *SE,* 20 November 1918.
92. *SE,* 11 December 1918.
93. *EE,* 22 November 1918.
94. *EE,* 3 January 1919.
95. *ELO,* 14 December 1918.
96. *EE,* 13 December 1918.
97. *SE,* 30 November 1918.

98. *ELA*, 21 December 1918.
99. *EE*, 20 December 1918.
100. Miliband, R., *Parliamentary Socialism* (1961), 64 and Marwick, A., *The Deluge* (1965), 264.
101. See Appendix, pp. 241-2.
102. *Labour Leader*, 2 January 1919.
103. *ELO*, 4 January 1919.
104. *Herald*, 4 January 1919.

CHAPTER 4

TRADE UNIONS: ADAPTATION AND GROWTH

East London had been notorious for the weakness and
instability of its unions up till 1914—its port 'the great
unmanageable',[1] its sweated trades 'the despair of all social
reformers',[2] and unionisation even of its larger factories
hampered by an over-supply of cheap labour. The war unexpectedly provided the period of prolonged prosperity
needed to break this vicious circle of disorganisation and
poverty. Government contracts flooded into the area, soon,
rising profits and full employment were providing the opportunity, and inflated food prices the incentive, to organise as
never before. By 1918 there were about 80 per cent more
trade unionists in East London than there had been in
1914.[3] For once, East London's trade union growth had
not merely equalled the national rate, but surpassed it.
Unlike those recruited during earlier mass strikes, most of
the new members came to stay. Though East London shared
in the national declines in membership during later periods
of high unemployment, there was never a complete reversion
to the chronic and destructive instability of the pre-war
years. One of the most hopeful signs for the future was the
fact that war-time recruits to trade unionism came from the
whole range of East London's established industries, rather
than merely from such temporary occupations as munitions
manufacture.

Trade unions exist to defend workers' living standards.
This fact has often caused a certain impatience amongst
high-minded socialists who believe their task is to steer a
feet-dragging majority of unionists within the Labour Party
along the path of political progress. But in fact the primacy
of the trade unions' economic aims made it far more difficult
(as well as more important) for war-time governments to

maintain an industrial than a political truce. A disciplined war economy was achieved through persuasion, threats—and concessions. The trade unions were rewarded by a fair amount of success in their efforts to obtain war bonuses, to secure protective guarantees in return for the temporary suspension of union practices, and to prevent full-scale industrial conscription. Their right to organise was re-inforced by arbitration legislation; their organised strength enabled them to retain even a *de facto* right to strike. It would be a mistake, therefore, to see the unions' role during the war as purely defensive. Trade unions emerged from the war stronger, in almost every respect, than when they entered it, and with a new-found confidence which was to spill over significantly into the political life of the labour movement.

Yet when the war began, few local or national union leaders foresaw any possible benefits. Alongside the war appeared the alarming spectres of trade dislocation and un-employment. The swift and unsatisfactory ending of a lengthy London building workers' strike was less a proof of patriotism than a battening down of the hatches in the face of economic storms to come. Past experience had proved, especially for the general unions, the disastrous results of unemployment. No doubt the prospect of diminishing membership and declining power encouraged the trade union leadership to resolve, on 24 August, 'that an immediate effort be made to terminate all existing trade disputes, whether strikes or lock-outs, and whenever new points of difficulty arise during the war period a serious attempt should be made by all concerned to reach an amicable settlement before resorting to a strike or lock-out.'[4] Opinions on the war itself, at this stage, were as confused among trade unionists as else-where in the labour movement. The 1913 Trades Union Congress had condemned arms manufacture and pledged the unions to 'do everything possible to make war impossible'.[5] Even the hysterical propaganda of the early weeks of war could not entirely efface memories of these resolutions, and of the fraternal presence of German trade unionists at the Congress. Ben Tillett condemned the war as 'absolutely wanton and brutal in every feature'.[6] Will Thorne, another unionist of great influence in East London who was later to

104

become a fervent patriot, wrote sorrowfully of the 'rudely shattered' hopes of internationalism.[7] From the earliest days of the war, trade union leaders were unanimously determined to continue to protect their members. At national level they joined forces with the socialists and co-operators on the WNC. Locally, union branches held emergency meetings to discuss relief arrangements for the families of men called to the war, and representation on the various committees being set up to deal with distress. The *Railway Review,* the popular weekly journal of the National Union of Railwaymen, reports the activity of East London Branches on 28 August:

Canning Town. Local Distress Committee was under discussion and steps are being taken to ensure the Trade Unions of this district being represented.

Poplar 1. We are represented on the local distress committee. Our branch distress committee has done good work in the short time it has been together for the wives and families of our 40 members who have been called to the front.

Poplar 2. Particulars of reservists called up sent to the Poplar Labour Representation Committee.

Royal Mint Street. Secretary instructed to write to City Council and Stepney borough for representation on Relief Committee.

Stratford 1. Decided to ask the West Ham Citizens Committee to co-opt three representatives from this branch.

Representation on local committees was an important political issue for socialists, and no doubt trade unionists who were also socialists shared this view. But the difference in view between political and purely trade union activists is illustrated by the disagreements which arose in West Ham. Several union branches objected strongly to the trades council assuming overall authority in the selection of 'labour representatives': they felt that individual unions should have been consulted instead.[8] Union organisation itself was undoubtedly the most important weapon of all in the battle against war-time distress. This message was driven home at every opportunity by union leaders. In December 1914 Thorne sharply criticised members who were contributing to the Prince of Wales fund at the expense of their union payments: 'What will our fellows, who are now in the fighting line, think when they return victorious from the battle field if they find that their mates who stayed at home have yielded to the enemy on the industrial field?'[9] The *Railway Review* urged NUR members to 'Keep Under the Old Umbrella—Needed Now as Much as Ever!'[10] The anxious tone of such promptings, especially by the unskilled unions, was the result of steep falls in membership during the early months of the war. Membership of the skilled unions was less volatile—especially since the wider range of benefits sometimes included unemployment pay— but in the long-term serious unemployment must inevitably weaken them too. By Christmas East London branches of the National Amalgamated Furnishing Trades Association and the Cigar Makers Mutual Association were in deep financial trouble.[11] But the worst was over. As employment improved, the tide of union membership turned also. By the spring of 1915 very few unions had failed to make up their losses of the previous autumn, and economic advance (rather than the exhortations of union leaders) had set going the huge expansion of trade unionism which was to continue throughout the war.

Trade unionists' failure to envisage such an expansion in 1914 was part of a general failure to anticipate the enormous demands which World War would make on the British economy. The government itself took many months to adjust. Gradually more and more East London workers found themselves directly or indirectly supplying the insatiable needs of the armed forces. Though it had no room for new national factories, East London made its contribution to the manufacture of weapons. The old-established London Small Arms Company (LSA), situated by Victoria Park, was producing a modest total of 250 rifles a week in July 1914.[12] Within a year output had been driven up to over 2,000 a week, through expansion of the workforce, the introduction of night shifts, and massive investment in the

KEEP UNDER THE OLD UMBRELLA--NEEDED NOW AS MUCH AS EVER.

latest equipment. Though the LSA's grand war-time total of 364,214 rifles was merely a small proportion of those manufactured elsewhere, this rate of production increase provides some indication of the scale and urgency of government demand. Other, larger munitions factories lay just beyond East London, drawing thousands of workers from within the area. Small arms and machine guns were produced at Enfield Lock; national projectile factories were built at Ponders End and on the Hackney Marshes; a national cartridge and box repair factory opened at Dagenham Dock early in 1916; while just across the river lay the giant Woolwich Arsenal.[13] The Arsenal's labour force rose from a mere 8,500 in June 1914 to a peak of 74,467 in May 1917. Over 28,000 of these workers were women.[14] Unfortunately it is impossible to calculate accurately how many of them commuted daily from East London, but scraps of evidence demonstrate that the number was large. There were complaints as early as November 1914 of the congestion in the two foot tunnels under the river. By 1917 three extra ferry services were in operation.[15] East Londoners were certainly among the thousands of Arsenal workers recruited into trade unions. In October 1915 the *Workers Union Record* announced 'the appointment of Brother G. Neal as collector in the Royal Arsenal, Woolwich, owing to the large number of Stratford men in the works'.

Munitions work could not be undertaken without the assistance of skilled engineers, and by January 1915 nearly all those who remained in East London were engaged on such work in one form or another. W.H. Beveridge soon discovered this when, as Assistant General Secretary to the Ministry of Munitions, he tried to increase the flow of men into armament factories. Urgent appeals for spare labour went out to every engineering firm in London, but 159 firms in East Ham, Stratford, Canning Town, Poplar, Shoreditch and Stepney could offer between them a mere 8 men who were free to move.[16] The only solution was to encourage sub-contracting of less complex processes to firms which could carry them out with unskilled workforces. This was exactly what the many small metal work firms in East London were hoping for, and soon the demand for munitions, with all the urgency and high profits and opportunities for union organisation which accompanied it, was permeating down to the lowest levels of the industry. Beveridge wrote despairingly of the difficulty of compiling complete lists of government suppliers: 'Sub-contracting goes to the third, fourth and fifth degree and the contractors will certainly not, as a rule, be able to give the names of the sub-sub-contractors.'[17] Although small foundries existed even in Whitechapel, Poplar and West Ham remained the centres of engineering. Eleven of the thirteen East London branches of the ASE were in these boroughs, together with six branches of the Boilermakers Society. The West Ham chemical industry also entered the sphere of munitions manufacture. The adaptation of a disused soda factory for TNT purification was to end, in January 1917, with the Silvertown Explosion.[18] Becton gasworks supplied the toluol needed for TNT.[19] From Henley's Telegraph Works and the Silvertown Rubber Company, two of the largest firms on the West Ham riverfront, came a large proportion of the government's rubber goods' requirements, from trench cables to aeroplane tyres and the first all-British magnetos.[20]

The ramifications of the industrial war-effort spread far beyond actual armaments production. Lists of government contractors published in the official *Labour Gazette* reveal the huge variety of other products which East London supplied to the War Office.[21] Over eighty items were produced by one or more firms in the area, ranging through the alphabet from 'aprons', 'armlets' and 'bedding' to 'weighing machines', 'wire rope' and 'wood boxes', alongside the mundane 'drill clothing', 'haversacks', 'paint' and 'tents' appear less predictable items such as 'embroidered bags', 'portable canvas mangers', 'toys' (?) and 'water testing cases'. Small East London firms often lacked modern machinery, but their adaptability and cheapness were important advantages from the government's point of view.

Under-payment was, of course, one time-honoured way of reducing costs. The war gave sweating a new lease of life in the early months. The government fixed flat rates for army clothing, but refused to fix a minimum amount to be paid in wages on each garment. Much of the sub-sub-contracting

109

took place (as in engineering) beyond the government's knowledge or control, and at appallingly low wages. In the autumn of 1914 Sylvia Pankhurst found women sewing eyelets for 1s 8d per 400 (giving a total weekly wage of under 6s), and finishing shirts for 2d per dozen (6s–7s per week).[22] Her revelations were soon confirmed by other investigators, such as the Stepney Public Health Committee and the *Toynbee Record*. 'Government sweating' extended beyond the clothing industry to firms making brushes, boxes, paper bags and many types of food and drink. During the war the long-standing obstacles to organising sweated workers in trade unions did not disappear. Although uniforms, food, and other non-military equipment were essential to the forces, the industries which supplied them were less thoroughly covered by war-time legislation than the armaments and transport industries. The demarcation line between 'munitions' and other army supplies was constantly shifting during the war, as the government found it necessary to bring more and more industries under its control, but the great majority of East London clothing, equipment and food firms were permanently excluded from the more stringent regulations of the Munitions Acts. They were not unaffected by the web of industrial controls, however. Even in the sweated industries there were new incentives to organise. Employees could make use of the arbitration machinery set up to regulate the munitions industries, and could sometimes share in the benefits obtained from official encouragement of employer-union consultation. From 1915 onwards labour shortages, high demand and high profits helped at least to moderate the difficulties facing union organisers.

Six months after the war began, East London's war production was in full swing. Business was not only 'as usual', but very much better than usual. Workers in trades threatened with long-term slackness, such as building and luxury dress-making, were adjusting to the situation either by enlistment or transfer to new occupations. The indoor workforce of the London tailoring industry had increased by 60 per cent. The food industries were 'very good with much overtime', and a shortage of workers especially in chocolate factories ('there being a great demand for chocolate in military camps'). Few East London carpenters remained unemployed, thanks to a flood of government contracts for beds, tables, benches and army huts.[23] Transport workers were seriously over-worked. By January 1915 congestion in the docks was so great that 'men were being drafted in from Southampton and parts of the east coast'; average daily employment was nearly 30 per cent higher than a year earlier.[24]

Unemployment vanished fastest of all in the industries directly connected with armaments. It is not surprising that the engineers were the first workers successfully to demand higher wages. War Office contractors in London granted them a general 7½ per cent increase in December 1914. However ASE members soon discovered that whether or not the increase actually appeared depended very much on their own efforts. At this date the industrial truce was a purely voluntary arrangement, even in munitions industries. The methods chosen by the ASE during the next few months to enforce the new wage rates demonstrated the union's readiness to break the truce. In February the ASE *Journal* urged members to 'immediately transfer their services to those firms who are paying higher wages'. East London members working for R. Legg and Sons, Eagle Wharf, passed on this threat, and found it 'had the desired effect'. In March fitters at the London Small Arms factory downed tools, after a constitutional approach to the management failed to elicit the increase. At the British Alizarine Company, Silvertown, an ASE official joined up all the non-union engineers before successfully negotiating the new rates, and double time for Sunday working.[25] By April the *Journal* was able to report that, despite a few continuing skirmishes with small firms, the 7½ per cent rise was 'now general'. A month later the employers had been pressured into promising a further over-all increase; the whole process of local threats and negotiations began over again.

It is easy to see why the government concluded in the summer of 1915 that a strong Munitions Act was necessary. Disputes in East London were minor, compared with the massive Clyde strikes, but even in the sweated industries employers were finding that unless they raised wages they could not keep the workers they needed to fulfil urgent government contracts. Wage increases provide a more telling index of industrial militancy than strike figures, since so many employers preferred concession to confrontation. Trade unionists regarded the industrial truce as a bargain, not a surrender. As soon as the bargain began to look one-sided, because employers were profiting from the war while workers struggled to pay higher prices, the truce ceased to function. Even the most patriotic union leaders did not consider it their duty to stand quietly by as real wages fell. A final attempt to shore up the truce by voluntary means—the Treasury Agreements of March 1915—foundered amid continuing unrest in the main armament centres. In July 1915 the Munitions of War Act established the framework of legal restrictions within which the trade unions worked for the rest of the war. Strikes in the munitions industries became illegal. Disputes must be referred to the Board of Trade, which would arrange arbitration. Those firms most closely involved in war production became 'controlled establishments', in which all union restrictive practices were compulsorily suspended. In return, workers received guarantees that wage rates would be safeguarded (increases being sanctioned by the Ministry of Munitions), and also that profits would be restricted. The movement of workers engaged on munitions manufacture was to be limited by leaving certificates, issued by the employers, without which no munitions worker could obtain a new job. To enforce this provision, and other regulations which could be dealt with at local level, munitions tribunals were established.

The trade unions had little choice about accepting the new Act. The military necessity for it was obvious. The only possible resistance would have been resistance to the war itself. In East London, George Lansbury and his supporters hastily formed a Trades Union Rights Committee in the hope of encouraging such resistance. More than four hundred trade unionists attended its founding conference on 5 July. Eighteen Committee members were chosen from fourteen trade unions, including several from the building industry, wood working, engineering and the railways.[26] Despite Lansbury's decision to stay on the side-lines, inevitably most of the Committee were political activists who shared his views. George Belt (Dockers Union) was the national secretary of the Herald League, Tom Quelch (National Union of Journalists) was a leading figure in the BSP, W.F. Watson (ASE) and J.V. Wills (Building Workers Industrial Union) were well known for their syndicalism. The treasurer of TURC was Joe Banks (NUR), secretary of Poplar trades council and LRC, and the Committee's manifesto on Trade Union Rights was drafted by William Mellor, less known for his membership of the NUJ than for his activities as a Fabian and *Herald* journalist. When the manifesto was published, some Committee members were immediately in hot water with their unions for having claimed to be 'representatives'. This was a bad start for an organisation seeking acceptance in the trade union world. However, TURC refuted press and union claims that it was a 'wrecking organisation' by describing its aims purely as propaganda. Its manifesto urged unionists to 'preserve what rights still remain, and refuse steadfastly to surrender another inch to our allied foes—the capitalists and the politicians', the war was 'being used as an excuse for the undermining of rights and privileges won by long years of hard and patient industrial effort'.[27]

At a propaganda level, such a manifesto could hardly fail to rouse some response amongst trade unionists alarmed and confused by the terms of the new Act. TURC made sure that it got a wide readership, by sending fifty copies to every trades council in Britain, and a dozen to every union branch for which they had an address. East London, as one of the areas best known to the committee, certainly received its fair share. Within a few weeks both Poplar and Bethnal Green trades councils had endorsed the manifesto. The Poplar trades council (with Banks's encouragement!) contributed 10s to TURC, and asked for manifestos to be distributed to all its affiliated branches.[28] But although the manifesto was quite widely welcomed, TURC was not a success. Its proposals were too vague, its political motives too obvious, its trade union status too uncertain. A TURC-organised lobby against the Munitions Act at the TUC failed to materialise. In 1916 TURC redirected its efforts into forming a London Workers Committee, on the Clyde

113

model. When this too failed to grow, for reasons which will be considered in Chapter 5, the organisation was finished. It quietly dissolved in January 1917.[29]

Meanwhile trade unionists had been coming to terms with war-time industrial legislation in other ways. They had discovered that, like much other labour legislation, the Munitions Act could be influenced in practice by union activity. If workers were strongly organised, they could make effective use of the arbitration machinery to defend their living standards. Though strikes in the munitions industries were illegal, negotiations were not. The economic and military situation still left the unions with good cards to play, and the more they increased membership the stronger their negotiating position became. Trade unions in areas like East London, where before the war it had been very difficult to recruit members, stood particularly to gain from the new situation.

By August 1916 nearly a hundred East London firms were controlled establishments, and arbitration was compulsory (though the 'dilution' of skilled by unskilled labour was not) in the many other firms covered by leaving certificate provisions. The number of arbitration cases steadily increased. Reports in the *Labour Gazette* make it clear that unionised workers were both more likely to make claims, and more likely to be successful. The arbitrators were realists who understood that successful settlements must be based on an accurate assessment of the balance of power between employers and workmen, rather than on abstract economic principles. If the union was strong, the award would be larger. This lesson not only recruited new members, but encouraged union branches and even separate unions to combine in support of joint wage claims. Industry-wide arbitration awards became increasingly common during 1917, and where no national arrangement existed, regional claims often grouped East London workers with those elsewhere in the capital. Only during the last few months of the war, when wages militancy was at its height and arbitration procedures had become very well known, can a few exceptions be found to the general rule of trade union representation before the arbitrators. Arbitration, like the strike weapon, was a last resort, the result of a breakdown in negotiations. During the war the unions won a great many concessions without resorting to it. The process of growth and adaptation can be demonstrated in more detail by a closer look at the war-time progress of some of East London's main unions.

Unions of traditionally low-paid unskilled and semi-skilled workers grew faster than any others. The Gasworkers Union was already the area's largest union in 1914, with nineteen branches extending over every East London borough. Membership was open to 'all persons engaged in any kind of general labour in any industry,'[30] and the 1916 change of name to 'National Union of General Workers' re-emphasised its broad appeal. Will Thorne was a pragmatist in matters of union organisation, despite his socialist beliefs. He accepted the Munitions Acts with equanimity because he foresaw the extent to which the new conditions could be turned to his members' advantage. Large numbers of arbitration cases were fought by the NUGW on behalf of East London members, and the union's *Quarterly Reports* record still larger numbers of wage claims settled by negotiation. Membership rose fast, especially in the controlled establishments. By 1918 the quarterly income of the biggest branches (Bromley East, Canning Town and West Ham) had quadrupled. The West Ham chemical industry was almost entirely unionised. Engineering labourers were another major source of recruitment: membership at the London Small Arms factory increased nearly six-fold between 1914 and 1918. Many of the new members were female 'dilutees'. But NUGW branches were consolidated in local industries which employed women in peace-time as well as in war. Branches formed in the sugar refineries and other food factories in 1911–12 won wage increases and new members, and union organisation in the Bryant and May match factory extended to the two other main match factories in the area. Even in trades where specialised unions existed, such as the tobacco industry and municipal employment, the NUGW negotiated and recruited successfully.

The NUGW expanded more rapidly in East London than it did nationally, though its national membership trebled.

The greater local increase can be explained by the union's historical roots in the area, and by the continuous, dominant presence of Will Thorne. Union propaganda and politics were inextricably mixed in Thorne's Sunday morning orations at Becton Road corner. His speeches and writings, and those of his supporters, were determinedly publicised throughout the length and breadth of East London. No other leader of a national union could match his reputation as the champion of the working man. It is not surprising that for many East Londoners the NUGW was *the* union, a focus for local loyalty as well as a powerful national organisation.

The importance of such loyalty is demonstrated by the contrasting history of the Workers Union in East London. Throughout the war the Workers Union devoted itself single-mindedly to making the largest number of new members in the shortest possible time. Its growth rate, in absolute terms, was unequalled by any other British union. Yet Workers Union organisers encountered considerable difficulties in East London. In 1914 the area was represented in the annual branch balance sheets by only three small branches, two of which were in their first year of existence. Two more were formed in 1915, but progress was so unsatisfactory during the following year that the district secretary decided to take over personal responsibility for the area.[31] Within a few months the situation had begun to improve: a new branch at Victoria Park recruited workers from the Hackney munitions factories, and Bethnal Green and Stepney engineering labourers joined up. In February 1917 a breakthrough was achieved at the Silvertown Rubber factory, when the employers agreed to negotiate with Workers Union representatives. 'This is probably the first time that a trade union official has been well received in this factory, and establishes a position which should encourage our members to go forward and bring in the many who do not belong to us yet.'[32] By June Canning Town was 'becoming one of our live branches. We have begun to reap the fruits of our propaganda in Silvertown, and a large number of new members have joined up. I hope the new members will keep it up. Further meetings are being organised to rope in those still outside.'[33] Whether the members would 'keep it up' was always a source of anxiety in the Workers Union, with its extremely high membership turn-over. However, 1918 was another successful year. The Workers Union was increasingly present at arbitration cases involving East London firms and the April issue of the *Trade Union Worker* recorded new branches at Mile End, Minories and East Ham, prophesying hopefully: 'If all our members in the East End make up their minds to double the size of our Union here during the next six months it can easily be done.'

There was certainly plenty of room left for expansion, as the soaring membership of 1919–20 proved. This probably explains why the Workers Union and the NUGW were able to co-exist peacefully in East London. Relations between the two unions were generally co-operative rather than competitive, even though branches of both unions occasionally existed in one factory.[34] Despite the achievements of 1917–18, the Workers Union lagged some way behind the older union in East London at the end of the war. The Workers Union's largest branch (Canning Town) claimed 1,000 members in 1918, which was considerably less than the 3,000 members in Bromley East NUGW. Branch balance sheets record much smaller sums paid into Workers Union branches than to those of the NUGW, despite the fact that the former had a popular Sick Fund, which encouraged a high proportion of the members to pay 6d instead of 3d weekly contributions.[35] The Gasworkers Union had already begun to organise labourers in most of the large East London factories by 1914, so it was able to build on solid foundations. The Workers Union was left mainly with the smaller factories to organise, and those where the employers were traditionally hostile to union activity. Even its exceptionally generous benefits, and its brash newspaper advertising campaign, failed to attract members away from the NUGW.

One of the main reasons for the Workers Unions' success nationally was its special appeal to women workers. Women members received similar benefits to men, despite lower entrance fees and subs, and there was even a special marriage dowry benefit (or a lump sum at fifty) in return for an extra 3d a week contribution. Though these terms attracted many

117

East London women to the Workers Union, the female membership of the NUGW expanded still faster. The National Federation of Women Workers, which had also been making determined efforts to unionise East London women before the war, shared the NUGW's advantage of a head-start. Women joined trade unions during the war for many of the same reasons as men. Labour shortages put a higher potential value on their work than ever before; after the introduction of conscription the number of women directly replacing men workers trebled to nearly one and a half million. Most of these 'substitutes' were employed in the munitions industries, and especially in the government's own factories, but there was also a rise in the proportion of women workers in such important East London industries as clothing, food, drink, tobacco and transport. It seems likely that there was less transfer of female labour to munitions manufacture in East London than in other places where few opportunities for female industrial labour had existed before the war. However the histories of local firms and trade union records show that thousands of local women found new employment in the Poplar and West Ham engineering and chemical works which serviced nearby armament factories.

Despite the efforts of the Gasworkers and the NFWW before the war, average women's wages remained less than half the level of men's in 1914.[36] Poverty, underemployment and home work were still more formidable obstacles to female than to male unionisation in East London, and the problems of the first weeks of the war threatened to eclipse the existing NFWW branches. The women at Morton's pickle factory, for example, were immediately placed on a two-day week because of the disruption to the firm's export trade, and could no longer afford union payments out of their reduced wages.[37] But as employment picked up, union membership recovered with it. The NFWW organised one of the first arbitration appeals under the 1915 Munitions Act, on behalf of female packing case workers in East and South London: higher time rates and equal piece rates for women 'substitutes' were the result. This success was the outcome of weeks of organisation, meetings being held for the workers at Poplar, Old Ford, Hoxton and Millwall.[38] Respect for the

NFWW grew as both the craft unions and the government gradually realised that the unionisation of women offered the best solution to male unionists' anxieties over dilution. In January 1916 an amendment to the Munitions Act, which NFWW representatives helped to draft, gave the government powers to fix the wages of all female and most male dilutees. The new Act depended, like its predecessor, on union strength for effective enforcement, and soon huge branches were built up in the big armament centres, including Woolwich. North of the river meetings were held for women workers on military equipment at Limehouse, Poplar and Tidal Basin,[39] and during 1917 the NFWW won a foothold in such important factories as the Western Electric Works at North Woolwich, Knight's soap works, and the GER workshops at Stratford.

The final year of the war saw bigger gains for the NFWW in East London than any previously achieved. One of the most striking successes was the unionisation of female ropeworkers. Early in 1917 these workers were included in the scope of government wage controls and promised £1 a week minimum wage, compared with previous earnings of 14s 6d for a 55½ hour week. The NFWW moved in quickly to recruit 170 women at Frost's, in Shadwell, and this firm was soon paying the new rate in full. The lesson was quickly learned. By May over 600 East London ropeworkers had joined the union, and forced uncontrolled as well as controlled firms to pay £1 a week.[40] Other improvements followed. In July the secretary of the ropeworkers' branch wrote to the *Woman Worker:* 'I have now pleasure in informing you that we have been given overalls and caps to work with, and a room to have our dinner.' However such concessions were resented by some employers, and when a new Ministry of Munitions Order fixed a higher minimum wage of 29s in 1918, several firms refused to pay. The NFWW promptly took them before the General Munitions Tribunal. Hundreds of women took a day off work to attend the hearing, 'somewhat to the dismay of the Tribunal clerks and Magistrates'. At a deferred hearing a few days later the audience reappeared, and 'kept up a pointed and picturesque running commentary on the evidence for the defence'.[41] They won their case, and the publicity they received can have done no harm to the NFWW's reputation in East London.

The *Woman Worker* naturally tended to emphasise the successes of the union rather than its failures. But branch reports also reveal that the NFWW shared the Workers Union's problem of a high turn-over in membership. For example, an arbitration award for workers at the Stratford Co-op Laundry is reported as follows:

> When the Stratford Laundry girls asked the Federation to get them a rise in wages, they expected to get it by return of post. This did not happen! And there were many grumblings because weeks went by without result. . . remember, girls, if the laundry is to continue to lead in the matter of wages, everybody must stick to the Federation and back up their Branch Officers.[42]

Annual Reports deplored the fact that many saw no point in continuing membership after their wage rise had been achieved. This impatience and inconsistency was inevitable among very poor workers who had no traditions of union organisation. The NFWW tried to combat it by turning its branches into social centres, organising outings, concerts and even elocution classes, as well as wage claims. The organiser of Poplar NFWW wrote enthusiastically of the 'spirit of comradeship' at a successful town hall dance: 'There is no better way of bringing the workers in touch with one another than by means of these social gatherings, which combine music and dancing with a certain amount of very useful propaganda.'[43] There was a danger that the organising of girls' clubs in Poplar and Woolwich would perpetuate the NFWW's heritage of middle class philanthropy, rather than strengthening its links with other unions. But the special benefit which the NFWW derived from the Trades Boards Act and war-time legislation perhaps indicates that female trade unionism could only flourish among low-paid workers in special circumstances. It needed its experienced committee women in high places as well as its grass roots support, so that until the branches became better-established in poor areas some division between the leaders and the led was unavoidable.

The threat of unorganised women to established wages and conditions was a serious preoccupation for many craft unions, especially in the engineering industry. By the end of the war a quarter of all engineering workers were women (nearly half in government factories).[44] The Amalgamated Society of Engineers' alarm over this female influx must be understood partly in terms of pre-war technological developments: war pressures merely accelerated the existing trend towards manufacture by machinery which could be operated by unskilled or semi-skilled labour. This trend could not be reversed in the long run, for all the government's guarantees on dilution, and meanwhile many hourly paid craftsmen found their wages falling behind the piece-rate earnings of repetitive machine workers. Dilution never became a painless process for the engineers. The strengthening of the ASE during the war was largely a defensive exercise, aimed at bringing all craftsmen into the union and fortifying it against the unskilled masses outside. Like other craft unions, it grew at only a moderate rate: its recruiting policy remained exclusive, and skilled workers had already been strongly unionised at the outbreak of war. Despite its refusal to admit the less skilled to its own ranks, the ASE actively encouraged their unionisation by the NFWW and NUGW. Relations with the Workers Union were strained, however: the Workers Union view that dilution had come to stay was fiercely opposed by the ASE, and it had even been known to entice away skilled men with its low contributions. At Woolwich Arsenal there was a complete breakdown of co-operation between the two unions in August 1915, when the ASE accepted a rise of 4s for skilled men only, after a joint wage demand.[45] The situation at the railway workshops in Stratford provides further evidence that tensions between skilled and unskilled unions were sometimes as severe as those between unions and the employers or the government. As an industrial union, the NUR was attempting to recruit all railway workers regardless of their craft. The ASE had to work hard to maintain and expand the GER membership. The NUR's refusal to acknowledge the engineers' privileged status encouraged both the employers and government arbitrators to refuse ASE claims for payment of full district

ELIZA COMES—TO STAY?

Another effect of the war— the A.G.M. decided to admit women members.

rates. In April 1915 a strike threat by engineers working on the Underground persuaded the management to pay up, but NUR opposition delayed a similar concession at GER for a further two years.[46]

Under the Munitions Acts engineering became the most tightly regulated industry in the country. Many engineers were employed directly by the government, most others worked in controlled establishments, and nearly all were tied to their work by leaving certificate rules. But the ASE was far from helpless. In August 1915 the London district organiser reminded members that 'all our usual machinery for dealing with grievances and matters in dispute can be continued, i.e. deputations of men to the foreman or management (failing satisfaction, calling in the union officials), the right to meet employers in conference, then after failure of the usual agreed procedure, we proceed to the Board of Trade'.[47] London rates had been pushed up by a minimum of 7s a week in union shops by January 1916—'not a bad investment for the operative engineers' contributions to our society,' as the ASE *Journal* commented.[48] Soon the union was attempting to defend its members against conscription, as well as against rising prices and the dilution threat. Briefly the government caved in to union pressure and agreed to allow the ASE and other skilled unions involved in munitions work to issue trade cards, or exemption documents, to their members. But the outrage of the general unions forced the abandonment of this scheme three months later. The ASE's disappointment was severe. Even in East London, where there was no militant shop steward's movement, feelings ran high. Mass protest meetings were called, and some engineers at the GER workshops and at Woolwich joined in the May 1917 strikes.[49] Though trade cards were not restored, the government was alarmed enough by the reports of its Commission on Industrial Unrest to make other concessions to the engineering unions. There were further generous bonus awards which the ASE vigorously enforced in East London during the last year of the war.

Throughout the war the ASE kept its door firmly barred to women, including those who became skilled engineers. Other unions faced up to the dilemma of women workers in different ways. In the transport industry trade unionism had also been a male preserve in 1914, mainly because very few women were employed until the war began. In July 1914 a mere handful of women worked on the railways as cleaners. When shortage of men caused their numbers to rise rapidly, and women took over the jobs of porters and ticket collectors as well, the NUR was forced to reconsider its policy. The 1915 annual conference voted to admit women. This was no great sacrifice of principle, as it would have been for the ASE, as the NUR had always been open to all grades and was aiming eventually to create a closed shop on the railways. But the admission of women was nevertheless viewed with a certain amount of curiosity and trepidation, as *Railway Review* cartoons suggest. The presence of 'lady members' in East London branches was a matter of comment for some time afterwards, until they came in such numbers that they were no longer newsworthy. Concern remained that women would be used to undermine men's rates. Though the government had agreed to pay female substitutes the minimum male rate for the job, this did not amount to equal pay. Female bonuses remained lower, and jobs were often deliberately reclassified so that it could be claimed the women were not directly substituting. Stratford 1 branch of the NUR reported a blatant case, in April 1917: 'We are still trying to get the minimum rate for some of our sister members. Strange things happen on railways. Male ticket collectors: female takes the position, same work, hours, and are called ticket takers. Some ask what is in a name; some are wondering whether it is cheap labour?'[50] Open hostility was expressed by Bethnal Green branch to 'cheap females' who were being promoted above experienced men at Liverpool Street Station.[51] The solution to the problem was generally agreed to be strong organisation of both men and women behind the equal pay demand. West Ham branch passed a uninamous resolution in support of this demand:

> no security for railwaymen will be possible in the future until the point shall have been established as a condition of railway service that no woman shall be employed in any capacity under any circumstances on railways in such a manner as to yield a greater profit to the companies than if a man were employed.[52]

Demands for equal bonuses for women were part of a continuous campaign for general increases in the war bonus. Government control of the railways meant that wage awards became national awards for the first time. Control was exercised through a committee of company managers, and if negotiations with the committee broke down the railwaymen had recourse only to direct negotiations with the Cabinet, since they were not included in the arbitration provisions of the Munitions Acts. By 1918 this top-heavy negotiating apparatus threatened to produce a major strike. But during the war the NUR succeeded in negotiating a total bonus of 33s (20s 6d for women), in seven stages. These increases were not won without a fight. The NUR had to mobilise the full strength of its membership behind each wage claim before it was achieved. In the week after the first war bonus was introduced (February 1915) Poplar 1 Branch joined up 21 new members; Poplar 2, 12, Royal Mint Street, 8; Bethnal Green, 47; Canning Town, 8, Stratford 1, 58; and Stratford 2, 323 ('the increase has moved 'em at last!'). Men had learnt the value of trade unionism from the facts of the wages increases, and could also now afford union subs more easily, as the *Railway Review* pointed out in an editorial on 'the stampede towards the branch room'.[53]

A similar pattern of wage demands and growth continued throughout the war. Union members did their best to persuade or coerce those who refused to join the NUR, whilst benefiting from its negotiating efforts. West Ham branch even demanded that the October 1916 award should not be paid to non-unionists: 'Agreed unanimously to individually impress this on the something-for-nothing brigade during the next few days. The limit to human endurance in this matter has arrived.'[54] Union recruitment meetings were regularly held, especially at the controversial GER works. 'There is much activity on the part of the craft unions to secure members, and same can only be counteracted by our members pursuing a vigorous policy in favour of the NUR', reported Plaistow branch in December 1917.[55] The success of the union's 'vigorous policy' can be seen in the East London membership figures, which until the end of the war

TOO SLOW.

THE RAILWAY SHOPMAN: "No, thanks! Your conveyance is a bit out of date. *That's* the method by which I mean to travel!"

continued to rise at a rate well above the national average.

Other public transport trade unions followed the NUR's war-time policy of opening its doors to all grades including women. Their bonus negotiations were complicated by the fact that there were many employers, and two main trade unions in fierce competition with each other. The Amalgamated Association of Tramway and Vehicle Workers organised the majority of tram workers, while the London and Provincial Union of Licensed Vehicle Workers had more bus and taxi drivers, and was attempting to break into the National Union of Vehicle Workers' field of commercial drivers. The rivalry between the unions seems to have done recruitment no harm, since in East London both the AATVW and the LPU managed to double their membership during the war. But it weakened their negotiating position (as the fiasco of the 1915 tram strike proved), and by the end of the war the majority in both unions was in favour of amalgamation. Their affiliation to the National Transport Workers Federation (the LPU in 1915 and the AATVW in 1917) helped to teach the value of unity, for in 1917 the Federation was able to achieve, through arbitration, the first-ever national wage award for bus and tram workers.[56]

At the beginning of the war such an award was unheard of. Separate bonus claims were made to all the different employers, and the outcome varied according to the strength of the union in the area. In its 1916 *Annual Report* the AATVW lists increases won by tram workers in its East London branch from local councils: war bonuses vary from 4s in West Ham and 3s in East Ham ('men only') to 2s in Ilford, while there were additional variations such as a 2s 6d merit award in Walthamstow and an extra 1s for married men in Leyton.[57] Women were lucky to get any bonus at all. Both the main unions were strongly opposed to female labour, and only the extreme shortage of male conductors and cleaners forced them to agree to women doing these jobs in 1915, 'subject to them doing exactly the same work, and at the same remuneration, and that their employment should terminate at the end of the war'.[58] All the old hostility was aroused once more when the question of women drivers was raised in 1916. They would be a danger to the public, claimed the editor of the *Licensed Vehicle Trades Record:* 'I suggest in all humility that nature never intended the nervous system of the ladies to be equal to that of the males.'[59] A blunter protest came in a letter from Shoreditch LPU branch, threatening to 'enforce our opinions to the full extent of our abilities'.[60] The *Annual Report* of the AATVW spelt out the real reason for opposition: 'they are. . . a menace to the male tram drivers, both now and in the future'.[61] As more women entered the union, they were able to add their own voices to the equal pay demand, and also to cast further doubt on the chivalry of the men. 'Is it really for the girls' sake only they are taking this trouble?' queried a Bow conductress in the *Record*. 'Isn't there just the thought, "If they don't take interest in the girls' wages etc. now, the men may suffer when this war is over"?'[62] From whatever motive, the LPU supported the unofficial bus strike in May 1918, which at last won equal bonuses for this section of women workers.

Bonus disputes often exacerbated the rivalry between the AATVW and the LPU. An interesting local example of this is provided by an article on 'The position in Poplar' in the *Licensed Vehicle Trades Record* (31 January 1917). The two unions agreed to put in a joint 15 per cent wage increase. Poplar council offered 2s, which satisfied the 'Blues' (AATVW), but enraged the 'Reds' (LPU), especially when they saw 'Blue' officials going among the men and women trying to persuade them to accept the offer. The 'Blues' refused to call a meeting, so the 'Reds' invited members of the rival union to attend their own meeting. It was unanimously decided to reject the offer and to apply for Board of Trade arbitration (even non-unionists voting in favour, according to the 'Red' reporter!):

> So much for the 'Blues'. As trade unionists they are not in it, as sick club men they might have an excuse, but as a mixture of both they are worse than useless; and no self-respecting man who thinks a workman should be a man and not merely a machine, would have anything to do with them.

The 'Red' triumph was completed when the arbitrators decided to award 3s 6d to the men. The LPU did not forget the women's case, however. At their next branch meeting they passed a resolution protesting at the inequality of the award, and demanding equal pay for women.

One branch of the East London transport industry escaped the problems of female labour. After an unsuccessful experiment in Liverpool in 1915, the idea of women dockers was abandoned, partly because of union intransigence, but also because they really were physically incapable of much of the work. The Dockers Union had, in fact, been open to women since 1889. However as the original aim of forming a general union of unskilled labourers became subordinated to the aim of unionising actual dockers, female membership remained very low. During the war there was some effort to expand the general branches. In a *Dockers Record* advertisement of September 1916, women workers are 'especially invited' to join at 2d per week; they had already been organised at munitions works, a toy factory, tin box factories and laundries. This revival of interest in women sprang from the usual motives. Ben Tillett wrote of women workers in the East London oil cake mills: 'In order to preserve the rates of pay for male labour, we have taken in hand the organisation of females in these mills.'[63]

The organisation of dockers remained the major concern of Tillett's union. The war went some way towards ending the instability of employment at the docks, and thus prepared the way for the move to abolish casualism in 1919–20. A brief period of dislocation was followed by a longer period of extremely good employment from December 1914 onwards. As the port began to suffer from over-congestion, rather than under-employment, war bonuses were easily won. The general 3s bonus of February 1915 advanced by stages to 32s at the end of the war. Though the government set up a Port and Transit Committee to supervise traffic through the docks, wage claims were handled through the normal procedures of the Munitions Acts. Membership of the East London branches of the Dockers Union reflects closely the level of activity in the port, and even the variations between different docks. Almost every branch made substantial progress between December 1914 and June 1915, the only exceptions being the small general branch of tin workers and the Haggerston branch. The income of the major dockers' branches rose impressively, for example from £232 1s 2d to £443 3s 7d at the Victoria and Albert Docks.[64] But few branches maintained their growth rate during 1916. Trade became less good and very irregular, so that although the union continued to press for wage rises dockers were forced to compromise by accepting war bonus awards rather than increases on hourly rates.

In the winter of 1916–17 a new problem faced the union. Trade improved slightly, and although 'at times hundreds of men have been idle for days', the government proposed bringing Transport Workers Battalions into the London docks to help out when there was a rush of work. The Dockers Union strongly opposed the proposal, which meant 'putting men into khaki and bringing them back to do their ordinary work under military discipline'. Dockers under twenty-six years old were being reviewed for military service, and it was feared that general industrial conscription in the docks would follow.[65] When the Battalions began work in February 1917 another of the union's fears was confirmed: 'A regrettable feature in the London District is the employment of soldier dockers at one dock while regular dock workers are unemployed elsewhere—or even at the same dock.' The union urged its members to work on Saturday afternoons, when necessary, and 'to accept work on ship or quay, although they may have only followed up one or the other; in this way we shall be able to retain the Dock work in the hands of Dockers, and, we hope, successfully stop the further introduction of soldiers or any Tom, Dick or Harry who may be sent under the National Service Act'.[66] The establishment of central call places, at the unions' request, encouraged flexibility of employment and for a period the Transport Battalions were withdrawn.

However in the spring of 1918 trade revived so dramatically that even the Dockers Union admitted, 'we have had difficulty in obtaining sufficient numbers of civilians to do the work'.[67] The supply of civilian dockers had been cut to the bone by conscription, and the return of the Transport Battalions was inevitable. In some cases dockers who had been recently called up had their notices cancelled, through trade union pressure, and the men were 'still retained in the port, where they are of much greater service to the country than they would have been if they had been put into the army'.[68] The civilian dockers who remained were more strongly organised than ever before. The number of 'perms' had been increased, and complete casualism had been virtually eliminated. A union claim for an 8d per hour total war advance in April 1918 produced an arbitration award of 7d—a result which was hailed as 'a triumph for the [Transport Workers] Federation and our Union in particular'.[69] It certainly stimulated membership, which in most branches rose above the 1915 peak during 1918 despite a decline in the number employed. Ben Tillett claimed that his union had made not merely substantial progress in numbers, but

very solid progress—that is to say, I believe the additional members will be solid and permanent. We have sought, not merely to get into our ranks additional members, but have consolidated as we have gone along, so on the surface it does not appear that we have progressed so far as certain kindred organisations, but time will tell.[70]

Unlike the thousands of dilutees recruited by other general unions in the munitions factories, dockers working in the Port of London in 1918 were likely to remain there, and to remain in the union.

The clothing industry had proved even more difficult to unionise than the docks before 1914. As we have seen, its ill-paid, unorganised workers were all too easily exploited by war profiteers when the first flood of government contracts poured into East London. The workers' delay, and in some cases failure, in taking advantage of labour shortages to raise wages was due partly to the weakness of the clothing unions, but also to the fact that they did not fully share the benefits which the Munitions Acts brought to other industries. Since clothing firms were not controlled establishments, there was no clearly-established, compulsory path through the unions to the arbitration tribunals. In fact the status of clothing workers under the Acts seems to have been a bit of a mystery even to the Ministry of Munitions itself. In July 1916 a girl who worked at Groom's factory in Limehouse was refused a job at a Park Royal munitions factory because she had no leaving certificate. When the case came to Sylvia Pankhurst's notice she phoned the Ministry, only to be told that the question was 'so complicated that no definite answer could be given'. A few days later a letter informed her that no leaving certificate was required.[71] Arguments took place at Committee on Production hearings about whether or not arbitration was compulsory.[72] In March 1917 the *Journal* of the Amalgamated Society of Tailors and Tailoresses reported an extraordinary incident of confusion. Members of the International Mantle Makers branch were arrested while picketing their East London workshop by police 'acting on their own initiative':

> The dispute arose out of a reduction in prices on Army work, and the police contended that it was an offence under the Law to impede or interfere with the production of war material; persistent efforts were made at the War Office to obtain a definite ruling on the question, but without result, responsible officials refusing to commit themselves to a definite statement which could be used in Court.

Eventually a magistrate released the men and referred the dispute to arbitration.

Voluntary resort to arbitration gradually became more common, as its advantages were recognised by the unions. Towards the end of the war several major arbitration awards were made to clothing workers, including (from October 1917) some national awards. The problem was for the clothing unions to recruit enough members to support such claims. Like other unions, they used arbitration successes as a persuasive argument to bring in the new members needed to enforce the higher rates, and to make future claims. 'Are you receiving the 20 per cent War Bonus?' asked the Amalgamated Society's *Journal* in December 1917. '*If you are not,* inform the secretary of the branch of the AST in your town at once. . . *Are you in a position* to maintain your present wages? If you are not a Member of the above Union your chances are very remote.' A United Garment Workers leaflet of July 1918 spelled out the same message: 'Join the UGW at once, thereby ensuring your being entitled to receive the increases of wages which have been granted by "the Committee on Production".'

Early in the war Sylvia Pankhurst's campaign against 'government sweating' had revealed how widely wage rates varied from firm to firm in East London. Finishing trousers, for example, was paid at a rate of 2s a dozen at Fifer's in Roman Road, but 3s a dozen at Mendes' in Bethnal Green Road. Finishing one soldier's coat, apart from the buttons, was worth 4d at Mendes', but only 2½d at Diamond and Beave's in the Cambridge Road.[73] There was no such thing as a district rate. Even three years later, when large-scale arbitration awards had (on paper, at least) gone some way towards achieving greater uniformity, local variations persisted. The result was that movements for higher wages tended to arise at different times in different factories. Isolated minor strikes occurred which, although they might lead to workers joining a union, were rarely the result of union leadership. In October 1914 women workers at Polikoff's refused to make soldiers' blankets at 1½d a dozen, when men were being paid more than twice as much.[74] Miss Squires, of the factory inspectorate, describes a similar event concerning a blouse firm making body belts for the troops, through a sub-contractor:

> The price offered was so low that the firm could not give them to their own inside workpeople and therefore gave them to outworkers in the East End. One after another these outworkers took back the work and refused to do it, the price paid being 8d per dozen, providing their own cotton at 3¾d a reel.[75]

The gradual rise in clothing workers' wages must have been the result of many such refusals.

Bigger strikes sometimes occurred in the same spontaneous fashion. The United Garment Workers Union told the Committee on Production, in June 1917, 'it has taken our local officials all their time to prevent unofficial stoppages of work in the trade. For a long period now we have had this shop and that shop threatening to shut down; we have had complaint after complaint from the War Office regarding important work being held up.'[76] Schneider's, of Durward Street,

Whitechapel, was one of the most important government contractors in East London. In October 1916 all its 500 employees came out on strike when the firm decided that in future they should pay for their own trimmings out of a very inadequate recent pay rise. There were other grievances, too, such as over-charging for cotton and insurance, a compulsory deduction of 3d per week for 'charities', and the behaviour of foremen who had to be bribed to keep up a regular supply of work to piece-workers. After an unsuccessful attempt to split the women strikers from the men with wage promises, the firm capitulated. All the strikers' main demands were met, including the sacking of blacklegs. It was even agreed (though perhaps not put into practice!) that 'in the event of a worker being dismissed at the instigation of the foreman or passer, the case be referred to a committee of the elected representatives of the workers for investigation. The decision of the workers' committee shall be final'. Although these workers had apparently made such strides towards organisation and collective bargaining, they did not link up with the UGW. Instead, they joined the syndicalist International Workers of the World.[77]

This fact illustrates another persistent obstacle to the effective unionisation of clothing workers. The workers' disunity was reflected in the trade unions themselves. The main Jewish clothing unions in 1914 were the London Jewish Tailors and the London Ladies Tailors, Machinists and Pressers, but East London also contained members of the Amalgamated Union of Clothiers Operatives, the London Society of Tailors and Tailoresses, the Amalgamated Society of Tailors, and such specialist clothing unions as the Waterproof Garment Workers, the Trouser Makers, and the Cap Makers. In 1915 the Amalgamated Union of Clothiers Operatives absorbed the London Society, the London Jewish Tailors and several smaller unions to form the UGW, with an East London membership of about 2,000. But damaging inter-union rivalry continued. The Waterproof Garment Workers soon broke from the UGW and went their own way. The Amalgamated Society continued to organise separate East London branches, with diminishing success which its journal blamed both on the departure of Jewish tailors for Russia and on 'unscrupulous and determined opposition from the Garment Workers'.[78]

When the Amalgamated Society's two main East London branches folded in 1917 some of the ex-members may well have gone to the UGW. However it seems likely that most left to join the London Ladies Tailors. This Jewish Union, led by the socialist Jacob Fine, seems to have been the most successful in the East London clothing industry during the war. It claimed a membership of 3,000 by 1918. Its 1916 balance sheet (printed in both English and Yiddish) shows that funds had increased by £616 8s 8d during that year alone, though money had been found for political and trade union affiliations, a journal, and a library. The year's expenditure of £336 6s 8d on 'strikes and lock-outs' proves that the union actively supported demands for wage increases, war-time or not. Fine was not opposed in principle to co-operation with English trade unionists, but the success of his union as an exclusively Jewish organisation demonstrates the difficulty of building a united clothing workers' union in East London. To many orthodox Jews Fine's views were anathema, so that he could not hope to organise more than a fraction even of the Jewish workers. In Stepney alone clothing workers numbered over 36,000 in the 1911 Census; it is clear that in 1918 only a small proportion of these belonged to any union. For a great many clothing workers, dependent on rises in Trade Board rates, or perhaps excluded even from this protection, the war-time struggle to keep abreast of price rises was a losing one. This conclusion applies equally to other poorly organised East London trades. Workers who did not join trade unions during the war were likely to find their wages falling even further behind than in 1914, as they were overtaken by the unionised workers' successes.

The foregoing survey of the main East London unions' progress has shown how wage rises were rewarded by increased membership, which in its turn strengthened future union demands. The unions drew in new members by demonstrating their strength in other directions too. Despite new legal constraints, many aspects of work conditions apart from pay remained negotiable, and more employers than ever before were willing to negotiate. Conscription itself became a union issue in the case of skilled craftsmen and the dockers. A union card could mean the difference between a secure, well-paid job at home and being sent to the trenches. After 1915 there was acute anxiety, especially among socialists, about the loss of trade union rights under the Munitions Acts, and the danger this would present in a post-war situation of high unemployment. Socialists in East London failed to launch a mass campaign of resistance to the Munitions Act. Their failure demonstrates not only the reluctance of many trade unionists to sabotage Britain's war effort, but also a considerable undercurrent of union self-confidence. Both at national and at local level, trade unions sturdily defended their interests through pragmatic adaptation to the requirements of the Munitions Acts, and determined use of their strong economic bargaining position. By methods of negotiation, arbitration, and above all improved organisation, the unions were able to build up their strength to such an extent that no government would be able indefinitely to prolong war-time controls and restrictions.

NOTES

1. Tillett, B., in Dock, Wharf, Riverside and General Labourers Union, *Annual Report* 1900, 6.
2. Lansbury, G., in *Bow and Bromley Worker,* September 1911.
3. National union membership rose by 57% during the war (*Labour Gazette,* January 1920). By the end of the war approximately one in three of the occupied population belonged to a trade union; in East London the proportion was still below this average, approximately one in four.
4. Resolution of the Joint Board of the TUC, General Federation of Trade Unions and Labour Party, quoted in Cole, G.D.H., *Trade Unionism and Munitions* (Oxford, 1923), 52.
5. TUC *Report* 1913, 339.
6. Dock, Wharf, Riverside and General Labourers Union (hereafter Dockers Union), *Annual Report* 1914, 5.
7. National Union of Gasworkers and General Labourers, *Quarterly Report* September 1914, 7.
8. *SE,* 22 August 1914 and *Railway Review,* 4 September 1914.
9. NUGGL, *Quarterly Report,* December 1914, 6.
10. *Railway Review,* 6 November 1914.
11. National Amalgamated Furnishing Trades Association, *Annual Report* 1914 and WNC 30/1/47-62. The WNC appealed to the government for emergency grants towards the expenses of unions paying unemployment benefit.
12. *Official History of the Ministry of Munitions* (1922), I, Part 1, 92 and 98, and XI, Part 4, 67.

13. Ibid., VIII, Part 2, 245.
14. Hinton, J., *The First Shop Stewards Movement* (1973), 179.
15. Thom, D., 'Women Munition Workers at Woolwich Arsenal in the 1914–1917 War' (MA thesis, Warwick, 1975), 116–117.
16. Beveridge Collection, Vol. I, item 2, 87–89.
17. Ibid., 115.
18. Watts, J.I., *The Fiftieth Anniversary–Brunner Mond and Co. 1873–1923* (1923), 55.
19. Everard, S., *The History of the Gas Light and Coke Co. 1912–1949* (1949).
20. Slater, E., *One Hundred Years, 1837–1937. The Story of Henley's* (1937) and Silvertown Rubber Company, *Silvertown* (1920).
21. Food and, of course, armaments were excluded from the monthly lists of new contractors. The lists give ample evidence both of variety and of individual firms' adaptability, but do not provide an adequate picture of East London's total contribution to War Office needs, since only direct contractors are named.
22. *Dreadnought,* 22 August and 28 November 1914.
23. *Labour Gazette,* March, June and July 1915.
24. *Labour Gazette,* January and March 1915.
25. ASE, *Monthly Journal,* March and April 1915.
26. Trade Union Rights Committee, *Trade Unionism and the Crisis* (1915), 4 and 14.
27. TURC Manifesto, *Herald,* 24 July 1915.
28. *Herald,* 31 July, 11 September and 4 December 1915.
29. *Herald,* 6 January 1917.
30. NUGGL and NUGW, *Rules.*
31. *Trade Union Worker,* July 1916 and Workers Union, *Annual Reports* 1914, 1915, 1916.
32. *Trade Union Worker,* February 1917.
33. *Trade Union Worker,* June 1917.
34. *Workers Union Record,* August 1916. A speaker told the Workers Union Triennial Conference that 'they in London were going ahead with the idea of amalgamation, and had come to a definite agreement with the Gasworkers Society. They never sent an application in to a London firm without first asking if they had any members employed at the works affected. They did not experience any difficulties over the recognition of one another's cards.'
35. Workers Union, *Annual Report* 1918.
36. Hamilton, M., *Mary Macarthur* (1921), 24.
37. National Federation of Women Workers, *Annual Report* 1915, 20–21.
38. Ibid., 20 and Women's Trade Union League, *Annual Report* 1915, 11.
39. Women's Trade Union League, *Annual Report* 1916, 10.
40. *Woman Worker,* March and May 1917.
41. *Woman Worker,* September 1918.
42. *Woman Worker,* March 1917.
43. *Woman Worker,* July 1918.
44. Cole, G.D.H., *Trade Unionism and Munitions* (1923), 186.
45. Hinton, J., op. cit., 181.
46. ASE *Monthly Journal,* May and June 1915, August 1916, September 1917.
47. ASE *Monthly Journal,* August 1915.
48. ASE *Monthly Journal,* January 1916.
49. ASE *Monthly Journal,* May and June 1917.
50. *Railway Review,* 27 April 1917.
51. *Railway Review,* 10 October 1915.

52. *Railway Review,* 8 September 1916.
53. *Railway Review,* 26 February and 5 March 1915.
54. *Railway Review,* 22 September 1917.
55. *Railway Review,* 18 December 1917.
56. Amalgamated Association of Tramway and Vehicle Workers, *Annual Report* 1917, xxii: 'it must be admitted by all reasonable men and women that without the assistance of the National Transport Workers Federation we should not have been so successful'.
57. AATVW, *Annual Report,* 1916, x.
58. London and Provincial Union of Licensed Vehicle Workers, *Annual Report* 1916, 5.
59. *Licensed Vehicle Trades Record,* 6 November 1916.
60. Ibid.
61. AATVW, *Annual Report* 1916, xvi.
62. *Licensed Vehicle Trades Record,* 28 February 1917.
63. Dockers Union, *Annual Report,* 1917, 8.
64. Dockers Union, *Half Yearly Balance Sheets,* December 1914 and June 1915.
65. *Dockers Record,* December 1916 and January 1917.
66. *Dockers Record,* February and March 1917.
67. *Dockers Record,* March 1918.
68. Ibid.
69. *Dockers Record,* May 1918.
70. Dockers Union, *Annual Report* 1917, 5.
71. *Dreadnought,* 8 July 1916.
72. e.g. Minutes of Proceedings before the Committee on Production, 6 June 1917, in the archive of the National Union of Tailors and Garment Workers. The case was between the London District Wholesale Clothiers Association and the UGW. The former argued that arbitration was not compulsory, but the latter claimed that a strike would have been illegal under the Munitions Acts.
73. *Dreadnought,* 24 April 1915.
74. *Dreadnought,* 3 October 1914.
75. Annual Report of the Chief Inspector for Factories and Workshops for the year 1914, Cd. 8051 (1915), P.P. 1914–16, XXL, 453.
76. Minutes of Proceedings before the Committee on Production, 6 June 1917 (op. cit.), 11.
77. *Dreadnought,* 21 October 1916.
78. Amalgamated Society of Tailors and Tailoresses, *Journal,* September 1917.

CHAPTER 5

TRADE UNIONS: POWER AND POLITICS

The last two years of the war saw the climax of union activity. The unions used their power not only to pursue familiar economic aims, but also to influence legislation and the government's plans for post-war reconstruction. Both at leadership and at membership levels, trade unionists became more closely involved in directly political demands than ever before. Politicisation was a complex process. Like the growth of the unions themselves, it proceeded unevenly, spasmodically, even unintentionally, yet with gathering momentum as the war neared its end. There was no straightforward inevitability about a transfer of trade union strength into Labour Party—still less, socialist—organisation and votes. Conflicts within the trade union movement sometimes spilled into the political arena; many trade unionists owed a traditional allegiance to Liberalism rather than Labour, and pre-war tensions between unionists and non-unionists inside the Labour Party did not suddenly disappear. But by 1918 the direction of change was unmistakeable. In East London post-war Labour victories were to be built round a solid core of union support, tempered and taught by war-time experience.

The most obvious sign of the unions' new political role was the ever-increasing frequency with which their leaders could be found hobnobbing with ministers and generally being taken into the government's confidence. The May strikes of 1917 raised serious doubts about existing labour policy. Ministerial willingness to consult and compromise in the aftermath reflected the government's respect for the unions' organised strength, as well as an urgent desire to buttress official union leadership against the threat of unofficial militancy. Union leaders' cordial acceptance of government overtures, and welcoming of much of the labour legislation of 1917–18, was freely interpreted as blindly patriotic 'treachery' by socialist and syndicalist critics. But there is little evidence to suggest that men such as Thorne and Tillett did in fact abandon the astute pragmatism which had always characterised their leadership. The government made genuine concessions in response to union demands and the recommendations of its own Commission of Enquiry into Industrial Unrest. Leaving certificates were abolished in October 1917. The withdrawal of the trade card scheme a few months later was a major victory for the general unions, while the government's retreat from plans to extend compulsory dilution to private industry offered some compensatory satisfaction to the skilled unions. Longer-term government acceptance of a new status for trade unionism was signified by the Trade Unions Amalgamation Act of 1917, and the Ministry of Reconstruction's proposals for Joint Industrial Councils. It was hoped that fewer, larger unions and the establishment of a national conciliating and negotiating structure would contribute to industrial peace. But for union leaders the proposals held a different promise. Amalgamation schemes were almost universally popular at this time, expectations centring on the larger wage increases to be won from united strength. The Whitley Councils were also supported with a view to trade union, rather than national, interests. The value of existing arbitration tribunals, especially to unskilled unions, had already been demonstrated. It is not surprising that a permanent scheme advocating 'complete and coherent organisation' and 'frank and full recognition'[1] found favour with those leaders whose main field of work was in poorly organised industries.

At local level the Whitley proposals, and other government measures, were generally greeted with much less enthusiasm. At Morton's pickle factory in Millwall women workers refused to co-operate with their employers' attempt to establish the lowest tier of the Whitley Councils, 'on the grounds that such a committee would be detrimental to their interests as workers, and that they were convinced it was a "set-off" against their respective unions.'[2] ASE shop stewards in the London area also decided that 'such Committees will be of no advantage to the workers, as their real purpose is to defeat the trade union movement'.[3] These attitudes owed less to the actual content of the Whitley Reports than to workers' gathering sense of grievance on a whole range of other issues. The government Commissioners who enquired into London and the South Eastern Area produced a succinct list of 'Causes of Unrest':

In order of importance these causes may be ranked more or less as follows:

A. Food prices—and in connection with this
B. What is called profiteering.
C. Industrial fatigue.
D. Inequality of Sacrifice.
E. Uncertainty as to the future.
F. Want of confidence in the Government and resentment at undue interference.[4]

Despite a few government concessions, none of these basic causes had been eliminated by 1918. Mistrust of the employers and of the government were inseparable: a degree of shop floor politicisation was the inevitable result.

The divergence between union leaders and rank and file members towards the end of the war has often been studied in the light of evidence from areas where it became extreme. In East London, though not absent, it posed no fundamental threat to the unity and effectiveness of the trade union movement. Revolutionary shop stewards never gained more than a toe-hold, and in 1918 the Labour Party was able successfully to mobilise trade union support from local militants and union leaders alike. Steep rises in membership and a new rush of wage rises in the final months of war suggest no loss of confidence in the official channels of union negotiation. In October 1917 the Ministry of Munitions gave an unintended boost to wage inflation throughout the country, with its 12½ per cent bonus to skilled time workers in government controlled factories. The 12½ per cent, and 7½ per cent granted to placate angry piece workers, became so widespread that all munitions workers, and even non-munitions workers, began to consider these percentages as a general entitlement. As usual, enforcement of the new rates depended on union strength. During 1918 the reports of unions and of the arbitration tribunals demonstrate the success achieved in East London. The ASE, NUGW and the Workers Union were particularly active. Amongst the beneficiaries were workers at the Gas Light and Coke Company, West Ham chemical firms, Tate's sugar refinery, the Millwall lead works of Locke, Lancaster and Johnson, the timber works of Burt, Boulton and Haywood, building labourers, rubber workers, woodworkers, and of course engineering workers. Even the tiny Military Cork Headdress Trade Union was able to extract 7½ per cent for members employed by Charles Owen and Co. of Bow.[5] Such achievements reinforced union leadership locally; there seemed little reason for disillusion with existing trade unionism.

Though East London did not become a centre of shop steward militancy, the area reflected changes in the role of shop stewards which were occurring nationally. The new economic conditions and industrial legislation of war-time had greatly stimulated workshop bargaining. Shop stewards were gradually evolving from minor branch officials, responsible mainly for collecting subs and checking cards, into influential representatives, permanently present in the factories and increasingly accepted by the management. Their usefulness was acknowledged by union executives. Rule changes by the NUGW, ASCJ and ASE in 1917–18 formalised the stewards' new responsibilities, and their role was further legitimised by a national agreement between the ASE and the Engineering Employers Federation. Reports in the ASE *Journal* show union officials helping East London stewards to enforce this agreement. In May 1918 the London district organiser visited the Silvertown Rubber Company: 'after a lengthy conversation on things in general, I was able to persuade the manager to have the shop steward in with me and so join in the discussion, which proved effective, and I am of the opinion that good will be the outcome of my visit to this firm for all concerned'.[6] A few months later the same organiser spoke to a mass meeting of all the employees at Becton, winning their support for a works committee scheme initiated by ASE shop stewards.[7]

Despite the growing importance of stewards in East London's larger and better organised factories, the area was far from producing the sort of shop stewards movement 'capable of leading the mass of the workers independently of the existing trade union authorities'[8] which James Hinton has described. Even at Woolwich Arsenal the powerful shop stewards committee remained obstinately non-revolutionary, due to continuing craft exclusiveness and a tradition of management union consultation. North of the river all-grades workers' committees were in their infancy, none being strong enough to provide a focus for shop steward activity over the whole area. East London's many small factories and wide variety of trades, as well as the immaturity of trade unionism, made it extremely difficult to bring together an area committee on the Clyde model. Yet political activists would not accept that it was impossible. The few London stewards who belonged to the national syndicalist movement were determined to put their beliefs into practice. The failure of TURC has been described. The London Workers Committee set up in January 1916 was briefly successful at Woolwich after the ASE district secretary (ex-leader of the Arsenal shop stewards) was prosecuted for inciting a strike, however the peaceful settlement of this dispute caused an immediate set-back. Not until the deep discontents of the winter of 1917–18 was there any real hope for a revival. On 9 March 1918 an article in the *Dreadnought* by the syndicalist engineer, W.F. Watson, announced the LWC's re-establishment. During the following months regular articles appeared beneath the heading 'Workshop Notes', giving news of Committee meetings and of the shop stewards' movement generally, as well as expounding Watson's political views at length. Despite their author's determined optimism, it is clear from these articles that the new LWC made little progress in East London or anywhere else. By November Watson was confessing dejectedly: 'When we think of the splendid organisation of our provincial comrades, and when we consider that to organise similarly London workers has always been the despair of those who have attempted it, we sometimes wonder whether it will ever be achieved.'[9]

Meanwhile, as the end of the war approached, union leaders were facing up to the future with a serious concern for their members' general interests which disproves the wilder syndicalist accusations against them. Even the strongest war supporters did not expect a guaranteed happy-ever-after outcome. Trade unions claimed a right to share in the tasks of post-war reconstruction from a consciousness of their strength, and of the importance of their contribution to military victory. Many held special reconstruction conferences, at which fundamental reforms were debated. Even the craft unions realised that their cherished restoration of pre-war practices did not provide an adequate solution to post-war problems. The future of trade unionists was bound up with the future of their industries, which in turn involved questions of national and international politics. When the *Railway Review* invited NUR branches to send in their own reconstruction programme for discussion at its November 1917 conference, the response was enormous. Out of hundreds received, West Ham's programme was one of the few to be published.[10] It began with three industrial demands: an end to the industrial truce, permanent union representation on the National Railways Executive, and higher pay for shorter hours. This was followed by a section on 'social and economic policy' which included recommendations for a Citizen Army, workers control of the food supply, protective tariffs for British industry, and the preservation of future peace by an international police force. Some of the proposals bear the stamp of National Socialist Party propaganda. Nevertheless the West Ham programme was typical of most in its attempt to link narrowly industrial demands to broader political issues.

How could the Labour Party take advantage of the new breadth of trade union concerns? To answer this question it is necessary to look back at the relations between the unions and the Labour Party earlier in the war, and to examine the relationship between trade unionism and socialism. In 1914 the national Labour Party was held together by a general belief in independent working class representation rather than by a shared political ideology. The exact mix of socialists and trade unionists within local Labour Party organisations varied considerably from area to area. In East London the more successful Labour Representation Committees depended very largely on local trades councils and trade unions.

Though the socialist societies were a vital element in the LRC's, socialist enthusiasm alone could not compensate for the weakness of trade unionism in the inner East London boroughs. The great majority of East London Labour Party leaders were well-known local men who were both trade unionists and socialists. A few, like George Lansbury, were best known for their socialism (though he was a life-long member of the NUGGL too). Most had been drawn to the politics of labour representation through their union activities.

When the war broke out it produced two conflicting results. On the one hand, the issue of war or peace divided the supporters of Lansbury from those of Will Thorne, the majority of trade unionists siding with Thorne in the early years. On the other hand, the war increased the number of bodies within which socialists and trade unionists could work co-operatively in defence of workers' interests. Suddenly they found themselves taking an active part in the management of local affairs, instead of struggling to win elections. Fortunately the problems with which war-time committees had to deal were those on which it was easy for plain trade unionists and more ideologically-motivated socialists to agree. The discussion and united campaigning on such issues took place not merely amongst labour committee members, but within the trades councils which had nominated them, and within the trade unions which sent delegates to the trades councils.

The lessons of rising food prices and profiteering, for example, were taken as seriously by the trade unions as by any overtly political group. Many union journals regularly reproduced the WNC's monthly prices memorandum. All trade unionists quoted its figures to justify wage demands, and joined in socialist demands for drastic government action to end price inflation. Meetings were held in East London to back such demands by the trade unions, as well as by the socialist societies and trades councils. The NUGW sponsored a protest meeting at Canning Town Public Hall in July 1916, at which a powerful array of West Ham councillors drove home the need for tighter government controls and for working class action to enforce them.[11] It seemed obvious

145

even to many workers who had no acquaintance with socialist theory that the capitalist profit-makers were responsible for the shrinking value of their wages. Union leaders did their utmost to popularise this view, which conveniently helped them to reconcile their patriotism with their inability to sustain the industrial truce. Some of the most strident denunciations of profiteering came from Tillett and Thorne. In his 1914 *Annual Report* Tillett described profiteers as 'mere carrion crows living on the dead and the dying. These thieves would not make decent scavengers. When the history of this war is written it will be shown that our army and country generally has been bled white by the most rapacious type of capitalist that has ever cursed the world'. The ready response to such attacks among the union rank and file is reflected in the flood of NUR branch resolutions against price rises published in the *Railway Review*. Forest Gate thought that price rises were 'entirely due to the greed of the owning classes'. At Stratford 1, 'The opinion of a good many brothers is that the "capitalist profiteer" is a greater enemy than the Germans'.[12] The joint trade union and Labour Party campaign against conscription also received warm support in East London. After it was introduced, union leaders helped to popularise the demand for 'conscription of wealth', and continued steadfastly to resist the threat of industrial conscription.

Like prices, profits and dilution, industrial conscription was an inescapably political issue which concerned the unions' vital interests. The reaction of socialists to war-time strikes often illustrates the difference between those who upheld workers' rights as a matter of principle, and those who defended them as a matter of survival. There was widespread support in the socialist press for the spring strikes of 1915. But as the connection between munitions supply and ultimate victory became clearer, attitudes modified. In March 1916 a *Herald* editorial described the Clyde strikes as

> disastrous and regrettable to all concerned. We in London are so far away, and our sources of information so limited, it is almost impossible to form an accurate judgement as to the rights and wrongs of the dispute. One thing is clear: the dispute must be ended and the

men got back to work at once. We who are pacifists dare not inter-
fere with the essential supplies needed by the Army and Navy until
the nation gives the word to 'stop the war'.[13]

Many patriotic union leaders agreed with this condemnation
(including Will Thorne and the ASE executive committee).
Yet it seems likely that rank and file trade unionists were
sometimes more sympathetic to the strikes than well-known
socialist opponents of the war and of the government. During
the May 1917 strikes the West Ham branch of the NUR
passed a resolution supporting the engineers 'in the trouble
forced upon them'.[14] In the *Trade Union Worker* the London
district organiser of the Workers Union made it clear that his
members' opposition was due to the trade card issue rather
than to any blanket disapproval of strikes as such.[15] Even the
ASE executive blamed the government, rather than the unofficial strikers themselves, for what had happened.[16]

The lack of understanding displayed by the socialist press
in its coverage of munitions strikes is part of a wider misunderstanding of trade union activity during the war. Despite
their support of union rights, socialist papers published
surprisingly little trade union news. They apparently did not
consider the unions' day-to-day fight back against government controls, through improved organisation, tough negotiating and the arbitration tribunals, as of any great importance.
The *Herald* gave the best coverage, printing weekly features
on trade union and trades council news which filled about
one and a half of the paper's sixteen pages. *Labour Leader's*
regular 'Trade Union Notes' were confined to half a page,
Justice managed about three quarters of a page on 'The
World of Labour', while neither the *Call* nor the *Dreadnought*
had any regular feature on trade unionism. Major strikes and
new legislation received extensive treatment, but none of
these newspapers conveyed anything approaching a comprehensive picture of trade union development during the war.
Editorial comment on union affairs dwelt mainly on such
public showpieces as the Trades Union Congress, and was
often confined to attacks on the union leaders' lack of
socialist politics. The political significance of their industrial
achievements went by the board.

The issue of the war itself threw into sharp emphasis the difference between pacifist perspectives and those of the bulk of trade unionists. Latent union prejudice against middle class theorists was re-aroused and found vigorous expression at the TUC and at Labour Party conferences in the early years of the war. There was hostility to pacifism in the branches, too. During 1915 East London NUR branches refused to accept speakers offered by the anti-war Union of Democratic Control. West Ham railwaymen resolved to 'agitate everywhere for the elimination of academic and bootless discussions by cranks, dogmatists, and pro-Russian pacifists until a conclusive and decisive victory is obtained'.[17]

Most East London anti-war socialists knew the state of local opinion too well to waste their time in 'academic and bootless discussions'. They devoted themselves instead to joint work with trade unionists on less controversial issues. George Lansbury, for example, kept his outspoken condemnation of the war mainly to the pages of the *Herald* until the last year of the war, when such views were less unpopular. In August 1914 he wrote: 'A militant trade unionism, stronger than ever on its defensive side, was never more wanted than at this hour.'[18] During the following years he gave local trade unionism every encouragement and support, and was often to be found amicably sharing a platform with a patriotic union leader. At food price meetings in Poplar Town Hall and Bow Baths, speakers alongside Lansbury included Ben Tillett and Jack Jones, as well as the anti-war unionists Robert Williams and Harry Gosling.[19] In March 1915 Lansbury and Jones jointly performed the symbolic ceremony of unfurling Bromley East Gasworkers' new banner. It bore the slogans, 'An injury to one is an injury to all', and 'Workers of all countries unite; you have nothing to lose but your chains.' Afterwards Lansbury presented Jones with an umbrella.[20] No doubt such friendly contacts were assisted by the fact that Lansbury himself was a loyal union member who had played an active role in the 1911–12 strikes. Even in war-time he found time for a little union organising, addressing a meeting of strikers at two Limehouse biscuit factories in January 1915.[21] When attacks were made on Lansbury's pacifism by Will Thorne and his supporters, he refused to retaliate. His mediating efforts have been mentioned, after the tables were turned in January 1918 and West Ham Labour Party threatened to ditch Thorne as their Member of Parliament.

Lansbury's cautious and sympathetic attitude to the trade unions contrasts with the impatience of Sylvia Pankhurst. Her growing enthusiasm for socialism did not lessen her emotional individualism. Early in the war her campaign against 'government sweating' might have allied her with the unions. But the low wages paid in the Queen's workrooms so angered her that the *Dreadnought* devoted more space to personal attacks on Mary Macarthur than to encouraging sweated women to join the NFWW. Sylvia evidently thought her own organisation could do more for such women than trade unionism: at the end of one report on wage increases at an East London clothing firm, obtained 'through our intervention', she urged other sweated workers to 'WRITE TO US FOR ADVICE'.[22] Though it printed local strike reports, the *Dreadnought* seldom drew any moral about the value of trade unions.

Sylvia of course claimed to be a supporter of the unions; but her own lack of experience and contacts in this field is very obvious, and not surprising when her status as an outsider was constantly re-emphasised by the presence of the middle class and aristocratic lady helpers on whom her relief work relied. Local trade unionists found it difficult to take her politics seriously, though some (including Ben Tillett) praised her charitable efforts. During the war she placed further strain on her already shaky alliance with the Poplar trades council, by scornfully criticising the efforts of other labour representatives on local committees, and denouncing patriotic union leaders in the *Dreadnought.* Attempts to improve relations with the unions were confined to those occasions when the WSF needed their support. For example, WSF speakers were sent to union meetings and all the East London unions circularised when the WSF wished to stage a demonstration on the adult suffrage question in August 1917. A few unions made formal promises of support, but very few members turned out to march with the WSF. There was difficulty in finding six volunteers to carry the Bow and

Bromley NUGW banner, and Sylvia admitted afterwards that the Bethnal Green trade unionists who were present came mainly to support their brass band.[23] Despite this disappointment, renewed efforts were made by the WSF the following month. Its application for formal affiliation to the Poplar LRC had run into union opposition. Lansbury wrote to Sylvia pointing out that the decision lay ultimately with local branches, and advising the WSF to get into closer touch with them. WSF members were urged at their next meeting to attend their branches in future; it was also suggested that greater use should be made of the unions as a field of propaganda.[24]

However the WSF's eventual admission to the LRC made no difference to its fundamental approach. As Sylvia Pankhurst's commitment to the revolutionary shop stewards' movement grew, her attitude to the LRC became deliberately casual. WSF delegates attended merely to press their own extremist resolutions. In April 1918 Sylvia remarked that 'the time might come when we could not continue in the Party'.[25] A breach began to look inevitable when the WSF decided not to take any active part in the general election campaign although it 'could not prevent members working for Labour candidates if they wished to'.[26] Sylvia herself turned down the offer of a nomination for a Sheffield Labour candidature, and wrote in the *Dreadnought:* 'When the Election has passed and the workers have settled down again to industrial organisation and active propaganda for the Soviets, we shall heave a sigh of relief.'[27] The contrast between this statement, and the vigorous efforts of the Poplar trades council to get George Lansbury elected, shows how far away from the local trade union movement the WSF had moved.

The eagerness of Sylvia Pankhurst and other British socialists to follow Russia's example, after the revolution, aroused doubts and hostility among pro-war trade unionists. They were soon further dismayed by Russia's decision to make a separate peace. Tillett reported scathingly to his members on the Leeds conference, which he claimed 'did not represent working class opinion and was rigged by a middle class element more mischievous than important'.[28] Socialist reporters had been particularly encouraged by the substantial number of union delegates both at Leeds and at the Brotherhood Church conference in August. But even trade unionists who were less hostile to pacifism than Tillett may have shared his fear that the proposed Workmen's and Soldiers' Councils would usurp union functions. The Dockers Union executive angrily condemned 'the creation of bogus organisations at the instigation of moneyed and middle class people whose mischievous exploitation of the labour movement is disruptive in character'.[29] Whatever union support there had been for the Councils at Leeds seems to have swiftly evaporated.

In the longer term the most important contribution of the Russian revolution to trade union politicisation was the encouragement it gave, directly or indirectly, to a reconsideration of war aims. A handful of union leaders had courageously opposed the war since in 1914; in 1917–18 peace demands came with increasing frequency from East London members. Pacifist socialists had failed to create a desire for peace. But when it came into independent existence their arguments were inevitably heeded, and progress made towards closer future collaboration within the Labour Party. NUR branch reports convey a vivid picture of the changing direction of union opinion. Early in 1917 the central concern of the West Ham branch was the fight for war bonuses. The 5s award in April was received with very luke-warm enthusiasm as 'the best of a bad job. As alternatives to acceptance West Ham members are quite frank in their views: hang the truce, and Conciliation Boards too!' The following month, as well as announcing support for the striking engineers, the branch put forward proposals for government control of the food supply and of industry. After the Leeds conference the West Ham railwaymen re-affirmed their earlier support for the war effort by praising the Seamen's Union's decision to refuse to take British socialist delegates to Russia. In August talk of a railway strike was dismissed as 'part of the sedulous propaganda of pacifists'. But the same report mentions that all West Ham members are now in favour of peace, if it can be obtained without negotiating with the 'upholders of Kaiserism'. The West Ham reconstruction programme reflected growing militancy on wages; it also contained proposals to guarantee future peace which suggest that even the patriots were tired of war-mongering.[30]

Other East London branches had never quite shared West Ham NUR's enthusiasm for the war, despite their rejection of the UDC's overtures. By the summer of 1917 their attitude to the anti-war movement was considerably more friendly. Stratford 1 branch (and possibly others, too) sent its own delegate to the Leeds conference, and after hearing his report agreed to finance a delegate to the London conference of the Workmen's and Soldiers' Council. At a July meeting, 'Miss Sylvia Pankhurst gave a very interesting lecture on "peace". . . It was agreed that this branch shall take part in the peace demonstration in September. The members who were present are heartily sick of the war and all that follows in its trail.' When the Brotherhood Church conference was broken up Poplar NUR passed a resolution of protest and demanded a government enquiry.[31]

Meanwhile, inspired by the renewed political discussion and by the hope of an early election on a much wider franchise, many branches began to set their political funds in order. In July 1917 Royal Mint Street held a special meeting on the subject, at which over £1 arrears was collected and the decision taken to circulate all the non-payers with a manifesto on the importance of the fund. Commercial Road branch held a similar meeting at Toynbee Hall in September, where members agreed to pay 1s per year. The NUR's reconstruction conference in November provided another stimulus to political activity; on 23 November Stratford 2 branch reported: 'Political fund increasing. We shall require a large political fund.' By the end of January 1918 96 per cent of the Commercial Road members were paying the political levy. NUR branches took an active part in selecting local Labour candidates. West Ham branch was so disgusted at the rejection of Thorne that it temporarily withdrew from the 'pro-German trades council'. Commercial Road sent two delegates to the April conference establishing Stepney trades council and Labour Party. Bow branch members were satisfied with the selection procedure in their area; on 28 February they invited George Lansbury, as parliamentary candidate, to attend and address their meeting.[32]

As peace approached, Lansbury and his supporters reaped the benefits of their continuous, close relationship with the trade unions. Despite the new Labour Party constitution's provision for individual membership, in East London no local Labour Parties yet existed which could be separated from the trades councils. The trades councils linked politics and trade unionism throughout the war, not merely because of their formal connection with the socialist societies in the LRC's but also because they had always considered the defence of unionists' broader interests as one of their major tasks. All the main war-time issues of relief, food prices, rents, wages, military service, pensions and reconstruction were discussed continuously in the East London trades councils. They were well prepared for their leading role in the political campaigning which led up to the 1918 election: by this date over half the local union branches were affiliated (considerably more than half in Poplar and West Ham). No socialist who had antagonised the union leaders on the trades council had the slightest hope of being elected in East London, or even selected as a Labour candidate.

Lansbury's early re-selection is a sign of his strong union support. At the South Poplar selection conference in May 1918 the unions completely dominated proceedings: the three men whom Sam March defeated were nominees of the Dockers Union, the ASE and the Stevedores Union, and union delegates made up a large majority of the selectors.[33] Walter Devenay, selected at Stepney, was London district secretary of the Dockers' Union. Alfred Walton, the Labour candidate for Shoreditch, was general secretary of the Coal Porters' Union. Even the West Ham upheaval, as has been indicated in Chapter 3, was not due to any weakening of trade union influence within the local Labour Party. The two men chosen by the selection meeting were both trade unionists, as well as anti-war socialists. During the election campaign many local union branches continued actively to back D.J. Davies against Jack Jones (including the Operative Bricklayers and the Coal Porters), though it soon became obvious that numerically they could not outmatch the NUGW. Will Thorne himself addressed the massive Canning

Town NUGW branch on Jones's behalf, and won a 3–1 majority in his favour.[34] Jones was in a particularly good position to play the trade union card. The *Stratford Express* pointed out that much of his local stature was due to the fact he had successfully represented so many Silvertown workers before the Committee on Production during the war.[35] Thorne's own union achievements, of course, were still more widely known in West Ham.

East Ham provides further evidence of the crucial role of the unions in the general election. Hine failed in East Ham North because the trades council vetoed his attempts, even going so far as to write to Workers Union branches, whose support he had claimed, warning them to have nothing further to do with the new, unofficial Labour Party.[36] Henderson's failure was due partly to the local jealous: of the trades council, and partly to political factors. In election week a fair number of East Ham union branches purchased space in the *East Ham Echo* to advertise their support for him. But it seems likely there was lack of active union enthusiasm for Henderson, though his campaign was financed by his own union, the Friendly Society of Ironfounders. There is no record of him visiting local union branch meetings, a task to which most other Labour candidates devoted considerable time and effort.

National union leaders redoubled their efforts in 1918 to persuade their members to vote Labour. Union journals and reports were full of news of political funds and union candidatures, and provide impressive evidence of the Labour Party's success in closing its ranks as the election approached. In March 1918 Ben Tillett issued a stirring call in the *Dockers Record* for support to that which

> during the next few years. . . might easily become the largest political party in the country. . . We trust that every member will take more than a casual interest in this question. We may have emphasised in the past the paramount importance of the economic factor, but that was in the days when not one in ten of our members had the chance to vote for a direct Labour candidate. Now that almost every member, including thousands of our women members, will for the first time have this opportunity, our views necessarily undergo modifications; now the industrial and the political must go hand in hand;

154

they are the two arms of the workers' movement, and if they pull together, as we hope and believe they will, the future is bright for the workers of the world; we may see in our day the realisation of many of the ideals which have been our guiding star for so many years.[37]

The renewed determination of union leaders to see the industrial and the political go hand in hand within the Labour Party was re-emphasised at the 1918 Trades Union Congress. A proposal for a separate anti-pacifist, anti-Bolshevik 'Trade Union Labour Party' was soundly defeated in favour of 'loyal co-operation with the Labour Party' in its existing form.[38]

How much effect did the advice of union leaders have on the political thinking of their members? This question is important, yet difficult to answer. The amount of political guidance offered by the leadership varied from union to union. On such subjects as profiteering union opinion was unanimous, yet on other subjects the nature of political comment also varied greatly, reflecting the view of individuals at the top of each union. Though many union leaders had socialist sympathies, few were prepared to jeopardise the industrial strength of their unions by overdoing the political propaganda. Some trade union reports contained very few references to politics (for example those of the AATVW, the London Society of Compositors, the Operative Bricklayers, the Friendly Society of Ironfounders and the National Union of Packing Case Makers), though most of these unions were affiliated to the Labour Party. The majority of reports contained an address to the members from the general secretary which combined industrial with political comment. Sometimes the political message was very general, emphasising the need for the working class to defend itself against the government and the profiteers. When the union secretary was also a leading figure in the Labour Party, members were often more specifically advised to take part in Labour Party politics. Some unions published regular parliamentary reports alongside those on the union's industrial achievement (for example the ASCJ and the NUGW). The NUGW was unusual, however, in actually enshrining its socialist principles in the union rule book.[39]

Many trade unions printed their own journals, which pro-vided the union leadership with wider scope to air their political views. Monthly or fortnightly editorials on industrial events could scarcely exclude political comment in war-time. Even the *Workers Union Record,* traditionally anti-political, was soon criticising the government's actions and making alternative proposals. London organisers of the Workers Union were so disgusted at the *Record's* political inadequacy that in January 1916 they founded their own *Trade Union Worker.* This newspaper, like the ASE *Journal,* devoted much space to political articles by guest writers such as Marion Phillips, Herbert Morrison and G.D.H. Cole. In the *Railway Review* and the *Woman Worker* politics was again a notice-able feature, but was never allowed to predominate. The *Licensed Vehicle Trades Record,* on the other hand, verged on becoming a socialist pamphlet. When its editor resigned to join the army in 1915 his job was taken over by George Sanders, a militant socialist and industrial unionist who announced: 'I want to make this something more than a mere trade journal, not a medium for slanging matches between individuals, but its columns always open for matters of general interest to everyone connected with our society',[40] This opened the way for a flood of political articles and long editorials attacking everything from profiteering to the Church, the monarchy and the war itself. Sanders did not convert all his readers. By 1917 criticism of his extreme politics was so widespread that the union executive was attempting to unseat him. A lively debate in the letters column revealed the wide range of opinions within the union on the subject of 'Socialism and Trade Unionism', Sanders persisting in his claim that, 'The doctrine of the Socialists is a matter that affects us, and its teachings do have an immediate bearing upon the whole of our members and their well-being.'[41] His 'open door' policy for opponents' views was perhaps unusual. But many union journals had a letters page which helped to ensure (and to prove) that leaders' opinions did not completely dominate the political education of members.

There can be no doubt that the political views expressed

in union leaders' speeches, and in trade union reports and journals, reached a wider working class audience than the more fully developed and coherent politics of the socialist press. The political ideas of union leaders were spread downwards by word of mouth through local organisers to the union branches, and from branch meetings to the factory floor. Examples have been quoted of branch resolutions on subjects like profiteering which closely echo the language of the union leadership. Copies of union reports were sent free to all branches and made available for members to read. A few union journals were free as well, including the *Dockers Record*. The evidence suggests that union journals were read by many members who were not regular branch attenders. Despite the problems of soaring costs and lack of paper, all union journals increased their circulation during the war. The journals of the clerical and postal unions had exceptionally large readerships, probably because their members were more literate than most. Sales equalled or even exceeded branch membership. Most other unions could not hope to match such figures. At the beginning of 1916 the *Railway Review* was selling about 60,000 weekly copies to its 300,000 members—'although we believe most of them see it'.[42] Progress was slow but steady until 1918, when the editor wrote of a 'magnificent spurt in our circulation', in September he reported 2,000 new readers gained within the past few weeks.[43] Even the *Licensed Vehicle Trades Record* won readers. In December 1917 the high circulation of the paper was dragged into the debate over politics and trade unionism: 'Let me assure our Friend that more journals are sold now at 2d than were sold three years ago at a penny, notwithstanding the fact that about ten thousand of our members have joined the colours in the interim.'[44]

The *Railway Review* was probably right when it claimed that its readership exceeded the number of paying subscribers. Other editors made the same complaint. George Sanders pointed out that circulation 'could have improved a lot if in some instances three or four members did not make one copy of the journal suffice. I stood at a garage recently and heard one purchaser say to another, "All right Bill, don't you buy one, you can have mine tomorrow".'[45] In a plea for more buyers, the editor of the ASE *Journal* pointed out that only about one sixth of the membership paid for the paper, but 'we may assume that our circulation is five times that of our issue—which is the proportion of readers allowed by the experts'. He went on to describe the results of this wide readership: 'The *Journal,* as an educational force has a compelling power which it is impossible to estimate; it plays a very large part in shaping the thoughts, activities and destinies of the men in our trade, and through them their fellow workers in kindred trades.'[46]

The journals of unskilled unions made great efforts to expand their readership (and attract new members) by introducing popular, entertaining features. The *Railway Review* was deservedly famous for its cartoons. Other humorous items in this journal included the weekly musing of Battersea Bowser, a cockney porter with a shrewish wife, and members' jokes and verses. The *Trade Union Worker* had a strong line in short stories, often with a political moral, but with plenty of romance and sentiment as well. The *Woman Worker* specialised in household hints, recipes, and competitions in crochetting and verse-making. It got a huge response when it invited branches to send in group photographs for publication. Like several other journals, it also published individual branch reports. These were a particularly important feature of the *Railway Review,* and great was the indignation among members when the editor decided to publish the reports only monthly in order to save space. West Ham branch accused him on 30 March 1917 of 'disturbing the most useful and popular feature of the *Review* to the detriment and inconvenience of its purchasing and most loyal supporters. In our opinion the proposed changes will make the organisation and detailed work of the branches more difficult than ever'. This last remark highlights the fact that branch reports provided the branches with more than merely the satisfaction of appearing in print. At a time when most members were working excessive overtime and were often unable to attend meetings, the reports helped them to keep in touch.

For those who did attend, branch activities provided a further opportunity to develop their political ideas. Even in the early years of the war political speakers were often invited to East London NUR branches. In February 1915 the West Ham branch heard a speaker from the local Patriotic Association on 'The Origin, Nature and Constitution of the British People', and in June invited members of other branches to hear Joe Terrett (of the Socialist National Defence Committee) on 'Secret Diplomacy and the Working Class'.[47] Plaistow was the only branch which accepted a speaker from the Union of Democratic Control in 1915. When they were accused, as a result, of being pro-German, they wrote indignantly to the *Railway Review:* 'Will other branches note that we do not uphold the principles of the UDC party, but invited them for criticism only'. In May Poplar 1 also braved criticism by inviting an ILP speaker, who confined his speech to 'The Case for a Labour Party'.[48] The NUR encouraged working class education outside the branch room. East London branches repeatedly expressed their support for the Central Labour College and its aim of 'independent' (i.e. socialist) working class education; in March 1915 Bethnal Green voted to raise 5s per quarter towards its maintenance. Branches encouraged members to read history and politics at home, too. Plaistow NUR opened its own branch library in 1916, and in 1917 Poplar 1 decided to subscribe to the Fabian library.[49]

The NUR was more heavily committed to education than most unions. But the Sunday afternoon classes in Stratford on economics and industrial history had attracted a wide variety of trade unionists in 1917, and speakers on general political subjects attended many other unions' meetings. NFWW members were probably less educated than most, yet invited Lansbury, Sam March and others to speak at their socials. The success of Poplar NFWW elocution classes suggests that political education aroused a lively response. The branch secretary reported to the *Woman Worker:*

> Our chief aim is practice for public speaking. Each member takes the chair in turn, and everyone who comes is obliged to speak, and at the end criticisms are made by Miss Berwicke, who is coaching us. We discuss 'Workshop Committees', 'Housing', and any sort of trade union or Labour question, and our interest is proved by the length of the discussion and the late hours at which we generally return home![50]

Members of more skilled unions, like the ASCJ, were encouraged to attend Workers Educational Association classes, and the WEA's 1916 campaign to establish 'What Labour Wants from Education' received warm support.[51] To varying degrees, most unions saw it as part of their job to extend members' interests beyond mere wages questions, thus consolidating support for trade unionism, but also helping to open the way for the Labour Party.

Those workers who regularly went to branch meetings and took an active part in trade union social and educational activities were undoubtedly a minority of the total union membership in East London. Reluctance to attend meetings outside working hours is a perennial problem of trade unionism, and it seems likely that war-time conditions of overwork, darkened streets and restricted licensing hours were an added deterrent. The evidence of branch reports is inconclusive. In March 1915 West Ham NUR reports 47 new members 'most of whom were present' at the meeting; in March 1917 Stratford 1 complains: 'We should like to see some of the new members attend the meeting room sometimes.'[52] The same branch had taken drastic measures to accommodate its expanding membership in October 1915: 'There will be plenty of room for all in the branch room now, as the billiard table is shifted, giving seating accommodation for over 200 persons.' This suggests that no more than a sixth of the membership of 1,200 were expected at any one meeting; however over 100 obviously were attending, which made a more sizeable meeting than the branch was accustomed to. In July 1917 the enormous branch of Stratford 2 was forced to exchange its normal premises for Water Lane School because of overcrowding.[53]

Among the unions generally, complaints of low attendances were more common than complaints of overcrowding. At Shoreditch branch of the LPU a mere 9 of the 96 members turned up to one meeting: this was considered exceptionally bad.[54] The only union providing definite information on attendances was the ASE, which published branch voting figures on various national issues in its reports. These demonstrate that attendances varied greatly, depending on the issue which was being discussed. Less than 10 per cent of the East

London membership were present to vote on benevolent fund levies in 1916 and 1917, but considerably more voted on affiliation to the TUC in 1918. The question of the government's manpower proposals in the same year brought out over 50 per cent of the members.[55] Probably the numbers were still higher if a local dispute was under consideration.

A *Railway Review* article on 'Non-Attendance at Branch Meetings' indicates which sort of members were good attenders:

> in the main the vast majority of our members are apathetic and in-different, due to the lack of class consciousness of their status in society, and the historical mission they as workers have to fulfil in order to achieve their economic emancipation. None of us imbibed the principles of Trade Unionism, etc., in our mother's milk; nevertheless one is bound to note that the most active of our members in each branch of our organisation are those who can claim to have some conception of first principles, due to hard clear thinking, and study; men who recognise their own individual responsibilities in the questions at issue which vitally affect the whole working class movement.[56]

The most assiduous trade unionists were likely to be those who had an interest in Labour politics, whether it had developed through their experience of unionism, or whether they had entered the union as socialists. This picture of a political minority dominating the activities of many union branches is certainly borne out by the branch reports in union journals, and by trades council reports. After following the activities of the East London NUR branches over a year or two it is easy to identify the political affiliations of each branch's leading members. West Ham subscribed to Will Thorne's brand of patriotic socialism; Forest Gate contained ILP supporters; Poplar 1 was guided by Lansbury's views and staunchly backed the local Labour Party. Branch resolutions, besides sometimes being influenced by the opinions of union leaders, often directly reflected the political commitments of the members who drafted them.

In a poor area like East London, trade unionism was likely to precede an interest in socialism, rather than the other way round. The fact that many union members did not regularly attend branch meetings, and looked upon their unions merely as a route to higher wages, does not lessen the political importance of trade unionism. Through their national leaders, local organisers, journals, reports, meetings and factory floor recruitment efforts, the unions introduced the idea of independent political representation to very large numbers of workers. The active 10 per cent or 20 per cent of members provided the foundations of East London's Labour voting strength after 1918. Unlike the mass of ill-paid, non-unionised labour, these men and women were open to political education and organisation, and were in a strong position to influence the thinking of their fellow-workers. Even one tenth of total union membership is a considerably larger number than the few hundred members of local socialist societies. The trade unions had always been inter-woven with the fabric of the Labour Party, at leadership and through the trades councils. The war strengthened these links. Industrial questions became more closely connected with questions of politics and government. State intervention in the economy and society also gave socialist policies a new relevance. Though all parties acknowledged the need for social reconstruction in 1918, only the Labour Party was preparing for an enthusiastic peace-time extension of inter-vention, unequivocally in the interests of the working class, and as far as possible under the control of workers and their organisations. This was becoming clear to the hundreds of trade unionists who had voted Liberal before 1914; it was clearer still to the many thousands of newly enfranchised and, in many cases, newly unionised workers who entered politics for the first time at the end of the war. Election results were soon to show how enormously the East London Labour Parties stood to benefit from the expanding influence of a trade unionism more deeply rooted than in any pre-war period.

NOTES

1. Ministry of Reconstruction, Committee on Relations between Employers and Employed, Supplementary Report on Works Committees, Cd. 9001 (1918), P.P. 1918 XIV, 953.
2. *Dreadnought,* 15 June 1918.

3. *Dreadnought,* 16 July 1918.
4. Commission of Enquiry into Industrial Unrest, No. 5 Division, Report of the Commissioners for the London and South Eastern Area, Cd. 8666 (1917), P.P. 1917-18, XV, 70.
5. ASE *Monthly Journal,* May 1918; NUGW *Quarterly Reports,* March and June 1918; *Labour Gazette,* July and August 1918.
6. ASE *Monthly Journal,* May 1918.
7. ASE *Monthly Journal,* November 1918.
8. Hinton, J., *The First Shop Stewards Movement* (1973), 16.
9. *Dreadnought,* 23 November 1918.
10. *Railway Review,* 26 October 1917.
11. *SE,* 26 July 1916.
12. *Railway Review,* 29 January and 5 February 1915.
13. *Herald,* 30 March 1916.
14. *Railway Review,* 25 May 1917.
15. *Trade Union Worker,* May 1917.
16. ASE *Monthly Journal,* June 1917.
17. *Railway Review,* 9 July 1915.
18. *Daily Herald,* 6 August 1914.
19. *Herald,* 6 February 1915.
20. *Herald,* 27 March 1915.
21. *Herald,* 30 January 1915.
22. *Dreadnought,* 10 July 1915.
23. WSF Members Meeting Minute Book, 19 March 1917-20 January 1920 (P 21), 13 August and 17 September 1917.
24. WSF Committee Minute Book, 1 June 1918-26 April 1918 (P 17), 13 September 1917.
25. WSF Members Meeting Minute Book, 19 March 1917-20 January 1920 (P 21), 15 April 1918.
26. Ibid., 15 November 1918.
27. *Dreadnought,* 30 November 1918.
28. *Dockers Record,* June 1917.
29. *Dockers Record,* August 1917.
30. *Railway Review,* 27 April, 25 May, 29 June, 31 August and 26 October 1917.
31. *Railway Review,* 6 and 27 July and 31 August 1917.
32. *Railway Review,* 3 August 1917 and 25 January, 22 February, 26 April and 24 May 1918.
33. *ELO,* 1 June 1918.
34. *SE,* 20 November 1918.
35. *SR,* 30 November 1918.
36. *EE,* 5 July 1918.
37. *Dockers Record,* March 1918.
38. TUC *Report* 1918, 252-261.
39. The stated objects of the union, in the NUGW *Revised Rules* 1917, included 'Number 9. To secure the return of members of the Union to boards of guardians, municipal or other local authorities, and to parliament, providing the candidates are pledged to the collective ownership under democratic control of the means of production, distribution and exchange.'
40. *Licensed Vehicle Trades Record,* 28 April 1915.
41. *Licensed Vehicle Trades Record,* 11 July 1917.
42. *Railway Review,* 28 January 1916.
43. *Railway Review,* 22 March and 20 September 1918.

44. *Licensed Vehicle Trades Record*, 1 March 1916 and 12 December 1917.
45. *Licensed Vehicle Trades Record*, 3 January 1917.
46. ASE *Monthly Journal*, July 1915.
47. *Railway Review*, 29 January and 11 June 1915.
48. *Railway Review*, 21 May and 23 July 1915.
49. *Railway Review*, 30 June 1916 and 27 April 1917.
50. *Woman Worker*, 7 August 1918.
51. ASCJ *Monthly Journal*, August 1916.
52. *Railway Review*, 2 March 1915 and 9 March 1917.
53. *Railway Review*, 22 October 1915 and 27 July 1917.
54. *Licensed Vehicle Trades Record*, 25 July 1917.
55. ASE, *Quarterly Reports* December 1916, 1917 and 1918.
56. *Railway Review*, 9 August 1918.

CHAPTER 6

THE JEWS AND THE WAR

'The Hebrew colony, unlike any other alien colony in the land, forms a solid and permanently distinct block—a race apart, as it were, in an enduring island of extraneous thought and custom.'[1] So wrote Major Evans-Gordon, Conservative MP for Stepney, at the height of the disquiet and mounting prejudice which preceded the 1905 Aliens Act. By 1914 open hostility towards the East London Jews had abated, partly because of the success of the Act in reducing the number of new arrivals. But although the *East London Advertiser* thought that foreign Jews were 'slowly, very slowly, coming under distinctly British influences',[2] their integration with the surrounding population was a prediction for the future rather than a fact of the present. To most East Londoners they remained 'a race apart', separated by religion, language, culture and employment. The progress which had been made towards acceptance was fragile. There was a grave danger that the outbreak of war would revive and accentuate all the old fears and suspicions of the alien population, for their experience of war would inevitably differ from that of the native gentiles.

The *Jewish Chronicle,* voice of patriotic Anglo-Jewry, opposed war until the very last minute. 'War breeds the feeling of prejudice, from which the Jew, placed as he is, is bound to be the keenest sufferer,' warned its editorial on 31 July 1914. But once war was declared the *Chronicle,* and most established British Jews, swung abruptly round to a stance of extreme pro-war patriotism. Reservations about Jews fighting fellow-Jews were brushed aside, and a commanding new slogan adopted: 'ENGLAND HAS BEEN ALL SHE COULD BE TO JEWS, JEWS WILL BE ALL THEY CAN BE TO ENGLAND'.[3] The sudden switch from pacifism to war-

165

fever reflects a deep-seated feeling of insecurity amongst the leaders of Anglo-Jewry, which increased rather than decreased as the war proceeded. They feared—rightly—that any suggestion that Jews were not 'doing their bit' would be seized upon by anti-semites. In earlier years, similar fears for the reputation of the Jewish community had caused widespread opposition to large-scale immigration, and anxiety over the poverty and foreign behaviour of the East London settlers. Now these same immigrants were the potential weak link in the solid front of Anglo-Jewish patriotism.

Vigorous efforts were immediately made to promote the views of the *Jewish Chronicle* among the Jewish population in East London. Success was not lacking in the early days. The *Chronicle* noted approvingly that among the crowds clamouring to join up outside the Whitechapel recruiting station were several hundred young Jews, 'more English than the English in their expression of loyalty and desire for service'.[4] A month later a special Jewish recruiting meeting at Camperdown House (the Aldgate headquarters of the Jewish Lads Brigade) produced 150 immediate enlistments. Most of the speakers were British Jews, including local politicians such as Sir Stuart Samuel (Liberal MP), G.A. Cohen (Conservative candidate) and J. Raphael, of the Whitechapel and Spitalfields Costermongers Union. A Stepney councillor remarked that 'there had seemed at first to be some very slight hesitation in coming forward because of the alliance between England and Russia', but apart from this ominous note the meeting was an impressive display of united Stepney patriotism.[5] It was the start of a propaganda campaign by the Jewish Recruiting Committee which brought many of the most distinguished British Jews to East London to urge its inhabitants that 'the responsibility and duty of the Jews was even greater than that of the Britisher, because it was their duty to fight for the liberty, justice and freedom they had in this land'.[6] By December 1914 nearly 300 old boys of the Jews Free School had enlisted. Stepney Jewish Lads Club had sent 107. Both the *East London Observer* and the *East London Advertiser* commented favourably on the fact that, relative to its size, the Jewish community was providing more than its fair share of volunteers. [7]

But even at this early stage of the war, such a picture of patriotic harmony is misleading. Many thousands of East London Jews turned a deaf ear to the recruiters. About half were ineligible for recruitment because of their foreign nationality. The great majority of the ghetto population was foreign in its habits and inclinations, even if British by birth. Britain's quarrel with Germany seemed no concern of theirs. The fact that Russia was fighting alongside Britain was an added disincentive, and religious loyalty (despite the exhortations of English rabbis) seemed also to dictate non-involvement in the war. The international nature of Jewry was a living reality for recent immigrants who shared their ghetto with hundreds of German and Austrian Jews. British attitudes towards foreigners (or those who until recently had been foreigners) were also frequently discouraging. Heightened patriotism went hand-in-hand with renewed xenophobia. The press use of the term 'German-Jew' encouraged popular confusion between 'enemy aliens' and other foreigners. The *East London Observer* was already sniffing out spies and saboteurs in Whitechapel, 'which has the unenviable distinction of accommodating more alien enemies than any other area in London'.[8] Even naturalised British subjects felt unsafe, after a number of 'enemy' Jews had had their shops looted. The *Jewish Chronicle* described how, with a pathetic faith in legality, they clung to their papers 'as if life depended upon their preservation'. Some displayed the precious naturalisation or birth certificate in a window 'between the miniature flags of the allied nations'; others hid it in the synagogue for greater safety. [9]

Some of the worst incidents of prejudice against foreigners occurred over the question of relieving economic distress. Complaints of discrimination in East London soon began to reach the War Emergency Workers National Committee. On 16 October Fred Knee of the London Trades Council wrote to inform the WNC of 'the curious manner in which Stepney of all places is behaving towards its distressed people who are not naturalised British subjects'.[10] Though the Bethnal Green and Shoreditch relief committees were prepared to assist aliens, in Stepney all foreign Jews were being referred

to the Jewish Board of Guardians. Soon after, a memorandum on the same issue from a Mr Cohen of the United
Furnishing Trades Union arrived at the WNC office. The
transfer of Jewish cases had in fact been requested by the
Board, and the practice had by now spread to other East
London boroughs. Cohen explained the demeaning nature
of the Jewish Board's investigations ('of such a character as
to make applicants feel that they are begging'), then concluded forcefully: 'I wish to state that the feeling of the
majority of Jews is so full of disgust at the methods and
general manner of the Jewish Board that they have repeatedly stated their preference to starve rather than apply to that
body.' The handing over of relief to the Board was 'a
dangerous precedent'.[11]

Since one of the main aims of the WNC was to defend
workers suffering war-time distress from Poor Law treatment,
it is not surprising that J.S. Middleton lost no time in taking
up Mr Cohen's complaints. Ben Cooper, Jewish secretary of
the Cigar Makers Union and a WNC member, was asked to
write a full report on discrimination, and on 21 November
Middleton communicated to the national secretary of the
Prince of Wales Fund his committee's demand for equal
treatment for Jews.[12] Meanwhile the WNC had received
further direct complaints from another source, the East End
Jewish Trade Unions War Emergency Committee. This committee had been set up on the initiative of the Jewish Bakers
Union in the first week of the war, and by October had
collected information on a number of cases of discrimination.
Jewish trade unionists were being kept off Stepney committees, though representatives of the Board of Guardians
were welcomed (an example of anti-trade unionism rather
than anti-semitism, in fact, since gentile unions received
similar rebuffs). Jewish women were being refused work at
the Stepney borough relief workshops. In another case, a
carpenter who was a naturalised British subject was refused
a government contract because he was Jewish. Some refusals
may have resulted from misunderstanding, but the evidence
strongly suggests that, in Stepney particularly, there was
considerable hostility to assisting friendly aliens as well as
enemies, and indeed Jews in general.[13] When the *Toynbee*

Record investigated unemployment in Stepney, in December 1914, it confirmed this impression.[14]

The misguided patriotic zeal of Anglo-Jewish philanthropists actively encouraged discrimination. Minutes of a Jewish Board of Guardians' meeting on 31 August 1914 reveal that this body not only offered to take over a large slice of the local borough relief committee's work, by dealing with 'all cases of foreign Jews', but also proposed intervening in the assessment of relief payments to British Jews. In the following six weeks the Board's cases more than doubled, from 796 in the same period of 1913 to 1,832; the cost rose from £770 to £1,716.[15] Wealthy Anglo-Jews were anxious to avoid accusations that East London immigrants were a burden on Britain. But costs were so high, and Stepney Jews' opposition to transfer to the Board's care so strong, that eventually subscribers to the Guardians' funds questioned the wisdom of such policies.[16] Other Jewish charities followed the Board's example at the beginning of the war. The Poor Jews Temporary Shelter assumed responsibility for all Jews who found themselves stranded in London as a result of the war. Within a few weeks the Shelter was filled to overflowing with Belgian Jewish refugees who had little hope of moving on after the usual 14–day permitted stay. After opening new premises in Poland Street and Great Alie Street, and running up a huge overdraft, the Shelter was eventually forced to appeal to the whole Jewish community for money and offers of hospitality. Under the Rothschilds' leadership £40,000 was raised between September 1914 and March 1915, and the refugee problem largely taken out of the hands of the East London organisation.[17] Meanwhile the Jewish Soup Kitchen in Butler Street joined in the campaign to spare the British public's purse by undertaking to double its usual relief to the poor in the winter of 1914–15.[18] The Jewish Society for the Protection of Women and Girls tried to overcome the discriminatory policy of the Stepney borough workrooms by opening its own, exclusively for alien Jewish girls.[19]

The East London press had a few perfunctory words of praise for Jewish philanthropy, but it is doubtful if it had any deep effect on local opinion, helping to combat anti-

alien and anti-Jewish prejudice. During 1915 it became clear
that the war would not be won easily. The *Lusitania* disaster
in May brought the mounting hatred of the Huns to
explosion point in East London. The three days of violence
which followed were directed at Austrians and Germans
(many of them Jews), but endangered all foreigners. The
police stood by helplessly while angry mobs smashed and
robbed their way through every East London borough.
'Most of the shops and houses were so ransacked that only
the bare walls remained', reported the *Observer*.[20] The
Advertiser warned that 'unless the movement can be speedily
checked, shopkeepers of other than German nationality will
be bound to suffer. It is difficult with so many foreign residents to make sure that a name which is Russian, Belgian, or
Serbian, will not be mistaken for German.'[21] The following
week, the columns of the East London press contained
curious genealogical advertisements, demonstrating the pure
Allied descent of shopkeepers with foreign-sounding names.

There was no repetition of the *Lusitania* riots. But prejudice against the East London Jewish population continued
to grow. Towards the end of 1915 military service emerged
as the most dominant issue separating the Jews from the
native population, the more so because accusations of 'shirk-
ing' were linked with fears that aliens and their offspring
were replacing British soldiers in jobs and businesses. Such
fears were fuelled by the evidence of growing prosperity in
the Jewish community. 'The working classes have had a more
prosperous time than for many years past', reported the
Jewish Board of Guardians in December 1915. Government
contracts had solved the unemployment problem and were
offering even unskilled boy and girl workers the chance to
earn 'abnormally high wages'.[22] A *Jewish Chronicle* reporter
who visited Whitechapel one Saturday night found evidence
of newly-acquired wealth in the brisk business of the luxury
trades. Jewellers' shops were 'crowded to the doors, so great
was the press of would-be customers. . . The cluster earrings
were selling like sandwiches on "Chometz Bottel" night.'[23]
Such reports (a variation on the 'fur coats and pianos' stories
about munitions girls) did not go unnoticed by anti-semites.
The *East London Observer* chose national registration in July

1915 as the pretext for the first of what later became a continuous stream of anti-semitic editorials: 'A great deal has been said as to Jewish effort in the War, but there is a strong local feeling that the "Jew Boys", as they are termed, who hang about street corners and public houses, the cheap foreign restaurants and similar places, ought to be made to do something for the country they honour with their presence.'[24]

The failure of the Derby scheme in Stepney focused further unfriendly attention on the Jews. In vain the Jewish Recruiting Committee requested War Office permission 'to make a special canvass in the Stepney Borough in particular, and in East London generally'. In vain the *Jewish Chronicle* pointed to the still favourable overall total of Jews serving, and the honours they had won.[25] The *East London Observer* continued to accuse, and the local support for its accusations is clear from its correspondence columns. An anonymous Stepney councillor wrote:

Since the war began I can honestly say that I have not come across a dozen Jewish soldiers. I have been told in many quarters that they are earning heaps of money in consequence of the shortage of men. If this is so, it is a despicable advantage to take, and the sooner it is brought to an end by conscription the better.

Jacob Fine, of the London Ladies Tailors Union, sarcastically offered to set the councillor right with a guided, fact-finding tour of the Jewish quarters—'or will he wait to change his own views at the next Municipal Election?' Undeterred, 'Stepney Councillor' delivered a new broadside the following week: 'Have your correspondents made enquiries as to the extraordinary increase in Jewish marriages that took place in East London soon after it was stated by Mr Asquith that single men were "to go first"?' A fortnight later he publicised the fact that only 2 out of 900 Jewish children at the Fairclough Street School had fathers on military service, compared with 52 of the 500 young Christians at St Paul's Church School.[26]

Meanwhile the Military Service Bill was becoming law. The behaviour of Jewish applicants to the Stepney military tribunal soon provided a far more potent source of anti-semitic propaganda. The tribunal's first session resulted in 29 refusals out of 33 cases, and a mass of bad publicity for the Jewish community.[27] Not only was doubt thrown on the honesty of the claims, but the attitude of both claimants and their supporters in the public gallery was disrespectful, and at times defiant. There were 'groans of protest' when one tribunal member suggested an applicant's sister should be sent out to work to support the family in his absence: 'The application was refused amid cries of "Shame!" and "A disgrace!" from the public. The Mayor said he would have to order the public out if such scenes occurred again. A voice: "A great farce".' Such scenes—and worse—continued to occur at every sitting of the Stepney tribunal. The mayor was repeatedly forced to put his threat into action. Since eviction of the public could, by law, only be a temporary expedient, it failed to deter: 'as they went they uttered catcalls and whistled "Britons never shall be slaves". Some unseemly language was also used. Outside a number of constables were engaged in keeping the public at bay.' Later in the same session, angry tribunal members were goaded into the unwise step of swapping insults with the re-admitted audience.[28] It was an undignified spectacle, calculated to damage the tribunal's reputation amongst the Jewish community, as well as the Jews' standing in the eyes of other East Londoners. The *East London Observer* could be relied upon to exaggerate every incident of disorder into an attack on the Jewish population as a whole. Its editorials fulminated against 'gross behaviour and obscene interruptions and unpatriotic displays' which 'might tempt one to suspect that German gold had been at work'.[29]

Despite editorial hostility, verbatim reports of tribunal proceedings in the local press provide evidence of the true reasons for many Jews' unwillingness to serve. Appeals were most frequently made on economic grounds. But there were more specifically Jewish reasons for the size of the Stepney tribunal's task. One man pleaded that 'he was opposed to warfare, his parents having left Russia so that he should not be conscripted'.[30] The tribunal was unimpressed, using the fact that he was a tailor making khaki uniforms to ridicule his plea, but there can be little doubt that fear and hatred of military discipline was deeply rooted amongst Russian Jews whose forebears had suffered so atrociously in the Tsar's armies. Even the *Jewish Chronicle,* amid its patriotic propaganda, sympathised with the immigrants' 'inclination to regard military service from the typically Russian viewpoint— as something to be escaped from, at all costs'.[31] Religious objections were also common. Joining the army would inevitably mean breaking the Sabbath, eating non-kosher food, and committing hundreds of other trespasses. For the priestly Cohens, who were forbidden to look upon dead bodies, to engage in warfare was an act of sacrilege. It was the tribunal's task to decide whether such objections were genuine: an impossible task even when those sitting in judgement shared the same religion as the applicant, and a mere charade when they were ignorant of the laws and customs of that religion.

There is no shortage of evidence that the East London tribunals were prejudiced against Jewish applicants because they were Jewish and 'foreign', as well as because they did not want to fight. During the summer of 1916 resolutions were forwarded to the government from the Stepney and Bethnal Green tribunals condemning the privileged position of aliens who were being 'allowed to strengthen their industrial position without any sacrifice'.[32] Emotive talk of alien shirkers and alien job-snatchers sometimes occurred even while the tribunals were discharging their judicial functions.[33] Such remarks were seized upon and highlighted in the local press. The government's obvious indecision over the alien question encouraged the expression of extreme views. In June it was decided to permit the voluntary enlistment of friendly aliens. In July appeared the first official threat of deportation, if 'voluntary' recruiting failed. But the legal and practical difficulties of enforcing such a policy made the government hesitate. As the deadline for beginning repatriation was postponed from month to month, the publicity and ill-feeling surrounding the issue grew to a crescendo.

But the Jewish opponents of military service were also starting to organise and to produce their own, self-defensive propaganda. At the beginning of the war Rocker had bravely persisted in publicising his anti-war position to the Yiddish-speaking population through his newspaper, *Arbeter Fraint.* Its forcible closure, and the trial of its journalists for an offence against the Defence of the Realm Act (DORA),[34] coincided with the emergence of a far stronger anti-conscription movement in East London. On 7 July 1916 the *Jewish Chronicle* reported that the Home Secretary's statement on military service for aliens had produced 'a great deal of agitation'; 'numerous conferences' had been held to discuss the matter, and a protest meeting was planned. The outcome of this activity was the Foreign Jews Protection Committee (FJPC). It brought together representatives from 22 Jewish organisations, including 7 socialist groups, 12 trade union branches, and various Friendly Societies.[35] Rocker's remaining supporters in the Yiddish Anarchist Federation and the Workers Circle were included, but the committee was not dominated by any one group. Support was drawn from all those in the Yiddish-speaking community who opposed the enforcement of military service on immigrant Jews. During the year of the FJPC's existence, evidence suggests that this support was very substantial. It was no mere paper committee. The FJPC organised petitions, deputations and mass meetings, and intervened in the meetings of other organisations. Despite the ad hoc basis on which it had been established it held together and, because many of its activists were socialists of one sort of another, assumed a politically educative role within the community.

The first action of the FJPC was to draw up a petition outlining its case, which was sent immediately to the Home Secretary. The proposal to repatriate friendly aliens who refused to enlist was 'a grave issue':

> However this may operate with regard to Italians, Frenchmen or men of other nationalities domiciled in this country, in the case of Jews born in Russia, who have taken refuge in this country from the unspeakable persecutions and hardships inflicted on them by the Russian government, the result can only be a violation of the right of asylum which has made Great Britain a nation honoured above all others. . . We cannot therefore do otherwise than place before you, Sir, the tragic impossibility of our position under the new proposals,

and to ask that, if it is no longer possible for the British Government to regard us, as heretofore, as refugees and exiles, then to let us go forth to some other land where conditions so repugnant to humanity and justice will not be imposed upon us, and where we may be sorrowfully at peace.[36]

The demands of this petition, and the manner in which they were expressed, reduced the *East London Observer* (and no doubt many of its readers) to a state of apoplectic fury. Herbert Samuel, the Anglo-Jewish Home Secretary, was equally unmoved. At the end of August he refused to receive an FJPC deputation, though it included the distinguished figure of Zangwill. He did, however, listen to the arguments of patriotic Jews, and agreed to postpone repatriation until a Special Russian Jewish Recruiting Committee had completed its efforts.

Meanwhile the FJPC itself was going from strength to strength. By October it claimed to represent 120 organisations![37] No doubt this was an exaggeration, but there is other evidence of the support for its stand. A spokesman of the English Zionist Federation, who was known to support the recruitment of foreign Jews, was shouted down at a mass meeting at the Pavilion theatre, Whitechapel. After two hours of uproar, and some fighting in the audience, he retired without obtaining a hearing.[38] A similar scene occurred at Premierland when a meeting was convened on the subject of forming a Jewish battalion.[39] Such obstructive tactics were welcomed (and may even have been organised) by the FJPC. But it also attempted to put across its case by rational argument. Abraham Bezalel, the FJPC's secretary, wrote a series of letters to the local press explaining why foreign Jews should not be forced to serve.[40]

By the end of the year it was obvious that voluntary recruiting had failed, despite the efforts of the recruiting committee, and despite added inducements such as free naturalisation after three months' service. Only a few hundred foreign Jews enlisted. The government would be obliged to act. Repatriation could not come quickly enough for many people in East London. Local tribunals continued to pass angry resolutions, local MPs harassed the government in the

House of Commons, and the editorials in the local press were more vitriolic than ever. In February 1917 the Bethnal Green tribunal instigated an East London conference on 'this obvious injustice'[41] which marked a climax of anti-alien hysteria. Delegates included Members of Parliament, councillors and tribunal members from every East London borough. Their demands for 'equal sacrifice' were familiar, but were expressed with extraordinary vehemence. The fact that so many leading figures in East London public life felt impelled to speak of the Jews in terms of open prejudice and hatred proves that the *East London Observer* was no isolated anti-semitic voice. The FJPC sent a telegram to the conference appealing 'to the chivalry of the English to defend them against insidious attacks'; the chairman refused to read it.[42]

But Jewish appeals for understanding and support were not always so contemptuously cast aside, even at the height of the anti-alien witch hunt. The Russian revolution was to bring the supporters of the FJPC into close collaboration with British anti-war socialists. Predictably, fear of Jewish economic competition and envy of their privileged position with regard to military service were reflected to some extent in the organised labour movement. Neither the TUC nor Labour Party conferences opposed the deportation threat. Yet, despite the patriotism of most union leaders, Jews won some sympathy for their case in the local trade union movement even before the revolution gave it a clearer political point. The Bethnal Green trades council backed up Jewish protests against discrimination in relief matters early in the war.[43] In February 1915 a London Trades Council resolution against the persecution of Jews in Russia was passed 'with only a few dissentients'. A major victory was achieved by East London Jewish delegates when, in July 1916, a special meeting on the aliens question decided to back the FJPC position. There was 'considerable discussion' but the majority was a substantial one (37 votes for, 19 against).[44]

The FJPC expected most support from fellow-socialists. Among British socialists, as among trade unionists, there were divisions and some hostility, since attitudes towards the Jews were largely governed by attitudes towards the war itself. As the pro-war and anti-war factions of the BSP battled for control in 1914-16, the arguments of the former became increasingly tinged with anti-semitism. An important reason was the fact that East London Jewish members played a major role in the opposition to Hyndman. During 1915 letters in *Justice* from Hyndman and Victor Fisher portrayed the BSP split as a movement of ill-educated East Enders, misled 'with all the acuteness of their race' by Jews: even Marx was criticised at one stage for his 'characteristic Hebrew detachment from national feeling'![45] Although several important BSP pacifists were Jewish (notably Joe Fineberg, of Stepney), the majority were not. However Jewish influence was very evident in the *Call,* which immediately took up cudgels in defence of the East London immigrants. When the government announced its intention to enlist or deport foreign Jews, Fairchild wrote: 'We protest with all the emphasis at our command against the cruel injustice about to be perpetrated by the British Government upon the Russians living in our midst. . . The Right of Asylum is sacred, it must be maintained!'[46] By October 1916 at least thirteen East London newsagents were selling the *Call,* mainly in Jewish areas.[47] Not surprisingly, its editor was in demand as a speaker at meetings against military service. The combined Russian socialist groups gathered 2,000 Jews at Premierland to hear Fairchild (together with Alex Gossip and David Carmichael of the London trades council) pledge his organisation to support the right of asylum.[48]

This determined stand alongside the FJPC is a contrast to the attitude of the other anti-war socialist groups, which had less direct connection with East London Jewry. A few of Rocker's old followers (including his wife's sister, Rose Witcop, and Joseph Leftwich, now on the executive of the Union of Democratic Control) were attracted to the ILP by its strong pacifism. But despite overtures from the Russian Social Democrats, *Labour Leader* failed to take up the defence of the immigrant Jews. ILP members who sometimes spoke at FJPC meetings seem to have done so on an individual basis. The *Herald* was also luke-warm in its attitude. In July 1916 Lansbury contributed rather a muddled editorial on the subject of conscription, maintaining that 'it is idle to insist on the mere theoretic "right of asylum" for under conscription Great Britain no longer offers that kind of asylum even to her own people.'[49] The WSF had not succeeded in setting up a Stepney branch by 1917, but Sylvia Pankhurst's devotion to her peace campaign naturally led her to identify strongly with the East London Jews who refused to fight. In February 1917 she was one of the main speakers at a rally organised by the FJPC. She told 2,000 Jewish workers, who once again filled Premierland, that 'To her the fight of the Jews Protection Committee on behalf of their compatriots was a fight for the freedom of every section of the British people.' William Mellor, *Herald* journalist and ILP member, was in the chair. The rest of the proceedings must have been a mystery to them both, as the other speeches were in Yiddish. They were 'accompanied by constant applause', and the whole meeting was 'characterised by scenes of great enthusiasm and determination', according to a report sent to the *East London Observer.* ('We cannot. . . vouch for the accuracy of this account of the proceedings,' remarked the newspaper snidely.)[50]

News of the Russian revolution reached East London barely three weeks after the Bethnal Green conference, just as the crisis over deportation was nearing its climax. The joint celebrations of the Jewish community and of British socialists have already been described. The joy and relief felt by Russian Jews is vividly conveyed by Rudolf Rocker, who had shared their life for so many years, in his description of his own reactions:

> I read the news over and over again till I was convinced that it had really happened. I felt a tremendous surge of elation and excitement. Surely the Revolution would bring this mad war to an end, and give the peoples peace at last! . . . I could see all my comrades in the East End rushing off to go to Russia! The Revolution had opened their native land to them! They would not hesitate one moment to give their services to the Revolution! They would kiss the Russian earth from which Czarist despotism had exiled them![51]

For varied reasons, almost all Jews shared his delight. Many were indeed eager to serve the revolution. Those who would have preferred to remain in England were at least able to

178

contemplate imminent deportation with less terror, though the FJPC continued to oppose it on principle.

The *East London Observer*'s first reaction to the revolution was that 'the momentous change in Russia removes once and for all the sententious objection to fight in the British army because England is the Ally of Russia, by whom their brethren have been persecuted and oppressed'.[52] The government evidently shared this view, for they decided to press ahead immediately with a Bill for enlistment or deportation. A deputation from the Bethnal Green conference was sympathetically received at the House of Commons during the week which followed the revolution, and a few days later Bonar Law announced the Government's intentions. 'This matter is only now awaiting for confirmation by the new Russian government. . . expected every minute by telegram', reported the *Observer* gleefully, under the heading 'Bombs for Aliens'.[53] Meanwhile, the government decided to placate its critics by organising a Home Office conference on the alien question. Police chiefs and 'local representatives of high position' were invited; 'the whole situation was discussed, specially in the light of disorders which might take place if the public opinion in East London is still further inflamed by delay and increasing pressure', and the most effective immediate action was agreed to be 'a great police round-up of the Aliens who are of military age and eligible. . . the onus of proving they are bona fide Russian subjects being thrown entirely on themselves'.[54]

The Bill on Alien Military Service was finally published in mid-May. 'Frantic opposition is being engineered by the Foreign Jews Protection Committee', reported the *Observer.*[55] In a letter published in the same issue, Abraham Bezalel explained why. If military service was owed anywhere it was in Russia, not Britain; even those Russians who wished to leave voluntarily were finding it impossible to book passages, and in the case of those deported no arrangements were being made for the transport of wives and children; some areas from which foreign Jews came, such as Roumania, had not yet been liberated by revolution, so all the old objections to service still existed. Deaf to such protests, and fearful of anti-semitic disturbances, the government chose the following week for its 'great round-up' of eligible aliens. This action was a blatant sop to the anti-semites, and bore some resemblance to an official pogrom. According to the *East London Observer*, over 600 men were temporarily detained. Nine were charged with not presenting themselves for military service, and a mere four were eventually handed over to the military authorities.[56] When Sylvia Pankhurst investigated Jewish complaints of indiscriminate arrests and police violence, she found Whitechapel residents who put the number of those temporarily imprisoned as high as 4,000.[57] There was universal indignation and alarm.

The FJPC immediately took up the issue of the police raid. But, as the Aliens Military Service Bill worked its way through Parliament, and East London suffered its worst air raid of the war, it became clear that they were fighting a losing battle. They were refused permission to hold a protest meeting in the Great Assembly Hall.[58] Soon after, the same hall was the scene of a huge anti-alien demonstration organised by the British Workers League and attended by the Mayor of Stepney.[59] On 18 July the government announced that a Convention had been made with the Russian government, arranging for friendly aliens either to join the British army or to be repatriated. The terms of the Convention were publicised in East London by Yiddish wall posters.[60] Those who chose repatriation must apply for a passage at the nearest police station by 9 August, and be ready to leave 'at any time after August 13th'. All appeals for exemption must be made to a special tribunal by the end of August. The Convention was not unexpected, but the prospect of its rapid legal enforcement threw the Jewish community into deeper turmoil. The worst blow was official confirmation of earlier fears that no transport to Russia would be offered to families. Even the *East London Observer* doubted the wisdom of this decision: 'Personally, we think it would be rather a good thing to get rid of the lot while the opportunity offers. Sooner or later this will have to be done. . . They cannot be allowed to starve.'[61]

It was by no means clear who would prevent their starvation. The problem of the families was one of the main issues before the emergency FJPC conference summoned a week after the Convention. Representatives of sixty-seven Jewish organisations attended, and the meeting lasted from 3 p.m. until 11.30 p.m. Opposition to service in the British army was as strong as ever. The FJPC announced that the Jews' 'main desire is to return to Russia with their families'. If they could not take their families they would be forced to stay, in which case 'we pledge ourselves to follow the glorious footsteps of the conscientious objectors'.[62] The government was aware of the danger of organised resistance. At the beginning of August it took steps to extinguish the FJPC. A detachment of police from Scotland Yard raided the Whitechapel Road headquarters of the Committee. Piles of documents were seized, and Bezalel and another leader arrested. They were taken to Leman Street police station 'on a charge of conspiring to defeat the Military Service Act as applied to aliens'.[63] By the end of the month, despite the protests of Israel Zangwill, Bezalel had been interned. He refused to give an undertaking as to his future conduct, and two months later was deported to his native Roumania.[64] This raid, and the enlistments and departures which soon began to follow, virtually finished the FJPC. Only one more public meeting was held under its auspices, to protest against government plans for a separate Jewish regiment.[65] However there was soon new evidence of how widespread its support had been. Over half of the eligible Russian Jews chose to return to Russia rather than to fight in the British army. Ten thousand of those who remained applied to the Special Tribunal for exemption.[66]

Due partly to this continued resistance, and partly to the ever-increasing losses and hardships of the war, anti-alienism remained a powerful force in East London even after the new Military Service Act had removed one of the chief grievances. In September 1917 there occurred the most serious physical violence against the immigrants since the *Lusitania* riots. Between two and three thousand Jews and gentiles fought a pitched battle in Blythe Street and Teesdale Street, Bethnal Green. Accounts varied, but the cause of the disturbance was alleged by English witnesses to have been insulting remarks made by Russian tailors to a group of soldiers in a pub. 'All sorts of weapons were used—bars of iron, flat irons, logs of wood, and pistols', claimed one eye-witness. Police reports confirmed that the violence had been considerable (though no shots had been fired), and at least one well-armed Englishman appeared in the dock the next day.[67]

Petty persecution and prejudice against foreign Jews was more widespread than ever during the last year of the war. Every new problem was blamed on them in the local press and elsewhere. The Yiddish press consumed scarce news-print; the aliens themselves wasted scarce food; the exodus of better-off aliens from the air raid danger zone to Maiden-head, Reading and 'Brightchapel' caused potential 'health problems' in those towns.[68] In February 1918 seventeen people died when thousands rushed to an air raid shelter, only to find the gates locked. Most of those involved were Jews. 'Cowardly Aliens in the Great Stampede' was the *East London Advertiser*'s unsympathetic headline above the inquest report. Great prominence was given to the fact that one dead man was carrying more than £600 in his pocket, and also to police allegations that young alien men were responsible for the panic.[69]

An excellent new pretext for anti-alien propaganda was provided by the problem of families left behind by Russians who chose repatriation under the Convention. The govern-ment, having forced them to stay, tried hard to evade respon-sibility for their upkeep. Jewish labour organisations, like the Workers Circle, did their best to look after deported members' families; however many were soon forced into applying to the Jewish Board of Guardians for relief. On this occasion the Guardians' sense of economy triumphed over their patriotism—or perhaps patriotism indicated the unworthiness of such families. All relief was refused. The Guardians did, however, urge the families' case upon the government, which eventually agreed grudgingly to refund to the local Poor Law Authorities the cost of a minimal scale of assistance.[70] Even this concession failed to reduce local hostility to the Russian dependents. The *East London Observer* suggested repeatedly that 'concentration camps with strict rationing and regular-ised labour' would be a more suitable alternative. The Poor Law authorities themselves joined in the protests. By April

1918 the Mile End Guardians were circulating a resolution against grants to Russian families. It received enthusiastic support from Stepney, Bethnal Green and Whitechapel. The St George's Guardians made their own complaint to the Local Government Board, claiming that extra administrative costs were falling on the ratepayers, and that the total cost was being inflated by cases of fraudulence.[71]

Even the old issue of military service for aliens was by no means exhausted. Jewish soldiers enjoyed a brief moment of glory in February 1918, when the first contingent of the Judeans (the all-Jewish regiment of the Royal Fusiliers) marched through the City and the East End before embarking. They were greeted by the Lord Mayor from the balcony of the Mansion House, and by a fine array of local dignitaries (including a number of old enemies, such as the members of the Stepney tribunal) at the Pavilion Theatre. The mayor of Stepney told them graciously that they would 'add lustre to the Jewish name'. Anglo-Jewry, as well as the government, was determined to squeeze the maximum publicity value from the occasion. A luncheon was laid on for the soldiers at Camperdown House. Many prominent Jewish patriots were present, and the Chief Rabbi himself gave the blessing, proclaiming that, 'In the great struggle in which they were to take their part, British ideals were consistent with Jewish ideals.' When the troops eventually departed, a Sepher Torah was borne before them. The *Jewish Chronicle* waxed ecstatic at the sight of 'the spirit of Judas Maccabeus' hovering over Whitechapel Road:

As these fine and soldier-like fellows stepped it to the strains of the music of a Guards Regiment they must have seemed to many to be trampling down in their progress a host of foolish fears and fictions. . . In a short while a band of Jews–'foreigners' and East End aliens, turned into a body of smart troops–looking, each one of them, every inch a soldier–and a hundred well-spun fables about the race have been blown into nothingness.[72]

Such hopes were soon dashed. As the Russian Jewish soldiers marched, the new Bolshevik government was concluding the peace of Brest-Litovsk with the Germans. Nine days after the Judeans' march the British government announced that 'in present circumstances' it had decided to cease recruiting Russian subjects under the Convention.[73] Soon the press and public attacks on East End immigrants were once again in full swing. As the *Jewish Chronicle* commented sadly, 'the old difficulty that existed before the famous Anglo-Russian Convention had been revived'.[74] In fact, the military service situation was now more complicated than ever. At the end of March, the King's Bench Divisional Court ruled that the Convention still existed, though the Russian Provincial Government had gone. The following week, less because of the court decision than because of the critical military situation, the government began to call up aliens once again, and the Special Tribunal recommenced work on the five thousand exemption claims still outstanding. Russian soldiers were to be sent to labour units or to the auxiliary services, rather than to the fighting line. Such preferential treatment naturally confirmed every popular prejudice against Jewish shirkers. Demands were soon being heard, not only for an end to relief for Russian families, but for the wholesale internment of Russians since their country was no longer fighting alongside Britain.[75] Belatedly, the government offered Russian soldiers the option of joining the Judeans, but their anomalous status continued to provide ammunition for anti-semites until the end of the war.

It is difficult to gauge the true depth of anti-semitism and anti-alienism in East London during the war. War created new tensions, and heightened those which already existed. Friends and enemies of the Jews seem to have been equally convinced that widespread anti-semitic violence would result. Any attack on aliens was likely to have religious and racial overtones, since 'Jew' and 'foreigner' were interchangeable words in most East Londoners' vocabulary. However, despite the encouragement of extreme anti-semites outside as well as within East London, for the most part attacks remained verbal rather than physical. Though prejudice flourished, violence was rare. The *Lusitania* riots and the Bethnal Green disturbance of 1917 remained isolated incidents, and a proposal to revive the British Brothers League in September 1918 produced very little response.

The development of closer contacts with British labour organisations during the war made some contribution towards defending the Jewish community against attack. Jewish trade unionism remained relatively weak, but it was stronger in 1918 than it had been in 1914. By the end of the war the London Ladies Tailors Trade Union was sufficiently well-established to join the United Garment Workers at the TUC. Though the Amalgamated Society of Tailors had failed to hold its Jewish members, both the former unions reported big increases in their East London membership. Like other unions, they had been able to take advantage of war-time labour shortages and arbitration procedures to win wage increases and consolidate organisation.[76] It had become common practice for Jewish and gentile unions to present joint cases to the employers through the Committee on Production.[77] This was the most tangible evidence of growing mutual respect, helped by the strengthening of the Jewish unions and by the fact that Jews were joining gentile unions in a wide variety of industries. During the war Jewish trade union branches preserved their uniquely close links with the socialist movement. Their delegates provided the backbone of the FJPC, where they worked alongside representatives of the Jewish socialist groups. By 1918 Jewish trade unionists were showing a growing desire for links with British socialist organisations too. The London Ladies Tailors, for example, made financial contributions to the BSP, and played an important role in founding Stepney Labour Party.[78] At the end of the latter's first year its affiliates included, apart from Jewish tailoring unions, Jewish cigar makers, boot and shoe operatives, bakers, costermongers, and furniture makers.[79]

The development of joint activity between Jewish and British socialists, like the movement towards greater trade union co-operation, was a two-way process. After the Russian revolution the desire for closer links was strengthened on both sides. Rapid progress was made towards political co-operation during the last eighteen months of the war. The BSP was clearly in the strongest position to develop its organisation among East London Jews. Roots put down years earlier began to grow. Shortly after the revolution the

185

Jewish Social Democratic Organisation decided to affiliate formally to the BSP. Joe Fineberg departed from his secretaryship of the Stepney BSP branch to take up a post under the Bolshevik government.[80] But reports from the Stepney and Bethnal Green branches in the *Call* demonstrate that Jewish involvement remained high. Interestingly, Jewish Social Democrats were as hostile to proposals for a Palestinian homeland (revived by the Balfour Declaration of November 1917) as were the British members of the BSP. At the 1918 BSP conference they condemned the scheme for 'raising false hopes and unrealistic aspirations amongst the Jewish workers', and thus obscuring 'the real issue of their class interests'. The only really effective way to fight anti-semitism was by linking the Jewish labour movement with those of other countries.[81]

In May 1918 Fineberg was guest of honour at a dinner organised at the Old King's Hall by the Jewish Social Democrats. The dinner marked the centenary of Marx's birth, and among the 150 guests were representatives of the Workers Circle and various trade unions.[82] However by this time it was becoming increasingly difficult for Bolshevik sympathisers among the immigrant Jews to advertise their politics openly. Left-wing newspapers of all sorts were being frequently raided and suppressed under the DORA regulations, and foreigners were particularly vulnerable. In March 1918 a new DORA order prohibited aliens from addressing meetings and from 'engaging in propaganda'.[83] A new wave of arrests and deportations began. By the autumn the *Call* was accusing the government of 'a systematised offensive against Russians in this country suspected of sympathies with the New Russia of the Soviets':

> Some of our comrades. . . were dragged out of bed in the middle of the night, given but a few moments to scrape together a few articles of clothing, and packed off for deportation without funds, with no opportunity of settling their personal and business affairs, or of preparing themselves against the severe climatic conditions now prevailing in the far North.[84]

This account is confirmed by a detailed description of the

case of Mr T. Goldevitch in the anarchist journal *Freedom*. He was taken to Leman Street police station at 7.30 a.m. on 23 October, and held in custody until the following evening when, without his family, he was 'entrained for the ship'.[85] Among those deported in October was the secretary of the Jewish Social Democratic Organisation. There was little the BSP could do to defend its foreign members, since the legal position of British Bolsheviks was also precarious. But they did their best, and the spirited protests of the *Call* must have boosted its popularity with the remaining Jewish socialists, many of whom were shortly to join the BSP in the Communist Party of Great Britain.

In the years immediately after the war the Communist Party and the Labour Party in Stepney were closely intertwined. The BSP belonged to both organisations for as long as possible. Apart from the BSP and the trade unions, the Herald League also helped to bring Jewish and British workers together in 1917–18, and to found the Stepney Labour Party. Its programme of meetings and activities in Stepney appealed to a wider audience than that of the BSP, and reflected the interests of a largely Jewish membership. Meetings were held in the Jewish Capmakers Union Hall. An extraordinary variety of speakers visited the branch, including members of the Labour Party, BSP, ILP and WSF. In September 1917 Bertrand Russell spoke at the Capmakers Hall on 'How to secure Economic Freedom'.[86] Often the subjects chosen were cultural, rather than directly political, though the branch also took a full part in open air propaganda work for socialism. Stepney Herald League was as concerned as the BSP about the Zionist movement. C.R. Buxton was invited to speak on 'The Jewish People and the Nationality Problem' in July 1918. 'Mr Buxton was about the only Gentile present, and he appeared to me about the only Zionist', reported D. Bloom, the newly-appointed branch secretary, in the next issue of the *Herald.*[87] League members obviously supported the BSP's position on this question. Since Fineberg was among the strongest supporters of Labour Party affiliation by the BSP, there was no difficulty in joint action here, either. In April 1918 Stepney Herald League announced proudly that it was 'giving a powerful hand in the formation of a local Labour Party'.[88] The new party offered the prospect of Jewish and gentile political co-operation on a much larger scale than within the existing socialist groups.

Despite the unfavourable circumstances of the 1918 election, in Whitechapel the Labour Party candidate managed to run the sitting Liberal MP a close second. The 'coupon' Tory was beaten into third place. Whitechapel was the only East London constituency in which a Coalition candidate fared so badly.[89] However it is only possible to guess at the role which the Jewish vote may have played in this result. Many Jews had no vote because of their alien status. Those who did were subject to conflicting pressures. Jews who had supported the war probably shared the general mood of loyalty to the Coalition government. The thousands who had opposed war had little reason to support a government which had so harassed the immigrant community over the military service question. Coalition candidates carefully avoided Jewish affairs in their election propaganda. The *East London Observer* failed in its attempt to make 'post-war alien problems' a major election issue.[90] Bloodthirsty attacks on the defeated Huns were commonplace, but (presumably because Jewish votes were in the offing) a great hush suddenly fell over the subject of friendly aliens settled in Britain. The *Jewish Chronicle* truly stated: 'There is no Jewish party, and there are no Jewish candidates, as such. Jews are to be found in all camps.'[91]

The Whitechapel constituency aptly illustrates this fact. One of its Jewish candidates, G.A. Cohen, stood as a Coalition Unionist, whilst the other, J. Raphael, represented the Whitechapel and Spitalfields Costermongers' Union, and was shortly after the election to become an enthusiastic supporter of the Labour Party. Cohen did issue a special appeal to Jewish voters, claiming to have 'their interests at heart'. But he also hedged his bets by advertising prominently the fact, 'I am a British-born subject, and my family has lived in England for about 200 years.'[92] Raphael seems to have played down his Jewishness, appealing to the electorate on a broadly populist platform.[93] Both the Jewish candidates came bottom of the poll, but it is unlikely this was due to anti-semitism. Kiley, the victorious Liberal, was known to be friendly to the Jewish community (he had abstained during the Second Reading of the Aliens Military Service Bill, the only East London MP to do so). Dr Ambrose, as we have seen, also had much Jewish support within the new Stepney Labour Party. Labour candidates received the general backing of the Jewish National Labour Council of Great Britain, which declared in its election manifesto: 'The Labour Party stands for the co-operation of Peoples, and who more than we, the Jewish People, understand more the great need of co-operation in the interests of humanity?'[94]

Though the 1918 election provides no clear-cut pattern of Jewish voting, there was undoubtedly some correlation between social and political changes which had taken place during the war. In many ways war had emphasised the difference between the East London Jewish community and the surrounding population. Anti-semitism revived and flourished amid war-time crises and hardships. But on the other hand, war also contributed to the gradual process of integration of the foreign Jews into East London society. The growth of trade union and socialist organisations, to culminate in the launching of Stepney Labour Party, was only the most obvious sign of this. War had provided new economic opportunities within the ghetto which, as religious leaders were only too well aware, tended to undermine traditional customs and beliefs. Military service, whether enforced or voluntary, had abruptly removed thousands of young Jews from the ghetto's influence. In the British army they mixed with gentiles, made new friends, and learnt new ways. In January 1919 a Stepney rabbi produced a report on the need for post-war religious reconstruction which provoked an anxious correspondence in the *Jewish Chronicle*, vividly demonstrating the war's effect on orthodox beliefs and behaviour. Stepney Green station was crowded every Saturday afternoon with young Jews 'making their way Westward to places of amusement'.[95] Reverend Arthur Barnett, still serving as a Jewish chaplain in France, wrote:

Generally speaking, I believe the effect of war on the Jewish soldier will have been to make him less Jewish in life and outlook. Men who before had lived a fairly Jewish life, will now, after these years of de-

Judaising tendencies and influences, find it difficult to recover their faded Jewish consciousness. Army life has produced a sort of Jewish anaesthesia.

This conclusion was based on his experience of ministering to East London Jews serving in labour units in France.[96]

The number of Russian Jews who returned to their homeland after the 1917 revolutions was considerable. They included not only internationalists and Bolshevik sympathisers, but also many traditionalists who had never wished to integrate into British society, having come to this country as refugees. Because of the war and the revolution, the stream of new arrivals, already restricted by the Aliens Act, was cut off altogether. The war was not solely responsible for either the political or the social integration of the Jews. Basically, this was caused by the fact that the foreign-ness of the ghetto could not outlive the original generation of immigrants. The halt to further immigration made integration inevitable in the long run. As a new, British-born, English-speaking generation of Jews grew up in East London the existence of separate Yiddish-speaking trade unions and political parties gradually became an anachronism. The war speeded up this process of change. In 1918 Jews began, for the first time, to enter the foreground of East London Labour politics.

NOTES

1. Evans-Gordon, W., *The Alien Immigrant* (1903), 7.
2. *ELA*, 18 July 1914.
3. *Jewish Chronicle*, 7 August 1914.
4. Ibid.
5. *Jewish Chronicle*, 11 September 1914.
6. B.S. Straus at a Premierland show of war films, *ELO*, 1 May 1915.
7. *ELO*, 12 December 1914 and *ELA*, 19 December 1914.
8. *ELO*, 29 August 1914.
9. *Jewish Chronicle*, 16 October 1914.
10. WNC 26/4/79.
11. WNC 26/4/81. Cohen's condemnation of the Board's procedures is borne out by oral evidence, especially that of Mr Fineman, who began work for the Board in 1922 when the old methods and attitudes were still very much in operation.
12. WNC 26/4/85 and 26/4/87.
13. Letter from I. Sharp to J.S. Middleton, dated 20 October 1914, and Middleton's reply, in Labour Party archives. LP/REL/14/ 212 and 213.

14. *Toynbee Record,* January 1915 quoted in *ELO,* 2 January 1915.
15. Jewish Board of Guardians Minutes, 14 October 1914.
16. *Jewish Chronicle,* 2 April 1915.
17. Poor Jews Temporary Shelter, unpublished 'History', Chapter 36, and *Report,* 1914–15.
18. *ELO,* 15 December 1914.
19. *ELO,* 2 January 1915.
20. *ELO,* 15 May 1915.
21. *ELA,* 15 May 1915.
22. Jewish Board of Guardians *Report,* 1915.
23. *Jewish Chronicle,* 19 March 1915.
24. *ELO,* 3 July 1915.
25. *Jewish Chronicle,* 29 October 1915.
26. *ELO,* 1 January, 8 January, 15 January, 5 February 1916.
27. *ELO,* 18 March 1916.
28. *ELO,* 1 April 1916.
29. Ibid.
30. Ibid.
31. *Jewish Chronicle,* 6 October 1916.
32. *ELA,* 20 May 1916.
33. e.g. at Shoreditch tribunal, *ELO,* 16 September 1916.
34. Rocker, R., op. cit., 318–321, and *ELO,* 5 August 1916.
35. *ELO,* 19 August 1916.
36. *ELO,* 5 August 1916.
37. *ELO,* 14 October 1916.
38. *ELO,* 29 July 1916.
39. *ELO,* 14 October 1916.
40. e.g. *ELO,* 14 October and 25 November 1916.
41. *ELO,* 27 January 1917.
42. Conference report in *ELO,* 3 March 1917. Text of FJPC telegram in *ELO,* 10 March 1917.
43. WNC 26/4/83.
44. London Trades Council Minutes, 10 February 1915 and 27 July 1916.
45. *Justice,* 3 and 10 June 1915.
46. *Call,* 13 July 1916.
47. *Call,* 5 October 1916.
48. *Call,* 26 October 1916.
49. *Herald,* 15 July 1916.
50. *ELO,* 10 February 1917.
51. Rocker, R., op. cit., 325.
52. *ELO,* 24 March 1917.
53. *ELO,* 7 April 1917.
54. Ibid.
55. *ELO,* 19 May 1917.
56. *ELO,* 26 May 1917.
57. *Dreadnought,* 26 May 1917.
58. *ELO,* 2 and 9 June 1917.
59. *ELA,* 14 July 1917.
60. *ELO,* 21 July 1917.
61. *ELO,* 28 July 1917.
62. Ibid.
63. *Jewish Chronicle,* 3 August 1917.
64. *Jewish Chronicle,* 31 August and 9 November 1917.

65. *ELO*, 25 August and 1 September 1917.
66. *ELO*, 22 September and 17 November 1917.
67. *ELO*, 29 September 1917.
68. *ELO*, 20 January and 10 February 1917.
69. *ELA*, 9 February 1918.
70. Jewish Board of Guardians Minutes, 27 September 1917 and correspondence in Minute Book, 27 September–6 December 1917.
71. *ELO*, 6 October 1917 and 19 January 1918; *ELA*, 13 and 20 April 1918.
72. Reports in *Jewish Chronicle*, 8 February 1918 and *ELO*, 9 February 1918.
73. *ELO*, 16 February 1918.
74. *Jewish Chronicle*, 15 March 1918.
75. e.g. a resolution passed at a conference of mayors of the Metropolitan boroughs, reported in *Jewish Chronicle*, 5 July 1918.
76. See AST, *Annual Reports* 1914–18, LLT and UGW, *Annual Reports* 1919.
77. e.g. Transcripts of Committee on Production cases, 6 June and 26 September 1917, in the archives of the National Union of Tailors and Garment Workers.
78. LLT, *Annual Report* 1919 and Minute Book 1922.
79. Stepney Labour Party, *Annual Report* 1919–20.
80. *Call*, 7 February 1918.
81. BSP, *Annual Conference Report* 1918, 13 and 14.
82. *Call*, 16 May 1918.
83. *ELO*, 9 March 1918.
84. *Call*, 31 October 1918.
85. *Freedom*, December 1918.
86. *Herald*, 16 September 1917.
87. *Herald*, 27 July 1918.
88. *Herald*, 13 April 1918.
89. See Appendix, pp. 241–2.
90. *ELO*, 23 November 1918.
91. *Jewish Chronicle*, 29 November 1918.
92. *ELO*, 23 November and 14 December 1918.
93. *ELO*, 14 December 1918.
94. *Jewish Chronicle*, 6 December 1918. The other four points of the manifesto were that Labour stood for progress, for good working conditions, for the abolition of conscription, and for a peace settlement including equal rights for the Jews.
95. *Jewish Chronicle*, 31 January 1919.
96. *Jewish Chronicle*, 28 February 1919. To his horror, Barnett found that his attempts to obtain a substitute for the daily bacon ration aroused protests among Jewish soldiers, who told him 'It's not so bad when you get used to it!'

CHAPTER 7

EAST LONDON LABOUR POLITICS, 1919

'It is the simple and dazzling fact that 1919 can be, and must be, the beginning of a veritable New Order, a radiant point of time to which our children's children will look back as to a Renaissance, a Resurrection, decisively marking the workers' passing out of slavery to freedom.'[1] George Lansbury's hopes were shared, to a greater or lesser extent, by most of his contemporaries in January 1919. Talk of reconstruction, of a fit land for returning heroes, was as widespread at Westminster as at socialist and trade union meetings. Many in the labour movement doubted both the government's will and its ability to change society by parliamentary decree. If they regarded reform as inevitable, it was because they were confident that their strengthened organisations would, either forcibly or peacefully, extract the sort of measures they desired. But the hopes of reformers and revolutionaries alike were to be largely frustrated. The war produced no fundamental transformation of society, either whilst it was in progress or immediately afterwards. The Labour Party, which had outstripped its political opponents in planning a better future, soon began to benefit also from workers' impatience and disillusion. The success of the Labour Party in the 1919 local elections and in the following years shows that the new political attitudes created by the war and its aftermath were less transitory than the government's war-time apparatus of economic controls, and its reconstruction promises.

The similarities between East London in 1919 and East London in 1914 were certainly more apparent than the differences, both at the beginning and the end of that year. Bomb damage had been slight, despite the serious alarm caused by this new form of attack. More houses were destroyed by the Silvertown explosion than by the 'aerial torpedoes'; and the area around the ill-fated Brunner Mond works was rebuilt during 1918 almost along the old lines (to the disgust of local socialists, who had hoped for something better). Over the area as a whole, there had been far less new building than during any normal five-year period, because of the overwhelming redirection of men and materials into the war effort. Neither were there any great new industries as a result of the war. Men who had left the district to work at Woolwich Arsenal, at the government dockyards, or in the new national munitions factories, poured back into East London's established industries in 1919. The 1921 Census shows very little change in the major occupations of the area, though local industrial histories demonstrate the amount of technological development and adaptation which had occurred within existing firms. Some new processes and machinery could be re-adapted for peace-time purposes; and enterprising manufacturers continued to exploit the new opportunities presented by the eclipse of German industrial interests and German imports. In the inner East London workshops, however, pre-war methods which had managed to match war-time demands survived virtually unaltered into the post-war decades.

Changes in popular attitudes are, by their nature, more difficult to chart than physical or economic changes. Studies of socialists, trades unionists and Jews have suggested some of the ways in which war altered East Londoners' outlook. The changing views of activists within the labour movement were, of course, more evident than the opinions of the less vocal majority. But such activists also had an importance disproportionate to their numbers. When East Londoners cast their votes at the end of the war, they did not act as isolated individuals. Their voting intentions were influenced by the web of social relationships within which they lived and worked. Both at work and in the local community, the minority whose views were strongly and clearly held played a vital role in forming the political opinions of their friends, neighbours and workmates.

The new strength of the unions was to be one of the most important factors in Labour's East London success, since they provided, as well as a channel for political ideas, the organisational and financial backbone of the party's election campaigns. In many respects the East London trade unions of 1919 were different from those of the pre-war years: they were not only larger, but also more demanding. After four years of full employment and rising wages, such conditions were considered as a right. Craftsmen still regarded the restoration of pre-war work practices as an essential preliminary to industrial reform. But organised workers had no intention of returning to pre-war economic uncertainties. There must be no going back to the uncontrolled capitalism of 1914. This general premise was accepted far beyond the socialist minorities who often drafted trade union and Labour Party reconstruction plans. 'Labour is no longer content to be an *Inarticulate, Servile Mass*', wrote Ben Tillett in the *Dockers Record* of February 1919. G.D.H. Cole, who had prophesied gloomily in 1915 that the Munitions Acts would reduce workers to 'a definitely servile status',[2] now summarised the war's effects on industrial organisation and opinion very differently:

> There can be no doubt that, despite all the legislation which has worked against Labour, despite the partial industrial conscription made possible by the Military Service Acts and the Munitions Acts, the organised Labour movement has emerged from the war far stronger and with a more assured status. . . never before has the extent to which the whole community depends upon the working class been so fully realised, either by the other classes *or by the workers themselves.*[3]

The new mood of self-assertion, of determination to defend war-time gains and of ambitions for a better future, was to be manifested in industrial and political action, as well as in countless articles and speeches, throughout 1919. It was matched by the equally determined and demanding mood of the 'returning heroes', who were soon to make their own voices heard in East London politics.

Within days of the Armistice thousands of workers' livelihood was under threat. The flood of government contracts to East London firms rapidly diminished to a trickle, and by the end of November unemployed workers from Woolwich Arsenal were demonstrating in Whitehall.[4] Army protests put paid to government attempts to make employment prospects the main criterion for early demobilisation. Soon 10,000 demobilised soldiers per day were joining the hunt for work: the numbers on employment exchange registers and receiving government out-of-work donations began to rise alarmingly. By the early summer of 1919 the worst of the crisis was over. All the major East London trades were picking up business again, the docks were employing several thousands more than a year earlier, and in tailoring there were even some labour shortages.[5] However unemployment continued to preoccupy union leaders. Bland official comparisons with the pre-war situation were unacceptable. Instead, trade unionists compared the government's apparent tolerance of a degree of unemployment with its ability to sweep aside economic obstacles during the war.[6] Women workers were particularly hard hit, despite the efforts of the NFWW to insist that ex-munitions workers and female 'substitutes' should be found other employment. In February 1919 the *Herald* reported that 'rope workers, rag pickers and jam makers from the East End' had been amongst those attending a national NFWW conference which demanded 'the Right to Work, the Right to Life and the Right to Leisure'.[7] Meanwhile the *East London Advertiser* complained that local women who received the out-of-work donation were refusing any new jobs not at 'the absurd wages they were paid on munitions'.[8] The NFWW did its best to prevent members being forced into low-paid work, with its campaign for continued government regulation of women's wages and for the extension of the Trades Boards. But a sharp drop in pay or no wages at all was the inevitable lot of most East London women by the end of the year.

Unemployment was used by the unions as an argument for a shorter working week. But shorter hours were also being demanded almost universally as part of the promised improvement in workers' lives. As the *Dockers Record* put it in January 1919:

> Now is the psychological moment. The men are coming back from the army and want jobs; the only way to absorb them readily into

196

industry is to reduce the number of hours to be worked—but this is a secondary reason. The basic reason for the claim is that 44 hours work is sufficient for any man.

Over six million workers had their hours shortened in the following twelve months.[9] The reduction in hours did not lead to any reduction in wages. On the contrary, the wartime struggle to keep abreast of inflation continued. Food prices had more than doubled during the war; after a brief respite in the spring of 1919 they began to climb still further. Government intervention in wage bargaining was extended in an effort to maintain industrial peace. But the most vital sanction against strikes—fear of leaving British soldiers at the mercy of German attack—had disappeared. During 1919 more workers took part in strikes than in any of the thirty years since government records began.[10] From the point of view of the Labour Party, an even more significant statistic was the continued rapid rise in trade union membership.

Many of the biggest conflicts of 1919—the Glasgow general strike, the threats of the Miners Union—occurred far from East London. But the battles elsewhere did not pass unnoticed. Early in the year a small group of revolutionary shop stewards, led by W.F. Watson, made a determined effort to direct London workers towards the Clyde example. The River Thames Shop Stewards Committee was one of the few successful inter-union rank and file organisations in East London. By the end of 1918 it contained stewards from most ship building and repairing trades in yards from London Docks to Tilbury.[11] Watson persuaded his fellow ASE stewards to affiliate in December, then the following month urged an immediate strike for a 15s all-round wage increase. He found an effective ally in the youthful Harry Pollitt, a Boilermakers' shop steward who was already building a reputation for Bolshevik oratory. On 26 January an estimated 8,000 of the 15,000 shipyard workers packed the Poplar Hippodrome, in as defiant a mood as the revolutionaries could have wished. Pleas by the union officials for a strike ballot were brushed aside, as Pollitt proclaimed: 'For four years men had gone "over the top" for something that was of no use to them. Let them fight now to improve their conditions. The example of the workers in the Port of London would inspire others to follow, and so they would go on together building the city of the future.' The enthusiasm which greeted this speech is proof of East London's share in the new industrial temper of 1919. Support for the strike was solid the following Monday morning.[12]

When the strike began to falter three weeks later, one of the main reasons was that Pollitt's vision of expanding class warfare had failed to materialise. The carpenters' and painters' unions recognised the strike, but predictably (since the formalities had not been observed) some of the main unions, including the boilermakers' and engineers', refused to grant strike pay. Representatives of the River Thames Shop Stewards Committee were sent hotfoot to Glasgow, 'to ascertain the position there and convey the greetings of the London men to their fellow-workers up North'.[13] But it soon became obvious that a national link-up of unofficial bodies could provide no substitute financial backing. An East London Workers Committee, hastily set up on Watson's initiative in January, failed to attract any substantial support. Since its headquarters was at 400 Old Ford Road (home of the Workers Socialist Federation), and the treasurer of its Emergency Feeding Committee was Norah Smyth (Sylvia Pankhurst's second-in-command), it is not surprising that it was distrusted as a mere front for Bolshevik politics. On 22 February a much-sobered mass meeting of strikers, conscious that work had already re-started in four shipyards, voted to re-open negotiations with the employers.[14]

A major disappointment during the strike had been the failure of the Glasgow 40-hours movement to spark off a confrontation between London engineers and the government. Early in February ASE shop stewards responded warmly to Watson's appeal to 'adopt *in toto* the programme of the Clyde workers', and his warning to the union executive (who had accepted 47 hours) that 'direct action may be applied to them if they persist in their autocratic opposition to the will of the rank and file'.[15] But plans for an unofficial 40-hour strike were scotched by the executive's swift counter-offensive: the entire London district committee was suspended and its members banned from office for two years.[16] By March the government felt sufficiently sure of the revolutionary stewards' lack of mass support to order a raid on the London Workers Committee's office. Watson was charged with sedition and removed from circulation by a six-month prison sentence.[17]

Though no successful revolutionary leader replaced him, militancy on economic issues continued. It was not without political significance, for it contributed to the class-consciousness on which the post-war Labour vote so largely depended. It also contributed to the local strengthening of union organisation. In the great majority of disputes the unions harnessed the impatience of their members behind official policy, and thus obtained credit for the many concessions won. Leaders like Thorne and Jones were bitterly hostile to 'anarchist' unofficial strikes. On several occasions during 1919 they intervened to hold East London NUGW members in check. But at the negotiating table their stand for better wages and conditions was as tough as anyone's. If negotiations failed they too were ready to use the strike weapon, for example in support of London chemical workers' August pay claim.[18]

Two national strikes in the second half of the year won unanimous support from the trade union movement in East London. In both cases it was claimed that the strikes were defending the cause of all trade unionists against the government. The National Union of Police and Prison Officers had grown rapidly since the successful 1918 strikes; the Police Act of 1919 was evidently designed to reduce it to a government cipher. 'If the government are successful in breaking the Police Union, WHOSE TURN WILL IT BE NEXT?' demanded police strike leaflets of July 1919.[19] Money poured in from other East London unions, the NUGW among them, to support the dismissed strikers' families. Though the strike failed, the plight of the sacked men remained an issue in the trade union world for the rest of the year, and a number of ex-policemen made well-publicised conversions to socialism. The national rail strike, from 27 September to 5 October, was the most important of the whole year for East London. Government tactics seemed to bear out socialist claims that the strike marked 'the resistance

199

of the railwaymen to the Government's challenge to organised Labour as a whole'.[20] An atmosphere of political confrontation was whipped up by a vigorous propaganda war, in which the national and local press uncritically backed the government, while the *Daily Herald* and the Labour Research Department offered substantial aid to the NUR. Few workers could remain indifferent in an area where thousands of railwaymen lived and worked.

The huge Stratford branches of the NUR gave a lead to all East London rail workers. A Central Strike Committee held daily meetings, circulated other organisations for support, and sent statements of the NUR case to the local press. Thousands of strikers and sympathisers crowded the Grove, Stratford, at 11 a.m. then again at 7.30 p.m. each day. One day they marched to a rally at Tower Hill, the next day to Victoria Park. The Bethnal Green NUR band helped to keep spirits high, as did the speeches of strike leaders, fellow-unionists, and Labour councillors (the Committee's secretary, Tom Kirk, was himself a West Ham councillor). West Ham trades council began to plan its own food distribution scheme, in conjunction with the Stratford Co-op. Thorne and Jones turned their usual Sunday meeting at Becton Road Corner into a demonstration of solidarity; NUR speakers were invited to the platform, and over £18 collected for the strike fund. The enthusiasm of East London trade unionists for the railwaymen's cause was further expressed in branch resolutions forwarded to NUR headquarters. The South Poplar Labour Party offered free facilities for NUR committee work and meetings; the Shoreditch Labour Party organised its own public meeting of support, at which speakers included representatives of Bethnal Green NUR and several other unions. The timing of the strike—less than a month before the local elections—was of course providential for the Labour Party. The government's eventual retreat from its 'definitive offer' was greeted in East London and elsewhere as a major victory, and the election campaign proceeded on the crest of this success.[21]

Few unions escaped some share in the strikes of 1919. *Annual Reports* for this year tell the same story again and again. As the Electrical Trades Union put it, 'Dispute Benefit is up in the skies', but the union had also made 'the greatest progress in any single year in our history.'[22] As during the preceding year, solid organisation alone often proved enough of a threat to extract the required results. The activities of East London branches in 1919 suggest an increasing awareness of this. The *Woman Worker* described Trades Boards as 'a short cut to full organisation' in May 1919. Soon union representatives made up almost the whole of the workers' side on the increasing number of Boards, and NFWW membership in East London was rising faster than in any other part of the country. Women unionists in factories also demonstrated increasing self-reliance. By May 1919 stewards' committees existed in the three Yeatman's factories at Wapping, and at the Meredith and Drew biscuit works in Shadwell, and an NFWW organiser who visited the Cubitt Town branch was delighted to find that 'they have absolutely controlled themselves from June of last year'.[23] Other East London unions consolidated their position by trying to impose a closed shop system. ASE organisers were busier than ever in the wake of the Restoration of Pre-War Practices Act.[24] At the docks a dispute between over-enthusiastic Dockers Union collecting stewards and their NUGW counterparts was resolved by a formal agreement to co-operate in the exclusion of non-unionists in future.[25] Meanwhile both skilled and unskilled unions persisted in war-time efforts to strengthen organisation nationally through amalgamation. The revived Triple Alliance of miners, railwaymen and transport workers represented an ultimate sanction. By the end of the year most organised workers placed full confidence in the power of such official union bodies.

The eclipse of the revolutionary shop stewards movement occurred all over the country, as a result of changing industrial circumstances and the opposing pressures of the government and the union leaders. In London it was more rapid and complete than elsewhere. Under other circumstances the imprisonment of Watson might have provided a positive fillip to the movement. His Bow Street trial became something of a show-piece, with both E.C. Fairchild and George Lansbury appearing as defence witnesses, and the defendant himself lengthily expounding his views from the

201

dock. However there was a marked lack of enthusiasm for the fund, the conference and the Hyde Park demonstration which remnants of the London Workers Committee attempted to mount in support of their martyred comrade. Worse was to follow. In mid-July Watson mounted an ill-judged appeal against his sentence, during which it became evident that he had accepted police money. Tortuous explanations were offered—some of the information he sold had apparently been deliberately misleading—but the affair fatally weakened any remaining faith which London stewards placed in the Workers Committee as a whole.[26] The failure of a body so over-burdened with revolutionary dogma was doubtless inevitable; the Watson fiasco merely accelerated its end.

Yet during the early months of 1919 the government had certainly feared that revolutionary politics would engulf trade unionism. The continent of Europe provided alarming examples. Lloyd George was driven to a series of desperate expedients in an effort to win back workers' support for his government. He was successful, to the extent at least of gaining a respite from major strikes in which to proceed with his reconstruction legislation. But in the longer term the manner in which he avoided conflict by postponement caused resentment and distrust, to be reflected in growing support for the Labour Party. Both the Industrial Conference, summoned to discuss remedies for labour unrest on 27 February, and the Sankey Commission, appointed a week later to investigate the miners' claims, received enormous publicity throughout the labour movement. Their proceedings, and ultimate failure from the workers' point of view, provided political education for millions. Anger over Lloyd George's delaying tactics was soon coupled with disappointment over the much-vaunted reconstruction programme. Laws were passed to protect workers from the worst effects of post-war industrial dislocation, but all too often the protection offered was only temporary. Much government intervention seemed reluctant: in contrast, official decontrol of trade and industry was proceeding with enthusiastic rapidity. A reduction in the excess profits tax confirmed this impression, and revived war-time accusations of profiteering.

THE "NEW WORLD" HE FOUGHT FOR.

A familiar expedient—the establishment of local price tribunals—failed to impress in East London. The usual squabbles over labour representation ensued. In Poplar, West Ham and Shoreditch retailers were successfully prevented from dominating the tribunals; in Stepney and Bethnal Green arguments continued until the November borough elections.[27] Nowhere did the tribunals exercise sufficient powers to tackle the roots of the problem, so that eventually their ineffectiveness merely added to general exasperation.

In retrospect it appears that the failure of reconstruction was far from complete in 1919. One of its principal causes—the economic recession of the 1920s—had not yet begun to operate, and several of the long-term reforms proposed by the Ministry of Reconstruction did in fact reach the statute book. Yet the belief that reconstruction was failing, and that it was the politicians' fault, was common among workers by the end of the year. This is demonstrated by reactions to the housing problem in East London. The importance of the 1919 Housing Act, coupled with rent restriction, for the future provision of cheap working class homes, was little appreciated. More immediate solutions were demanded. The reality of the housing crisis was demonstrated week after week by the local newspapers, which published columns of 'Apartments Wanted', many offering the attraction of 'no children', and some the more direct bribery of a £5 or a £10 'bonus'. The subject re-appeared on the letters pages, in the form of protests or special pleading. A soldier wrote from hospital to the *Stratford Express* to say he had nowhere to go when discharged.[28] In the *Hackney Gazette* a woman whose husband and sons were on their way home from war service described her hopeless search of the surrounding streets for a larger home.[29] Another West Ham soldier had been looking for a house for nine months, since being returned to England as a prisoner-of-war, and was now threatened with eviction from his two rented rooms:

> I beg to suggest that it is such things as these that cause the spread of Bolshevism. I should be glad if one of your numerous readers would advise me what to do, also whether I can be forcibly ejected. I should also like to know what the Prime Minister is doing towards

redeeming his promises of making this land of ours a place fit for 'heroes to live in'.[30]

During 1919 the LCC and the borough councils began to prepare housing schemes. But progress was painfully slow. Susan Lawrence, Poplar's Labour LCC member, hammered the slothfulness of her political opponents on the County Council, while Herbert Morrison urged local Labour parties to place housing at the forefront of their election campaigns.

Fortunately for the Stepney Labour Party, a major housing row developed on their doorstep just as the autumn campaign was gathering steam. A Brick Lane landlord proposed to demolish a large number of houses, mainly inhabited by Jewish families, so that he could sell his land to a cinema company. On the day after the news broke Stepney trades council discussed the matter. The following day Labour Party activists began holding highly successful open-air meetings at the corner of Osborne Street, to attack the demolition and the passivity of the LCC and the borough council which had made it possible. Sympathetic members of the Discharged Soldiers Federation and the National Union of Ex-Servicemen joined the platform, and for several evenings running 'a vast crowd' cheered on speeches which broadened the issue from housing shortages to profiteering, and from profiteering to the importance of voting Labour. East End evictions soon became front-page news in the national as well as the local press. A hastily-summoned 'official' meeting of tenants, attended by councillors, LCC members and the local MP, failed to calm the situation and to win back the political initiative from the Labour Party. Clement Attlee used the occasion for a further attack on the Coalition government and its local supporters. Progressive councillors made some notably lame apologies, while the Tory mayor damaged his political cause still further by criticising poverty-stricken tenants who had been persuaded by £50 bribes into accepting eviction ('if they did not look after themselves, how could they expect the authorities to look after them?'). A week later the same hall in Hanbury Street was crowded for an all-Labour meeting on the housing question, at which Morrison warmly congratulated local

Labour Party members for their resourcefulness.[31]

Another national issue which influenced political opinion in East London, though in this case completely outside the sphere of local government, was the government's foreign policy. The 1918 general election had been won largely on the strength of Lloyd George's prestige as the architect of victory. But in 1919 the peace-making process became gradually overshadowed by fears that Allied intervention in Russia might herald a new war. Such fears were most acutely felt and most widely publicised by socialists who sympathised with the Bolshevik government. Though few now believed in following Russia's example, many more were reluctant to assist in overthrowing the Bolsheviks, and the great majority of the British labour movement opposed any further warfare. East London was strongly represented at a 'Hands off Russia' conference organised jointly by the London Workers Committee and the WSF in January.[32] The policy of 'direct action' against intervention received further support later in the year at conferences of the Labour Party, the Triple Alliance and the TUC, and was ardently proclaimed at the socialist street corner meetings which revived and multiplied in East London now that the danger from patriotic mobs had passed. The anti-intervention campaign extended its influence far beyond the membership of the WSF and BSP. Resolutions demanding 'the withdrawal of all troops from Russia' were passed by the West Ham, Bethnal Green and London trades councils,[33] and in July Poplar and Stepney trades councils held a joint demonstration against intervention, in Victoria Park.[34] West Ham trades council and the local ILP organised a further protest meeting in the West Ham Lane recreation ground. Several councillors were among the speakers, and the 'large attendance' included contingents from the Plaistow branch of the Dockers Union, from Leyton NUR, and from the Discharged Soldiers Federation.[35] There was even a brief anti-intervention strike at the docks.[36]

Such successes prove that there was much more opposition to a full-scale Russian war than there had ever been to the war against Germany. But although Russian intervention contributed to the unpopularity of the government in East

London, for most workers the political impact of the issue probably did not equal that of the housing shortage, rising prices, and other problems nearer home. Only the Russian and Polish communities felt their fate to be directly bound up with the Russian revolution. Anti-semitic attacks continued unremittingly in 1919, and the enemies of the Jews exaggerated the political sympathies of the ghetto to such an extent that every inhabitant was condemned as potentially a dangerous Bolshevik. East London arrests and deportations fuelled existing prejudices. In April 150 Russians were despatched by the government to Odessa: 'The majority of these Bolsheviks have black criminal records and are regarded by the Home Office as a grave danger to the community', commented the *Eastern Post*.[37] A second round-up in May resulted in 100 further deportations of 'alien undesirables', 16 of whom were identified as known Bolsheviks.[38] East London court reports make it clear that deportations were often due to the prejudice of magistrates, rather than to the seriousness of the offence. Any political connection was eagerly seized upon, whether relevant to the case or not. For example a case of illegal gambling by members of the International Workers of the World was reported by the *East London Advertiser* under the heading 'Bolshevism in East London'. The magistrates solemnly told the prisoners, 'You have set yourselves out to wage warfare on the social and moral life of the world', and recommended deportation.[39]

East London Jews were unpopular both for their religion and for their nationality. Local Boards of Guardians increased their protests against the maintenance of repatriated Russians' families. Stepney council debated resolutions calling for the internment or repatriation of all naturalised or alien enemy foreigners, and for a ten-year total ban on immigration.[40] The hostile attitude of local authorities was more than shared by the government, which introduced a tough new Aliens Restriction Bill in April. Stringent though it was, the Bill failed to satisfy many MPs, and parliamentary debates plumbed new anti-semitic depths as proposed amendments condemned enemy and friendly aliens without distinction. Will Thorne and Jack Jones were amongst the Labour members who spoke up in the Jews' defence: though sworn enemies of Bolshevism, they shared a justified fear that the Bill would prevent immigrants from pursuing normal political and trade union activities within the British labour movement.[41] A London trades council deputation was despatched to the Home Secretary, after a Jewish UGW branch voiced the same fear, and it was eventually agreed to exclude trade union officials from some of the Bill's sedition clauses.[42] The propaganda surrounding the new Act probably hardened anti-semitism where it already existed. But it also provided Jewish voters with new evidence of where their political friends lay.

During 1919 the East London Jews became deeply involved in another question closely related to the Russian revolution: the fate of Jews in anti-Soviet Poland. The Allied governments were known to support a regime which was cruelly persecuting its large Jewish population because of their alleged link with Bolshevism. On 26 June British Jews held a Day of Mourning against the pogroms in Poland. The event originated in East London, and it was East London which observed the occasion most solemnly. Shops, schools and places of entertainment closed as Jews flocked to the synagogues for Yom Kippur services, and to the West End to join the 100,000-strong demonstration. In the evening, East London Jews held their own meetings. Jewish socialists and trade unionists were to the fore, but sympathetic messages were received from non-Jewish labour organisations, and George Lansbury moved the main resolution at the meeting sponsored by the London Ladies Tailors in the Pavilion Theatre. His speech linked the Russian and Polish questions firmly together, and his presence epitomised the new relationship which had developed between organised Jewish workers and the Labour Party.[43]

As disillusion with coalition policies grew, the views of most East Londoners were captured in a *Railway Review* cartoon entitled 'The Awakening—The morrow of the General Election'. A haggard coalition supporter, surrounded by empty bottles of Lloyd George Dope, clasps his head in horror as he contemplates a future of 'conscription, profiteering, national factories and shipping handed to private firms, unemployment, no housing'.[44] Even in the first shock

THE AWAKENING.
The morrow of the General Election.

of disappointment after the general election, many Labour supporters foresaw this rapid about-turn of political opinion. The new year began with determination rather than dejection, for the local and national disarray of the Liberals, the large new electorate, and the hard-won war-time experience of political organisation and action all gave the Labour Parties of East London good reason to believe that they alone could offer voters a convincing alternative to Tory-dominated coalition politics. The history of the local election campaigns in 1919 shows Labour seizing its chance, but illustrates the problems as well as the possibilities. The pre-war obstacles to electioneering in poor areas had not disappeared overnight; in fact the larger electorate accentuated them. They are graphically described by Annie Barnes, a Stepney woman who joined the Labour Party in 1919 after an apprenticeship in the ELFS: 'the people were so ignorant, they had no real idea what an election was at all. People took advantage of them because they didn't understand, and they just voted for what they were told. We had hard work to explain that Labour was a new party which was for the people, and that we were going to bring better conditions. . .'[45] At the end of the war the problem of political apathy was unusually severe. Labour's road to power on the local authorities was not always to be an easy, straightforward one.

Amid the excitement of the general election, the Labour Parties in London had received a characteristic message from Herbert Morrison:

> The silent visionary with a card index beside him and a joyful heart within is not less important than they who move in the limelight. Build well, organise thoroughly, keep the machine in being—for in March it will be required again for L.C.C. elections. . . The Parliamentary election will be held on December 14th; rest on the Sabbath if you will, but get going for L.C.C. contests on December 16th.[46]

His determination to regard the general election and the local elections in the same light—as steps in Labour's progress towards government—was shared in East London. Early in January Labour Party activists began dusting themselves down and preparing for the next round of action. Bethnal

Green Labour Party, which had been too ill-prepared to run a candidate in the December election, announced its intention of contesting all the local LCC seats. Labour Party meetings in Bow and Bromley and Poplar came to the same decision. Delegates were selected to attend a Special Party Conference, summoned by the London Labour Party for 1 February, to decide the party's LCC election programme.[47] Meanwhile Morrison had appeared in person at the January meeting of the London trades council, his considerable powers of persuasion extracted £100 for the election fund, and a promise to support only those candidates officially endorsed by the London Labour Party.[48] By the beginning of February East London provided its full share of these. Bethnal Green had chosen two BSP members, Vaughan and Fitt, to contest the South West division. Sam March had joined Susan Lawrence as a South Poplar candidate. Two more well-known unionists, Sumner of the NUGW and Cruse of the Toolmakers (also a BSP member), were preparing to contest Bow and Bromley. Stepney's new Labour Party had decided to run four candidates, including Attlee of the ILP and the Jewish trade unionist, Isaac Sharp.

The single-mindedness of Labour organisation, in which socialism and trade unionism successfully combined, provided a contrast to the confusion of its opponents. Early in the war a political truce had been declared at the LCC which in April 1917 hardened into a formal coalition between Progressives and Municipal Reformers. Both parties had reasons for wishing to prolong this arrangement into the era of reconstruction, but political disagreements impeded negotiations, and a formal electoral pact was not reached until 24 February, barely a fortnight before polling day.[49] The Labour threat was clearly a major reason for the pact; it is a sign of the increased respect for Labour in East London that the coalition arrangement was almost universally applied there. Municipal Reformers were allowed a clear run against Labour in the divisions of Stepney and Bow and Bromley which they already controlled, whilst the Progressives were given a free hand in the remaining divisions. Only in Shoreditch did Progressive and Municipal Reform candidates confront each other, as well as a Labour candidate.

It was as if the bitterly fought pre-war contests between the two parties had never occurred. A comparison of the Progressive and Municipal Reform LCC election manifestos demonstrates how the pact blunted the edge of both parties' propaganda. The manifestos contained almost identical promises of improvements in housing, health, transport and education, of more equitable rates distribution, and of good treatment for LCC employees. The Municipal Reformers claimed their programme would be 'attractive to all classes and antagonistic to none', whilst the Progressives vaguely promised to 'have regard for progress not politics'.[50] Meanwhile, in East London, Municipal Reform publicity consisted largely of anti-Labour abuse: advertising and speeches dwelt incessantly on the party's pacifist and Bolshevik links.

The majority of local Labour candidates had indeed been opponents of the war, and a number were strongly sympathetic to Bolshevism. This seems to have done little damage to their chances. The March election, like those later in the year, was to be decided over the issue of social reconstruction rather than patriotism. Labour's policy proposals were far more radical than those of the other parties, including abolition of the rates system, public ownership of land and industrial capital, the municipalisation of all service industries and food supply and distribution, the confiscation of empty West End mansions to house poor families, and the introduction of a state health scheme. As Progressives and Municipal Reformers pointed out, most of these proposals went beyond the existing powers of the LCC! But the strength of Labour's programme lay in its appeal to workers' desire for change, rather than in detailed practicality. Those who studied the small print were a minority. The London Labour Party made the basis of its election demands clear when it claimed that 'organised Labour in London is standing alone for the welfare of all London against those types of private greed and monopoly which are out to exploit the community in the interest of the few'.[51]

The resources of the political parties were very unequally matched. During the election campaign the East London Labour Parties were heavily dependent on the doorstep activity of their supporters. This was due not only to the

NOT ADVISABLE TO REPEAT.

How some important Labour Candidates were expected to win
at the last election!

new respect for card indexes imparted by Herbert Morrison, but to Labour's inability to finance more expensive propaganda methods, such as newspaper advertising. The Municipal Reform manifesto appeared weekly in the local papers for a month before the election, along with advertisements for individual candidates, and the free publicity of highly partisan editorials. The socialist press (especially the *Herald* and the *Call*) did its best for Labour candidates, advertising their policies and urging readers to offer their help at East London committee rooms 'at any time between 9.30 a.m. and 11 p.m.'.[52] Public meetings had traditionally been another of Labour's cheaper alternative methods of presenting its candidates to the public. But in the circumstances of February 1919, when bad weather and influenza added to the wisespread political apathy, successful meetings proved impossible. Instead, voters had to be reached through patient canvassing, and through their union branches. There was a certain amount of ingenious improvisation to suit local circumstances. Langdon-Davis and Sharp 'issued printed appeals to Mile End electors in Yiddish'.[53] Susan Lawrence made the most of her official support from the NFWW. As the *Woman Worker* reported, 'The great feature of the election was a parade of Federation workers bearing sandwich boards (made in the office) with inscriptions of a stirring character. They created a veritable sensation; particularly on the day of the election, when, greatly daring, they walked down Chrisp Street.'[54] Charles Taylor, the Labour candidate in Shoreditch, successfully fought his campaign on a fund of less than £30. He was a powerful open-air speaker, and 'for two days before the poll he simply walked up and down the crowded streets calling people together by means of a muffin bell, and by this method was able to arouse interest in his fight'.[55]

Taylor was elected with a majority of ten votes over his nearest rival, the second Progressive candidate. Other Labour victors in East London were Bryan at Limehouse, March and Lawrence at Poplar, and Sumner and Cruse at Bow and Bromley. Attlee was narrowly defeated, Sharp and Langdon Davis did moderately well at Mile End, and only the Bethnal Green candidates (without the benefit of recent general election organisation) suffered bad defeats.[56] The Labour Party was exultant. The results provided the first clear evidence that the hoped-for post-war swing to Labour was actually occurring. Though the turnout was appallingly low (ranging from 10.8 per cent in Shoreditch to 20.1 per cent in Bow and Bromley), Labour organisation and propaganda had to a large extent counteracted the pacifist smear which proved so damaging at the general election. Moreover, as Lansbury pointed out, the 1919 victories were the first to be won independently by Labour on the LCC.[57] Four Labour candidates defeated Progressive opponents, and Progressive backing for Municipal Reformers in Bow and Bromley did not save their seats. This Progressive collapse could not be blamed entirely on short-term tactical errors; it reflected the fundamental crisis of post-war Liberalism, shorn of effective leadership, relevant policies, and traditional working class support. The *Call* concluded triumphantly: 'The results show that the General Election is no guide to municipal elections, and should encourage the Labour and Socialist forces to enter on the remaining local elections with redoubled energy.'[58]

The Poor Law Guardians elections were only a month ahead, on 5 April. Before the war these elections had rarely been fought on openly political lines in East London, except in Poplar and West Ham where socialist Guardians were a force to be reckoned with. Apart from in Poplar, polls at the Guardians elections were generally lower than at any others. Even in 1919, they did not appear to offer the East London Labour Parties a very promising prospect. However the London Labour Party refused to be deterred. Its manifesto for the Guardians elections appeared within a few days of the LCC results. After arguing that the Poor Law was in fact due for abolition, the manifesto boldly declared that 'the chief business of a Guardian of the Poor is to help the poor'. Detailed recommendations to this end included generous out relief, widows' allowances, good education for workhouse children, and transfer of control of Poor Law infirmaries to local hospitals.[59]

In Bethnal Green the entire existing Board of Guardians decided to stand again as 'Coalition' candidates, in an effort to avoid the expense of an election. One local paper described the situation as 'a gross scandal',[60] it was sufficient to deter the inexperienced local Labour Party from entering isolated opposition candidates. Shoreditch also took no part in the elections; seven Guardians already supported Labour policies, and the local Labour Party was probably too short of money to attempt to win more seats. In all the other Unions, however, Labour set to work once more on the basis of the London Labour Party manifesto. When the results were declared, the number of votes proved to have been even lower than in the LCC elections. Nevertheless the Labour Party had kept up the momentum of its advance in East London. For the first time it controlled the Poplar Board of Guardians, with fifteen of the twenty-four seats. The Stepney result was even more remarkable; fourteen of the eighteen seats went to Labour, compared with not a single seat before the war. Four of the new Mile End Guardians were Labour men, while even the Whitechapel Board, renowned as one of the meanest in the country, was joined by one Labour Guardian.[61]

Labour victors in both the LCC and the Poor Law elections quickly made their presence felt. The publicity their activities received was a useful bonus for Labour candidates in the forthcoming municipal contests. The local press carried lengthy reports on LCC debates at which the new councillors harried their opponents on every aspect of workers' welfare, drawing telling examples from East London. Reports on Poor Law Guardians' meetings provided equally educative reading. At the first meeting of the new Stepney Board, Labour used its already sweeping majority to co-opt a defeated Labour candidate as chairman. It also decided that future meetings should be held at 6.30 p.m.—'the majority of the members were labouring men, and therefore could not sacrifice their work to attend meetings held in the afternoon'.[62] Soon the Labour Guardians were really beginning to test their powers. They raised out-relief to a 'generous' level, ended the 'favouritism' displayed in past appointments; and tried to force all the Sick Asylum managers appointed by the outgoing Board to resign.[63] Mile End meetings were no more peaceful, though here Labour was merely a vociferous minority. After preliminary skirmishing over the low wages at which workhouse girls were sent into service, and the excessively generous war gratuities paid to senior staff, the Labour Guardians forced the Board to end profiteering by seeking lower tenders for Poor Law contracts, and succeeded in getting the Superintendent Relieving Officer (a friend of an old-established Guardian) dismissed for proven inefficiency.[64] In Poplar the Labour majority went about their work with equal determination. When the new rates were fixed in September it was revealed that Poor Law expenditure was £40,000 above that of the previous year. One Municipal Alliance councillor angrily remarked, 'that increase should show the ratepayers of Poplar what they might expect in November if the same class of men were elected as were returned for the Guardians in April'.[65]

The borough council elections, to be held on 1 November, were a major preoccupation of all the political parties, especially after Labour's spring successes. *'Get ready to sweep the board!'* ordered the *London Labour Chronicle* in June. Labour propaganda in East London was continuous throughout the summer and autumn. Socialist street corner orators who disagreed violently over the merits of Bolshevism spoke with one voice on the merits of Labour's municipal election programme. The West Ham Labour councillors were formally reunited at the end of April, and Thorne's 'Becton Road University' had never been more popular. By August Thorne was introducing new borough council candidates from his Sunday morning platform. Herbert Morrison was well aware of the importance of securing 'living contact with the trade union rank and file': in more boroughs than ever before the Liberals were trying to persuade trade unionists to stand as Progressive candidates in a renewed attempt to woo back labour support.[66] The Labour Party's much greater success in politicising East London unionists was demonstrated by widespread socialist-trade union collaboration in the establishment of local Labour Halls. The trades councils of West Ham, East Ham and Poplar were all raising money for this purpose during 1919. In June the West Ham trades council despatched collecting sheets to seventy local union branches, with a target of £5,000 in 1s shares: 'If every trade unionist would subscribe 5s, they would have a hall second to none in the Kingdom, the Town Hall included'.[67] Only the mass membership of the unions could provide the sort of funds required. In return they expected to use the hall as a social centre and branch meeting place. But the local Labour Parties planned to develop the halls as political centres too. Speeches made at the opening of the East Ham Labour Hall on 4 October dwelt both on the rail strike and on the usefulness of the hall for the municipal election campaign.[68]

The energy of the local Labour Parties continued to outmatch that of other political parties. Local Liberal and Conservative Associations had grown rusty during the long period of coalition. Both parties had difficulty in adjusting to the new task of appealing to a mass electorate; they were also handicapped by internal wrangling over recent boundary changes. However the danger of poor organisation did not go completely unforeseen. By the summer there were signs that coalition complacency was coming to an end. In July the Poplar Municipal Alliance 'resumed active operations' at an office in Bow Road.[69] In August the Union of Stepney Ratepayers (USR)—theoretically 'non-political and unsectarian', but in practice closely associated with Toryism—launched a Special Election Fighting Fund Appeal. Speakers at the Stepney Ratepayers' annual general meeting were truculently anti-Labour: 'They were not the only pebble on the beach. The middle classes had got to be organised to make their influence felt, and to some extent the USR would be able to supply that organisation.'[70] The East Ham Ratepayers Association was also astir. Despite the urgings of the *Stratford Express,* Municipal Alliance organisation in East and West Ham apparently still left a lot to be desired by the autumn. On the other hand, the *Express* found shortly before the election that, 'In both Boroughs, more especially perhaps in West Ham, the Socialist Party are well-organised, determined, full of fight, and with followers keen.'[71]

The London Labour Party's municipal election manifesto expressed more clearly than ever the party's commitment to fundamental reforms, while those of Municipal Reform and

Progressive candidates were once again confusingly similar. However, as in earlier contests, the paper promises of the various parties were less important than what the electors believed the parties to represent. Labour's political independence, and its simple appeal to the many poor against the rich few, were reinforced by the pattern of East London municipal candidatures. Confrontations between Labour candidates and anti-Labour candidates seeking both Liberal and Conservative support were very common. No separate Progressive candidates stood in East Ham, West Ham, Poplar or Shoreditch. This contrasts with the 1912 borough elections, when thirteen Progressives stood independently of the Alliance in Poplar, and a full card of Progressives contested Shoreditch. Even in Stepney, where the Progressives made a point of announcing their independence from the USR and the Municipal Reformers, they mustered only thirty-seven candidates for sixty seats. There is more than a hint of coalition in the fact that the forty-five USR and Municipal Reform candidates left the Progressives a clear run in four wards, and stood only one candidate against their three in two others. In return, the Progressives left the way clear for USR candidates in four wards. Four Stepney Progressive councillors showed their revulsion against coalitionism by moving over to the Labour camp. Only in Bethnal Green did the pre-war pattern reassert itself, with twenty-eight Progressives standing against thirty Municipal Reformers. Meanwhile the local Labour Parties did their utmost to fulfil Morrison's prophecy of 'a Labour fight for every Borough Council seat in London, quite regardless of the convenience of any other political party'. In Poplar, Stepney and East Ham Labour contested every seat; in West Ham every seat but one; in Shoreditch every seat but four (three of which were to be fought by 'Progressive-Labour' candidates—perhaps the only true remaining Progressives who matched the pre-war Liberal ideal). Even in Bethnal Green, where Progressivism had been so successful that not a single Labour candidate stood in the 1912 election, there were now twenty-eight determinedly independent Labour men.[72]

Much of the election propaganda of Labour's opponents breathed social harmony and class reconciliation (private

USR outbursts apart!). However information published about the candidates' addresses and occupations backed up Labour's claim to be the only party representing East London workers.[73] In Stepney, for example, almost all Labour's candidates were local men; large numbers of USR candidates lived outside the borough in pleasanter suburbs like Woodford and Leytonstone, while some had addresses as far afield as Leigh or Westcliffe-on-Sea. None of the USR men were Jewish. Though Jews had no single political affiliation before the war, the majority in Stepney voted Liberal. This tradition was continued by seven Jewish Progressive candidates. A new feature was the presence of no fewer than ten Jewish Labour candidates, one of them the ex-Progressive councillor and veteran president of the Costermongers Union, A. Valentine. In 1912 Lewis Lyons had been the solitary Jewish socialist candidate. Candidates' occupations are even more revealing than names and addresses. A total of twenty-seven Labour candidates in Poplar were employed as manual workers, including seven dockers, five railwaymen, four engineers and four labourers. Another four were paid officials of trade unions or of the local Labour Party. The remainder consisted of four married women (three of them wives of the above workers), two clerical workers, one journalist, one schoolmaster, one grocer, and George and Edgar Lansbury. Municipal Alliance candidates in the same borough, on the other hand, included only four who could conceivably be described as manual workers. There were seven clerical workers. The rest consisted of a mixed batch of traders, managers and professionals. A similar picture is presented by East Ham and West Ham candidates. In speech, appearance and manner, Labour's candidates must have provided a considerable contrast to those of other parties. Pre-war experience had shown that workers did not automatically vote for the candidates who most resembled themselves. But in the post-war climate of heightened class-consciousness, when Labour's election appeal was based firmly on its pledge to defend workers against profiteers, class differences between candidates took on a new importance.

Despite the centralised political leadership of the London

Labour Party, election campaigns in different parts of East London were far from identical. This was a source of strength, for though national issues and criticism of central government played a part in every campaign, Labour candidates were often at their most effective when demonstrating their response to such issues in the local context which both the voters and the candidates knew best. The political emphasis of each campaign was affected by a variety of local circumstances, not the least important of which were the nature of the local Labour Party itself, and the nature of the opposition which it faced.

Stepney Labour Party's speedy intervention in the Brick Lane housing scandal has already been described. Here was an unusually powerful local issue which dominated Labour electioneering in the borough. As J. Cahill, a Mile End candidate, told one open-air audience, 'it was whilst they had people to represent them who did not care in the least about their interests that such things would still occur'.[74] J. Raphael, standing in Whitechapel itself, was soon ferreting out other distressing eviction stories and publicising them in polemical letters to the *East London Observer*. Early in October Raphael took up a new cause: that of local eel sellers whose trade was being damaged by steep price rises. He was invited to chair a mass meeting at which an 'eel sellers' protection association' was formed, and a protest despatched to the Food Controller.[75] As a leading member of the Costermongers Union, Raphael's involvement is not surprising; but it provides a further example of the overlap of trade union and political questions, for the eel sellers' plight could be linked to Labour's wider opposition to profiteering—no doubt to the benefit of Raphael's municipal candidature. 'Housing, not cinemas' and 'War on Profiteers' were two of the main slogans in the Stepney Labour Party's necessarily brief newspaper advertisements towards the end of the campaign. There was little danger of the combined resources of the USR and the Municipal Reformers swamping Labour's message, despite their far more lavish purchase of advertising space. According to the *Observer* on 25 October, 'no fewer than fifty helpers' were working for every Labour candidate; a Labour spokesman was already predicting thirty-two victories.

In Poplar, the election campaign was keenly fought on both sides. The Alliance and the Socialists were old foes, and the November fight had many of the characteristics of earlier contests in the borough. The Alliance campaign was officially organised by Sir Alfred Warren, war-time Mayor and new Conservative MP for Leytonstone. Equally prominent was Lansbury's old opponent Reginald Blair, who as chairman of the Labour Municipal Society was one of the generals of the Municipal Reform campaign. The *Eastern Post* commented on Lansbury's close personal involvement in the election.[76] In an effort to counteract Municipal Reform advertising, he managed to raise a £200 donation from the *Herald* to the London Labour Party for last-minute publicity.[77] The *Herald* itself took up the party's cause with vigour. As a national daily, it was well-placed to link Labour's local government proposals to attacks on the coalition government. The Poplar election campaign probably produced more debate on national issues than any other in East London. But improved grass roots organisation was to prove as important for Labour's success as the political battle between the MP and the would-be MP for Bow and Bromley. Afterwards W.H. Lax, the well-known Methodist minister, paid tribute to local Labour supporters who, 'For weeks and months before the election. . . flooded the constituency with literature and plastered the walls with attractive posters', and on election day managed to bring 'practically everyone' to the poll.[78]

In contrast, Bethnal Green Labour Party had no tradition of good organisation and hard-fought electioneering. Though the major pre-war problems of strong Progressivism and weak trade unionism had diminished by 1919, the party's comparative failure at the LCC and Poor Law elections shows that local organisation took time and experience to develop, as well as favourable political circumstances. By November Bethnal Green Labour Party had recruited an important new body of helpers—the local Discharged Soldiers Federation, under the direction of Ernest Thurtle, who was George Lansbury's son-in-law. The Federation provided not only potential voters, but also a valuable basis for propaganda on the government's apparent failure to keep its promises to returning soldiers. Joe Vaughan, who had been a leading socialist and trade unionist in the borough throughout the war, was another major figure in the campaign. Open-air speaking was his chosen method; money for a printed election address was raised by passing round the hat at the end of each meeting.[79]

Like Bethnal Green, Shoreditch had a strong pre-war Liberal tradition. The November 1919 Progressive-Municipal Reform coalition helped Labour by simplifying the choice facing voters. The *Hackney Gazette*—no friend of socialism—reported that the sight of erstwhile political enemies 'joining forces and fraternising with all the ardour of life-long friends and allies' was 'naturally breeding much contempt' in the borough.[80] Addison had easily defeated an Asquithian Liberal and the Labour candidate at the general election. But when he addressed a town hall meeting in the week before the municipal contest, he faced a largely hostile audience who were inclined to support Labour Party hecklers' attacks on coalitionism in general and the government's record in particular.[81] The Shoreditch Labour Party had a new problem to reckon with, in the presence of twenty-four Discharged Soldiers Federation candidates contesting wards which Labour hoped to win. Social reforms were the main issue of the Federation campaign; however the outcome of the election proves that Labour's campaign on similar issues was far more effective. Their principal slogan was 'Down with the Profiteers!', to which the coalitionists (evidently aware which party posed the main threat) replied with the slogan 'Kill Bolshevism and Socialism disguised as Labour'.[82] Cheap improvisation was once again the order of the day. On the night before the poll the local Labour Party held a torchlight procession led by the candidates and 'assisted by an "orchestra" of muffin bells'.[83]

West Ham Labour Party was in a stronger position than any other in East London before the November elections. A by-election win in March 1919 had given Labour a virtual majority on the borough council, a Labour mayor was already installed; and the borough had two Labour MPs. It was impossible for the Municipal Alliance to win votes by depicting Labour men as wild revolutionaries, closely linked to Bolshevism and pacifism. Thorne, Jones and their supporters were respected public figures, well-known for their patriotism as well as their socialism, and were now publicly supporting those Labour candidates who had opposed the war. An effort by the Municipal Alliance to revive old wartime quarrels failed ignominiously. The local Discharged Soldiers Federation turned down their offer to give Federation candidates who stood against Labour pacifists a clear run; instead, the chairman of the North West Ham Federation branch (H.J. Rumsey, DCM, MM) chose to stand as a Labour candidate.[84] Rumsey had played a prominent role in the recent rail strike, offering the Federation's support to the mass meetings of strikers at Stratford. Some Federation members disapproved of his openly political stand. Having failed to win over the Federation, the West Ham Municipal Alliance did its best to exploit this disagreement by publishing an advertisement attacking Rumsey's actions. Again, their attack badly misfired. The Federation branch reunited in its own and Rumsey's defence, and the rail strike was re-emphasised as a major political issue.[85] West Ham Labour Party had done much to organise the strike locally. A week after it ended the president of the NUR attended a Labour Party meeting in Stratford, to promise his reciprocal support to three local election candidates.[86] Undoubtedly the rail strike did more to strengthen Labour's cause than to weaken it—a fact which Alliance and Municipal Reform parties in several East London boroughs seemed unable to grasp.

Another target chosen by the Municipal Alliance was the Stratford Co-operative Society. The Co-op's business enterprises were flourishing in November 1919, and membership had risen to over 47,000. Though expansion continued to occur outwards into Essex rather than inwards to East London, in West and East Ham, at least, the Co-op was potentially a powerful political force. It was deeply divided over politics however. During 1918 a group of Liberal co-operators did their utmost to prevent the recently elected socialist president from committing the society to Labour's cause. Though they were briefly successful at the time of the general election, the socialists regained the initiative in the spring of 1919. Co-op committee elections were due on 27 October. Neither the Liberals in the society nor the divisive propaganda of the Alliance could prevent a big majority of members from re-electing a socialist committee, approving loans made to railwaymen during the strike, and voting £150 towards local election expenses.[87] As the *Stratford Express* pointed out, this result indicated the probable outcome of the municipal contest the following week.[88] In East Ham the Labour Party benefited even more directly from co-operative support: T. McGiff's Becton candidature against a Moderate and a Federation man was financed by the Co-op, though he appeared on the election lists as 'Labour'.

The East Ham election campaign provides an extreme example of local idiosyncracy. No fewer than three of the six contested wards found themselves with two opposing Labour candidates! This was mainly due to the exclusive and quarrelsome attitudes of the local trades council, encountered by Henderson at the general election. At Manor Park a survivor of the patriotic North East Ham Democratic Labour Party stood against Allwright, Labour's champion on the pensions committee. In the Central East ward the official Labour candidate was confronted by a nominee of the local Dockers Union. In the Central West ward a highly personal contest developed between Webster, the official Labour candidate, and Albin Taylor of the National Union of Corporation Workers, who claimed he had been unfairly deprived of the official candidature. Feelings grew as heated over this issue as over the more serious political arguments elsewhere. Eventually the quarrel came to a head at a public meeting called to discuss another of East Ham's election curiosities— the 'burning question' of Sunday cinema opening. The local Cinema Association attempted to make the question a major campaign issue, after the council decided to refuse permission for Sunday shows. They financed a town hall demonstration, which Albin Taylor agreed to chair. Not unnaturally, official Labour candidates accused Taylor of political opportunism; under the leadership of Allwright, they disrupted the meeting with speeches from the floor, choruses of the Red Flag, and attempts to storm the platform. It is clear that strong feelings about Taylor, rather than about cinemas, prompted the disturbance.[89] When local clergymen circulated all the election candidates for their views on Sunday opening, they found three official Labour men in favour (including Webster), and three against. According to the *East Ham Echo,* the clergy subsequently went to considerable lengths to win votes for anti-cinema candidates.[90] But neither the cinema issue nor the clerical intervention seems to have had a decisive effect: Labour winners in East Ham included two 'pro' and two 'anti' candidates, while an independent 'Cinema Candidate' failed completely.

'The fight has really resolved itself into one between the Labour Party and those who are not of the Labour Party', commented the *Stratford Express* on election day.[91] The remark applied not only to West Ham, but to every East London borough. Labour had dominated the campaign almost as much as it was to dominate the results.[92] Despite 'cold and dispiriting' weather and low polls, 1 November 1919 proved a day of dreams come true for the party's supporters in East London. It won control of the councils of Shoreditch, Bethnal Green, Stepney and Poplar with huge majorities. Only nine seats were being contested in West Ham and six in East Ham, but Labour victories in the former confirmed the party in power, and even in the latter four of the seats fell to Labour. Among the winners were many socialists well-known for their opposition to the war, including Joe Vaughan of Bethnal Green, Ben Gardner of West Ham, and Thomas Edey of Stepney, whom we last encountered being stoned by an angry crowd of patriots in August 1914. Equally successful were Labour ex-servicemen such as Rumsey of West Ham, Miller of Stepney and Thurtle's Bethnal Green contingent. Alongside them stood the trade unionists and committee men who had defended Labour's cause on the Home Front: Allwright obtained the highest vote of any East Ham candidate. His victory speech reflected the spirit which united such varied candidates: 'It had been a hard struggle for four or five years to bring about the position they were in that night. He stood clear as a Labour man—to represent no politics, nothing else but Labour alone.'[93]

An outstanding feature of the election results is the

NOVEMBER 1st—WHAT A DRAUGHT!

solidity of party voting in almost every ward. Only very exceptionally did the individual merit of candidates appear to influence the result. Labour's sweeping victories were undoubtedly due to voters choosing to support 'nothing else but Labour alone'. Progressives and Municipal Reformers failed spectacularly, whether they stood as separate parties or in coalition. One group suffered an even more disastrous defeat—the independent candidates of the Discharged Soldiers Federation in Shoreditch, Stepney and East Ham. In the Central East Ward of East Ham a Federation candidate came a poor second (with 714 votes to the Moderate winner's 1,447); he was helped by the presence of the Dockers Union candidate, which split the Labour vote. This was the best result the Federation achieved. At Mile End West three Federation men came in last, behind three Labour winners and three defeated Progressives. At Shoreditch, where the Federation made its biggest effort, its candidates were grouped together at the bottom of the poll in all the wards they contested.

The failure of the Federation requires some explanation, for it had been widely predicted that ex-servicemen would change the face of politics when they came home from the battle front. Generous treatment of returning heroes was regarded as the yardstick of successful reconstruction by the civilian population as well as the ex-servicemen themselves, and in 1919 every political party was eagerly wooing their votes. Inevitably the ex-service organisations had political links from the outset. Liberal MPs had helped to set up the National Federation of Discharged and Demobilised Soldiers in March 1917, while Conservatives sponsored the Comrades of the Great War, established to restore the political balance shortly afterwards. Nationally, the Comrades were the largest organisation in 1919, but in East London the Federation held sway. The *East Ham Echo* reported in January 1919 that a meeting attempting to set up a local Comrades branch had been invaded by hostile Federation members claiming to represent the only organisation 'run by the men and for the men'.[94] Strong Federation branches already existed in East Ham, South West and North West Ham, Poplar, Stepney, Bethnal Green and Shoreditch. Their attitudes and activities during 1919 present a microcosm of the disagreements and debates within the Federation as a whole. Despite general agreement on democratic reforming aims—officers were excluded—the Federation lacked a basis of agreed strategy. It could not decide whether to act as a politically neutral pressure group, whether to seek independent political representation, or whether to place its weight behind one of the existing political parties.

Although they failed as an independent force at elections, the Federation branches undoubtedly played a significant role in East London politics. Their varied activities brought together large numbers of men who might not belong to any other organisation, and involved them in discussion of social and political change. Early in the year several branches already claimed over a thousand members; by the autumn demobilisation had swelled these totals to between two and three thousand. Recreational activities attracted members, as did the desire to prolong comradeship and share memories. But the main incentive was the Federation's determination to defend its members' interests, and those of dead soldiers' dependents. East London members were prominent in the Federation's national campaigns, and reports in the *Territorial Service Gazette* show that branch meetings debated general political issues like housing, unemployment and profiteering, as well as such purely ex-service matters as pensions. Federation members' views on these issues frequently coincided with those of the Labour Party. But locally as well as nationally there was disagreement about the desirability of closer formal links between the two bodies. A motion to affiliate to the Labour Party was defeated at the Federation's Whitsun conference: Poplar branch approved but Bethnal Green strongly disapproved and announced itself 'determined to reverse the verdict at the next opportunity'.[95] Events during the next few months made it harder than ever for many East London branches to maintain the official 'non-party' line. An anti-Bolshevik campaign by the Federation leadership provoked a strong protest from South West Ham. An executive circular warning Federation members to remain neutral in the rail strike was ignored by some branches and obeyed by others.

The borough election campaign found the East London branches still divided. Bethnal Green Federation joined forces with the local Labour Party: no fewer than eleven of the new Labour councillors were Federation members too. South West Ham Federation decided to back Rumsey's candidature early in September, but his actions during the rail strike seem to have later cooled their enthusiasm. Rumsey's own branch had difficulty in making up its mind whether to support him or not. At least one Labour candidate in Stepney, I. Miller, was also an active Federation member. When his branch refused to support him, he resigned and wrote an angry letter to the *East London Advertiser* accusing the Federation of blacklegging in the rail strike. Shoreditch and East Ham Federation branches openly opposed the Labour Party by running their candidates against it. The East Ham decision was no doubt influenced by the fact that the Liberal MP Sir John Bethell was the branch's main patron. The Federation's poor showing in the election was blamed by the *Territorial Service Gazette* on lack of organisation: confused and unoriginal policy was also a factor, no doubt. By November 1919 it was becoming clear to the majority of East London ex-servicemen that their political future lay with the Labour Party rather than with the ex-service organisations. The breakaway socialist National Union of Ex-Servicemen briefly won some support in the area at the end of the year. But the election results show that the de-politicisation of the ex-service bodies, soon to culminate in the formation of the British Legion, was already starting. The Labour Party was left to reap the advantages of the political education which Federation branches had begun.

Another, still larger, group who failed to make their expected independent impact at the 1919 elections were the new women voters. The East London Federation of Suffragettes had been fighting to bring local women into politics since 1912. But the Workers Socialist Federation of 1919 was in no position to mobilise East London women, partly because of its hierarchical structure and partly because of its eccentric politics. WSF Minute Books reveal that by the end of the war the organisation had virtually lost its earlier basis of local support. The emergency relief work of 1914–15 had increased Sylvia Pankhurst's tendency to take undemocratic short cuts: the easiest way to get things done was to do them herself, and the easiest way to finance her activities was through appeals to wealthy outsiders. Such methods persisted when the WSF reverted from charity to politics. Elected committees containing local women proved unstable and unreliable; soon the main business of the WSF was being transacted by a small Finance Committee, which between November 1918 and July 1919 consisted of Sylvia and Norah Smyth alone.[96] The shift of emphasis to provincial propaganda in 1917–18 reflected the failure of the East London branches. An attempt to revive the Bow branch during 1919, under Norah Smyth's direction, proved equally unsuccessful.[97] Though the WSF had drawn large numbers of local women into protest demonstrations on such issues as food prices during the war, it had not managed to build a continuous, self-reliant organisation.

From the outset the ELFS was closely linked to the Labour Party and especially to the Lansbury family. However Sylvia's changing political beliefs after the Russian revolution gradually drove the two movements apart. The annual conference of the WSF in June 1919 condemned 'the futility of Parliamentary action, and the confused and artificial character of the Labour Party', and looked forward to the establishment of a separate Communist Party.[98] The WSF's incongruous affiliation to the Poplar Labour Party could not continue indefinitely. On 20 July its members unintentionally provoked a crisis by making an unscheduled appearance at the Labour Party's meeting against Russian intervention, commandeering a trades council lorry as a platform, and haranguing the crowds on the virtues of Sovietism. The following week Norah Smyth received a curt letter from Poplar Labour Party informing her that the WSF had been expelled.[99]

The WSF's failure had little to do with other parties' efforts to provide a political counter-attraction for women voters. All the major parties paid lip-service to women's new importance at the end of the war. In March 1918 the pre-war Bow Conservative Ladies group was revived as a fully-fledged Women's Unionist Association, under the

presidency of Mrs Blair. A month before the borough elections the Mile End Liberal, Labour and Progressive Women's
Association was inaugurated. A certain amount of Progressive
and Municipal Reform election propaganda was directed
specifically at women voters, but the Women's Associations,
where they existed, were expected to provide loyal support
rather than an active, independent, political force. The
Labour Party's female supporters were almost as passive as
those of the other parties. A minority of educated socialist
women upheld working women's cases in the higher echelons
of the labour movement. Like Sylvia Pankhurst, they found
difficulty in persuading working class women to organise and
fight for themselves. The pages of *Labour Woman,* with its
lengthy, academic articles and moralistic tone, are an eloquent
reflection of the gap between women leaders such as Marion
Phillips, Beatrice Webb and Mary Macarthur, and the East
London women who were expected to follow.

Inevitably current beliefs about women's inferiority
permeated local Labour Party organisation. The party was
inseparable from the trade unions, which in most cases enforced male superiority in the workplace as a matter of
principle. Though large numbers of women joined unions
during the war, membership did not make them men's
equals. Many were temporary employees, and the male trade
unionists who backed their 'equal pay' demands did so in
the interests of the men whom the dilutees replaced. Even
those unions which welcomed women members rarely encouraged them to assume any initiative in organisation or
policy. It is not surprising that the Labour Party was as overwhelmingly male, in terms of national and local leadership,
as the trade union movement itself. When candidates were
selected for the borough elections in East London the Labour
Party chose as few women as the other parties. Four of the
nine female Labour candidates (out of a total of a hundred
and eighty-two!) were the wives of well-known Labour
activists. No Labour women candidates took part in the
contests in East or West Ham, or in Bethnal Green, though
the Progressives and Municipal Reformers had two women
candidates each in the latter borough. In Stepney each party
ran one woman. In Poplar and Shoreditch there were four

Labour women, facing respectively one and five female coalition candidates. Despite this sprinkling of women candidates, reports of women's speeches or of female audiences are entirely absent from the local press.

East London women's lack of participation in electioneering suggests one possible explanation of the low polls which were a marked feature of all the 1919 elections. Women formed 40 per cent of the electorate. They were by far the largest group of new, inexperienced voters, and the most lacking in political traditions and education. On the other hand there is no direct evidence that they were more reluctant to vote than men. Dependence and ignorance in fact made it very likely that women's attitude towards the act of voting (as well as their choice of party) would mirror that of husbands, fathers, brothers. Many of the motives which drew men to the polls to vote Labour were shared by women as well. In addition, women who were in a position to make an independent political choice had reasons of their own for voting. War-time price rises and food shortages, and the postwar housing crisis, were their direct concern, and the departure of men to the war had often forced them to cope singlehanded for the first time with these and a range of other difficulties at home and at work.

Since a mass female abstention is unlikely, some other explanation of the low polls must be sought. It is not hard to find. Contemporary writers agreed that war-weariness, at every level of society, produced political apathy. To many East London workers, voting in elections seemed less important than the struggle to defend war-time wages, conditions and full employment. Industrial organisation and action were more direct methods of achieving these aims than the ballot box. Other circumstances discouraged voting during 1919. Four elections followed rapidly upon one another. Though this helped the Labour Party's campaigning to develop and sustain momentum, it meant a sudden surfeit for new voters, and for old voters who had lost the habit during the war-time years of political truce. Coalitionism had weakened the party machinery of Conservatives and Liberals. It had also, perhaps, led to a certain loss of faith in party politics generally.

Because of Labour's startling victories, there was a widespread assumption in the spring that low polls had benefited that party and damaged the others. 'Labour has caught London napping', complained the *Hackney Gazette.* 'The municipal Gulliver has been electorally bound by the Lilliputians of politics.'[100] Retrospective admiration of Labour's superior organisation abounded. But by November there was less confidence in the view that Labour victories were merely an unfortunate accident. The *Stratford Express,* a firm supporter of the West Ham Municipal Alliance, admitted in the aftermath of the borough elections: 'it is not at all unlikely that if every elector had gone to the poll the proportion of Labour votes amongst non-voters would have been more or less the same as amongst those who did their duty on Saturday'.[101] This view was justified by later election results. By 1922 the percentage of electors who used their votes was recovering strongly, though it seldom equalled the high percentage of voters among the smaller pre-war electorate. The Labour Party did not suffer from the higher polls. In the general election of that year East London chose nine Labour MPs; this total rose to thirteen in 1924, when voting figures were better still. Despite some setbacks in the 1922 borough elections, in 1925 the Labour Party re-asserted its majority control on every council in East London; turnout was higher than at any local election since 1913. To the present day the Labour Party expects to benefit, rather than to lose, from a big turnout, because its traditional supporters are more reluctant to use their votes than those of other parties. There is little reason to believe the situation was different in 1919, when so many working class voters worked longer hours, were ill-educated, and were unaccustomed to possessing the vote.

The East London Labour Parties needed their superior organisation, their hundreds of canvassers, and the assistance of the trade unions to bring out the voters who achieved the 1919 victories. Good organisation was no coincidence: it was a result, as well as a cause, of political strength. The war-time growth of trade unionism, and the war-time activity of socialists, had enabled the Labour Party to establish a solid base in East London in a period when the other main parties relaxed their efforts. By 1919 the politically active minority within the labour movement was large enough, for the first time, to act as a catalyst impelling thousands of East Londoners to vote Labour. Changes in workers' outlook were as responsible for this development as the efforts of the Labour Party. Events on the home front and on the battle front had made workers both more aware and less tolerant of social inequality, and created high expectations of post-war reconstruction. The Labour Party embodied such expectations in its policies, then consolidated its war-time gains because the government failed to fulfil them. Few East London workers had any clear-cut socialist aim of abolishing capitalism. But they voted Labour in 1919 in the simple belief that the Labour Party stood for their interests, whereas the Coalition government and its local supporters represented the opposing interests of the employers and profiteers. A leading member of the London Municipal Society commented aptly after the November debacle: 'It was a class fight, pure and simple, and anybody of any standing at all was suspect.'[102] The war had not created the social antagonisms which underlay politics in 1919; but it had certainly focused attention on them, and in doing so, altered political attitudes. At the end of the war East London refused to return to the fatalistic acceptance of poverty and helplessness which had characterised the area in 1914.

NOTES

1. *Herald,* 4 January 1919.
2. Cole, G.D.H., and Mellor, W., *Trade Unionism in War-Time* (1915), 1.
3. *Daily Herald,* 30 June 1919.
4. NFWW, *Annual Report* 1918-19, 13.
5. *Labour Gazette,* June 1919.
6. e.g. United Patternmakers Association, *Annual Report* 1919, 5.
7. *Herald,* 22 February 1919 and NFWW, *Annual Report* 1918-19, 13.
8. *ELA,* 18 January 1919.
9. *Labour Gazette,* January 1920.
10. Ibid.
11. *Call,* 6 February 1919.
12. *Dreadnought,* 4 and 18 January and 1 February 1919.
13. *Call,* 6 February 1919.
14. *Dreadnought,* 22 February and 1 March 1919.
15. *Dreadnought,* 8 February 1919.
16. ASE, *Monthly Journal,* February 1920.
17. *Dreadnought,* 15 and 29 March 1919.

18. NUGW Executive Committee Minutes, 11 August 1919.
19. National Union of Police and Prison Officers leaflet in the TUC Library.
20. *Labour Leader*, 2 October 1919.
21. *SE*, 4, 11 and 18 October, *Dockers Record*, November 1919, ASE *Monthly Journal*, October 1919, NUGW Executive Committee Minutes, 2 October 1919, and *Hackney Gazette*, 6 October 1919.
22. Electrical Trades Union, *Annual Report* 1919, 3 and 4.
23. *Woman Worker*, May 1919.
24. e.g. visits to the Small Arms factory, the CWS factory at Silvertown, Woodward's engineering works at Millwall and Lyle's sugar refinery; in every case the employers were attempting to prolong dilution.
25. NUGW Executive Committee Minutes, 19 November 1919.
26. *Dreadnought*, 19 July 1919 and *Call*, 21 August 1919.
27. *Hackney Gazette*, 24 September 1919 and *ELO*, 11 October and 22 November 1919.
28. *SE*, 28 June 1919.
29. *Hackney Gazette*, 25 August 1919.
30. *SE*, 16 August 1919.
31. *ELO*, 6, 20 and 27 September 1919.
32. *Dreadnought*, 1 February 1919.
33. *SE*, 1 February 1919, London Trades Council Minutes, 13 February 1919, *Daily Herald*, 24 May 1919.
34. *ELA*, 2 August 1919.
35. *SE*, 26 July 1919.
36. *Dreadnought*, 12 and 26 July and *Daily Herald*, 27 July 1919.
37. *Eastern Post*, 12 April 1919.
38. *ELA*, 15 May 1919.
39. *ELA*, 30 August 1919.
40. *ELO*, 15 February and 10 May 1919.
41. *ELO*, 19 July 1919 and *Jewish Chronicle*, 24 October 1919.
42. London Trades Council Minutes, 8 May 1919 and *London Labour Chronicle*, August 1919.
43. *Jewish Chronicle*, 13 and 27 June 1919 and *ELA*, 28 June 1919.
44. *Railway Review*, 21 March 1919.
45. Barnes, A., *Tough Annie* (1980), 30.
46. *London Labour Chronicle*, December 1980.
47. *Herald*, 4 and 25 January 1919.
48. London Trades Council Minutes, 16 January 1919.
49. See Young, K., *Local Politics and the Rise of Party* (Leicester, 1975), 113-118.
50. *ELO*, 8 and 15 February 1919.
51. *London Labour Chronicle*, March 1919.
52. e.g. *Call*, 27 February 1919 and *Herald*, 22 February 1919.
53. *Eastern Post*, 8 March 1919.
54. *Woman Worker*, April 1919.
55. *Herald*, 15 March 1919.
56. Results in *ELO*, 8 March 1919 and *Hackney Gazette*, 10 March 1919.
57. *Herald*, 15 March 1919.
58. *Call*, 13 March 1919.
59. *London Labour Chronicle*, April 1919.
60. *Eastern Post*, 15 March 1919.
61. *London Labour Chronicle*, May 1919.
62. *ELO*, 26 April 1919.

63. *ELA,* 7 June 1919.
64. *ELA,* 28 June, 9 and 16 August, 6 and 27 September 1919.
65. *ELA,* 27 September 1919.
66. *London Labour Chronicle,* July 1919.
67. *SE,* 21 June 1919.
68. *SE,* 8 October 1919.
69. *ELO,* 12 July 1919.
70. *ELO,* 4 and 11 October 1919.
71. *SE,* 25 October 1919.
72. Election candidates and results in *Hackney Gazette,* 3 November 1919, *ELO,* 8 November 1919 and *SE,* 5 November 1919. For results see also Appendix, pp. 239–40.
73. *ELO,* 25 October 1919 and *SE,* 29 October 1919.
74. *ELO,* 6 September 1919.
75. *ELO,* 25 October 1919 and *ELA,* 1 November 1919.
76. *Eastern Post,* 25 October 1919.
77. *London Labour Chronicle,* December 1919.
78. *ELO,* 8 November 1919.
79. *Eastern Post,* 25 October 1919.
80. *Hackney Gazette,* 13 October 1919.
81. *Hackney Gazette,* 29 October 1919.
82. *Hackney Gazette,* 20 October 1919.
83. *Daily Herald,* 3 November 1919.
84. *SE,* 22 October 1919.
85. *SE,* 11, 15, 18, 25 and 29 October 1919.
86. *SE,* 15 October 1919.
87. *Co-op News,* 1 November 1919.
88. *SE,* 25 and 29 October 1919.
89. *EE,* 31 October 1919 and *SE,* 29 October 1919.
90. *EE,* 31 October 1919. Non-conformist and Anglican clergy combined in this enterprise.
91. *SE,* 1 November 1919.
92. Results in *ELO,* 8 November 1919, *Hackney Gazette,* 3 November 1919 and *SE,* 5 November 1919. See Appendix, p. 239.
93. *EE,* 7 November 1919.
94. *EE,* 24 January 1919.
95. *Territorial Service Gazette,* 28 June 1919.
96. There is evidence of a certain amount of local discontent with the Pankhurst method of organisation. For example, at the General Meeting on 15 January 1917 Mrs Walker and Mrs Boyce pointed out that 'no report was given of what was done with a penny', and that 'the organisation of the Branches was not democratic enough and that there was dissatisfaction on that account'. Interestingly, the report of this meeting was cut from the Minute Book and survives as loose pages among later material in the Pankhurst collection (P48). Another example is the criticisms made by Mrs Casey at the Finance Committee meeting on 12 September 1918 (WSF Finance Committee Minute Book 31 May 1917–6 November 1919 (P19)). Soon after Mrs Casey left the WSF, and no local woman could be found to take her place on the committee.
97. The Minute Book of the WSF Bow Branch, 7 January–30 May 1919 (P20), shows that membership varied from two to ten. Norah Smyth was the secretary; she wrote the minutes and took almost all the initiative in the branch's activities.

98. *Dreadnought,* 14 June 1919.
99. WSF Committee Minute Book, 22 May 1918–24 June 1920 (P18), 7 August 1919.
100. *Hackney Gazette,* 5 November 1919.
101. *SE,* 8 November 1919.
102. *London Municipal Notes,* December 1919.

Political Affiliation of Borough Councillors
1900–1925

Borough	Political Affiliation	1900	1903	1906	1909	1912	1919	1922	1925
Shoreditch	I							1	
	L	14	26	2	23	4	32	10	26
	M	28	16	31	19	25	7	28	6
	P			9		13	3	3	10
Bethnal Green	L	7	2		11	8	24	14	17
	M	23	28	30	19	22	6	10	9
	P							6	4
Stepney	I	10	24	6	21	3			3
	L						42	27	40
	M	32	15	39	39	34	5	33	11
	P	18	21	15		23	13		6
Poplar	I	3		2	5		1		
	L	7	11	9	9	8	39	39	36
	M	19	15	23	20	29	2	3	6
	P	13	16	8	8	5			

I = Independent
L = Labour
M = Municipal Alliance, Municipal Reform, Moderate, Ratepayer or Conservative
P = Progressive, Liberal or Liberal-Labour

Political Affiliation of Borough Councillors (continued)

Notes

1. Results are taken from the local newspapers.

2. Only a rough idea can be given of borough councillors' political affiliations, since in local elections candidates rarely stood under a party political label (except for Labour candidates), and voting habits within the councils were fairly flexible. A wide range of opinion is represented by each of the categories 'P' and 'M', which cannot be directly identified with the Liberal and Conservative Parties. Nevertheless it is fair to assume that the majority of 'P' were Liberals, and the majority of 'M' Conservatives. Both groups were politically opposed to 'L', as represented on this chart. Labour candidates who stood as Progressives have been counted as such in the totals given.

3. Borough election results for West and East Ham are not strictly comparable, as in these County Boroughs a proportion of the councillors were re-elected every year. The local newspapers give less clear information about political affiliations here. West Ham affiliations are stated as follows:

Borough	Political Affiliation	1909	1912	1919	1922	1925
West Ham	L	17	19	30	36	45
	M	16	25	18	24	15
	P	3	4			

240

Results of Parliamentary General Election, 1918

Shoreditch

C. Addison	Co Lib	9532
R. Sievier	U	3414
A. Walton	Lab	2072
H. Chancellor	Lib	1524
T. Warwick	Nat P	504

Bethnal Green N.E.

E. Cornwall	Co Lib	4448
W. Steel	Nat P	2312
W. Shadforth	Health	1127

Bethnal Green S.W.

M. Wilson	Co U	4240
E. Thurtle	NFDSS	1941
H. Meyler	Lib	1933

Limehouse

W. Pearce	Co Lib	5860
D. Sheehan	Lab	2470
C. Rodwell	Nat P	1455

Mile End

W. Preston	Co U	6025
W. Devenay	Lab	2392
C. Sanders	Lib	1119

Whitechapel and St. George's

J. Kiley	Lib	3025
R. Ambrose	Lab	2522
G. Cohen	Co U	2489
J. Raphael	Coster	614

Bow and Bromley

R. Blair	Co U	8109
G. Lansbury	Lab	7248
M. Dalton	Lib	988

South Poplar

A. Yeo	Co Lib	8671
S. March	Lab	4446
W. Allen	NFDSS	4339

Plaistow

W. Thorne	Lab	12156
A. Lupton	Ind	657

Silvertown

J. Jones	Lab	6971
T. Carthew	Co U	4259
D. Davis	Lab	2278

Results of Parliamentary General Election, 1918
(continued)

Stratford

C. Lyle	Co U	8498
C. Masterman	Lib	4821

Upton

E. Wild	Co U	8813
B. Gardner	Lab	3186
J. Nicholson	Lib	2380

East Ham N.

J. Bethell	Co Lib	9436
W. Mann	Nat P	6748

East Ham S.

C. Edwards	Co Lib	7972
F. Hamlett	Ind	5661
A. Henderson	Lab	5024

Lib	=	Liberal
U	=	Unionist
Co U	=	Coalition Unionist
Lab	=	Labour
Ind	=	Independent
Nat P	=	National Party
NFDSS	=	National Federation of Discharged Soldiers and Sailors

Sources: F.W.S. Craig, *British Parliamentary Election Results 1918-1949* (Glasgow, 1969), and local newspapers.

Political Parties of MPs Elected at General Elections, 1900–1924

Constituency	1900	1906	1910 Jan.	1910 Dec.
Haggerston	Lib	Lib	Lib	Lib
Hoxton	Con	Con	Lib	Lib
Bethnal Green N.E.	Con	Lib	Lib	Lib
Bethnal Green S.W.	Con	Lib	Lib	Lib
Limehouse	Con	Lib	Lib	Lib
Stepney	Con	Con	Con	Lib
Mile End	Con	Lib	Con	Con
St George	Con	Lib	Lib	Lib
Whitechapel	Lib	Lib	Lib	Lib
Bow and Bromley	Con	Lib	Con	Lab
Poplar	Lib	Lib	Lib	Lib
West Ham N.	Con	Lib	Lib	Lib
West Ham S.	Con	Lab	Lab	Lab
Romford (includes East Ham)	Lib	Lib	Lib	Lib

Constituency	1918	1922	1923	1924
Shoreditch	Lib	Lib	Lab	Lab
Bethnal Green N.E.	Lib	Lib	Lab	Lab
Bethnal Green S.W.	Con	Lib	Lib	Lib
Limehouse	Lib	Lab	Lab	Lab
Mile End	Con	Con	Lab	Lab
Whitechapel and St George	Lib	Lab	Lab	Lab
Bow and Bromley	Con	Lab	Lab	Lab
South Poplar	Lib	Lab	Lab	Lab
Stratford	Con	Lab	Lab	Lab
Upton	Con	Con	Lab	Con
Plaistow	Lab	Lab	Lab	Lab
Silvertown	Lab	Lab	Lab	Lab
East Ham N.	Lib	Con	Lab	Con
East Ham S.	Lib	Lab	Lab	Lab

Con = Conservative
Lab = Labour
Lib = Liberal (includes Coalition and National Liberals)

243

1. East London Parliamentary Divisions before 1918

2. East London Parliamentary Divisions after 1918

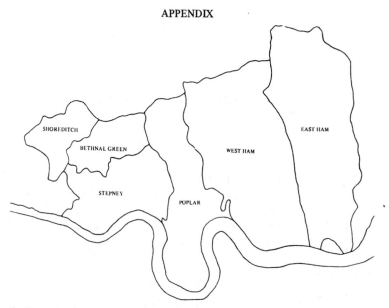

3. East London Boroughs

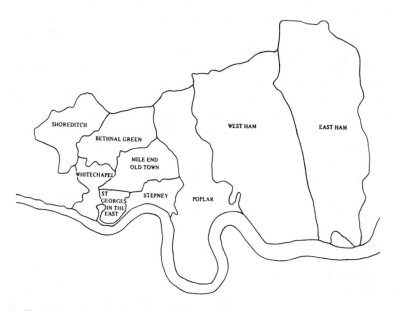

4. East London Poor Law Unions

RECOMMENDED READING

It is hoped that the following suggestions will be helpful to the general reader. A comprehensive bibliography can be found in my thesis, 'Labour Politics and Society in East London during the First World War' (PhD, London, 1978). Sources are also listed in detail in the Notes to this book.

Introduction

G. Stedman Jones, *Outcast London* (1971) and P. Thompson, *Socialists, Liberals and Labour* (1967) are essential background reading to a study of East London politics in the early twentieth century. Thompson's views on Labour and Liberalism should be contrasted with those of P. Clarke, *Lancashire and the New Liberalism* (1971). M. Pugh, *The Making of Modern British Politics 1867–1939* (1982) provides an excellent general introduction to the politics of the period. Relating more specifically to the labour movement, H. Pelling, *Popular Politics and Society in Late Victorian Britain* and K. Burgess, *The Challenge of Labour* (1980) set the pre-war scene. R. McKibbin, *The Evolution of the Labour Party 1910–24* (1974), gives a useful national perspective covering the war years. Like so many authors, E. Hunt, *British Labour History 1815–1914* (1981) ends at the beginning of the First World War; but his book is a valuable corrective to misconceptions about working class unity and the extent of workers' pre-war political and industrial organisation.

1. East London in 1914

The pre-war social and economic history of East London has been well served both by contemporary and by modern writers. Charles Booth, *Life and Labour of the People in*
246

London (1887–1902) provides the sixteen-volume bedrock. E.G. Howarth and M. Wilson, *West Ham, a study in social and industrial problems* (1907) is another product of solid research. The colourful descriptions of W. Besant, *East London* (1903) and J. London, *The People of the Abyss* (1904) are inevitably superficial in comparison, and often seem more concerned with the myth than the reality. East London inhabitants make their own voices heard in G. Lansbury, *My Life* (1928), R. Rocker, *The London Years* (1956), and E.S. Pankhurst, *The Suffragette Movement* (1931). G. Richman's interview-based *Fly a Flag for Poplar* (1974) and a number of more recent autobiographies by elderly East Londoners offer further authentic first-hand evidence. Outstanding among these are A.J. Jasper, *A Hoxton Childhood* (1969) and A. Barnes, *Tough Annie* (1980). The Jewish community has produced its own life stories, as well as the incomparable novels of Israel Zangwill and the modern researches of L. Gartner, *The Jewish Immigrant in England 1870–1914* (1960) and W.J. Fishman, *East End Jewish Radicals 1876–1914* (1975). J. White, *Rothschild Buildings* (1980) is a fascinating account, based on oral research, of life in one Whitechapel tenement block.

2. Into War: Labour and Local Government 1914–16

E.S. Pankhurst, *The Home Front* (1932) is the only book to give a detailed local account of civilian war experiences. Sylvia's own role is writ large, while that of representatives of the labour movement is treated dismissively. It is necessary to read the local and socialist press to redress the balance. The records of the War Emergency Workers National Committee (in the Labour Party archive) are another important source. A. Marwick, *The Deluge* (1965) provides a readable account of national developments on the Home Front. The activities of the war's opponents are described in J. Rae, *Conscience and Politics* (1970) and M. Swartz, *The Union of Democratic Control in British Politics during the First World War* (1971).

3. Towards Peace: Labour Politics 1916–18

Local and socialist newspapers are once again an essential

source for political developments in East London. The BSP's internal conflicts are described in W. Kendall, *The Revolutionary Movement in Britain 1900-1921* (1969). C. Wrigley, *David Lloyd George and the British Labour Movement* (1976) gives an interesting insight into the relationship between central government and the leaders of the labour movement. A centralist view on Labour Party reorganisation is given in J. Winter, *Socialism and the Challenge of War* (1974), and on the 1918 electoral reform in M. Pugh, *Electoral Reform in War and Peace 1906-18* (1978).

4. Trade Unions: Adaptation and Growth
On the whole neither trade union history nor trade union biography has yet attracted the historians it deserves. The First World War receives meagre coverage in most histories of individual unions and in the autobiographies of unionists such as Ben Tillett, *Memories and Recollections* (1931) and Will Thorne, *My Life's Battles* (1925). Trade union journals, reports and financial records are often not easy to interpret, or even to obtain (the TUC library and the Modern Records Centre at Warwick University have the largest collections), but they provide the only possibility of reconstructing local detail. East London's industrial contribution to the war can be reconstructed from histories of individual firms, from the War Office contract lists in the Board of Trade's *Labour Gazette,* and from the government's *Official History of the Ministry of Munitions* (1918-22). Two useful modern books covering the war period are J. Hinton, *The First Shop Stewards Movement* (1973) and A. Clinton, *The Trade Union Rank and File* (1977).

5. Trade Unions: Power and Politics
Trade unions records and the union and socialist press here again provide the backbone for an account of the unions' political role, supplemented by the secondary sources mentioned above.

6. The Jews and the War
The books of L. Gartner (op. cit.) and W.J. Fishman (op. cit.) set the pre-war scene. For the war years it is necessary to

turn to such primary sources as the records of the Jewish Board of Guardians (at the Jewish Welfare Board) and the Poor Jews Temporary Shelter (also retained by its modern equivalent, of the same name). The records of the War Emergency Workers National Committee contain some interesting material, as do those of the London Trades Council (in the TUC library). The reports of the (usually anti-semitic) East London press must be contrasted with those in the *Jewish Chronicle* and in *The Call,* the socialist paper most closely in touch with the Jewish anti-conscription movement.

7. East London Labour Politics, 1919

Though several aspects of post-war reconstruction have recently been researched, the published results shed little light on the East London situation. Reconstruction is generally viewed as a problem facing politicians and administrators in central government, rather than as a powerfully felt demand from the labour movement. Once more primary sources provide the only detailed evidence from an East London viewpoint. The local, socialist, trade union, and Jewish press are usefully supplemented in 1919 by the *London Labour Chronicle* (journal of the London Labour Party) and the *Territorial Service Gazette* (journal of the Federation of Discharged Soldiers and Sailors). G. Wootton, *The Politics of Influence* (1963) deals interestingly with the early history of the ex-service organisations. A general overview of post-war politics is given in M. Pugh (op. cit.). Labour politics are treated in more detail (though still with quite insufficient attention to extra-parliamentary events) in R. McKibbin (op. cit.) and R. Miliband, *Parliamentary Socialism* (1961). C. Key, *Red Poplar, Six Years of Socialist Rule* (1925) is a retrospective view of Poplar's post-war municipal socialism in action.

INDEX

Addison, Christopher 95
Allwright, A. 53-54, 225, 226
Amalgamated Association of Tramway and Vehicle Workers 127-128, 155
Amalgamated Society of Engineers 10, 109, 111, 113, 121-123, 124, 140, 142, 143, 147, 153, 156, 158, 160, 197, 198, 201
Amalgamated Society of Tailors and Tailoresses 132, 134-135, 185
anti-semitism 8, 16, 18, 166, 168, 170-172, 176, 177, 179-180, 184, 186, 188, 189, 207-208
arbitration 104, 110, 112, 114-115, 117, 118, 125, 131, 132, 133, 136, 138 n.72, 185
arbitration tribunal 131, 140, 142, 147
Asquith, H. 29, 57, 171
Attlee, Clement xvii, 33 n.63, 205, 211, 214

Banks, Joe 58, 61, 76, 113
Becton 11, 29, 91, 92, 109, 116, 142, 200, 217, 225
Besant, Walter 1, 2, 9
Bethnal Green xvii, 1, 4, 6, 9, 14, 16, 23, 24, 25, 26, 30, 50, 58-59, 62, 71, 80, 90, 95, 99 n.6, 113, 116, 124, 125, 150, 159, 167, 173, 176, 178, 179, 181, 183, 184, 186, 200, 204, 206, 210-211, 214, 215, 219, 222, 226, 228, 229, 230, 232
Beveridge, W.H. 108, 109
Bezalel, Abraham 175, 179, 181
Board of Trade 112, 123, 128
Boilermakers Union 10, 109, 197, 198
Booth, Charles 1, 5, 9, 16, 20

Bow 12, 27, 36, 37, 40, 71, 76, 79, 80, 86, 87, 90, 94, 128, 148, 149, 152, 211, 214, 215, 222, 231
British Brothers League 17, 18, 184
British Socialist Party 15, 23, 24, 26, 30, 39, 44, 56, 58, 62, 69-72, 73, 75, 76, 77-78, 79, 81, 84, 86, 88, 91, 92, 93, 99 n.6, 113, 177, 185-187, 206, 211
British Workers League 72, 96, 180
Bromley 12, 27, 71, 80, 86, 87, 90, 94, 115, 117, 148, 150, 211, 214, 215, 222
building industry 50, 110, 112
building workers 11, 104, 113, 142

Canning Town 11, 44, 105, 108, 115, 116, 117, 125, 145, 153
carpentering, woodworking 7, 111, 112
chemical industry 11, 109, 115, 118
chemical workers 11, 199
Clarion Club, Clarion Fellowship 24-25, 44
clerks 11
clothing industry, tailoring 4, 5-6, 7, 110, 118, 131, 135, 196
clothing workers 5-6, 84, 131-135
Clyde 44, 111, 197, 198
Commission of Enquiry into Industrial Unrest, 1917 123, 140, 141
Committee on Production 133, 138 n.72, 154, 185
conscientious objectors 57-58, 61, 62, 63, 64, 181
conscription 55-57, 62, 69, 71, 118, 123, 135, 146, 171, 177-178, 208

250

unemployment, unemployed 4, 11,
13, 15, 21, 30, 38, 40, 48-49,
50, 52, 103, 104, 106, 111, 169,
170, 196, 208, 229
Union of Democratic Control 148,
152, 159, 177
United Garment Workers 132-135,
138 n.72, 185
Upton 11, 96

Vaughan, Joe 62, 211, 223, 226

Walker, Melvina 81
Wapping 16, 201
war bonus 45, 55, 104, 123, 125,
127, 128, 129, 130, 131, 132,
141, 151
War Emergency Workers National
Committee 38-39, 43-44, 48-49,
52, 57, 64, 84, 105, 145, 167-
168
War Office 40, 41, 47, 109, 111, 133
war pensions committees 53, 58, 225
Watts, Alf 58, 76, 77
West Ham xvii, 2, 4, 9, 10-11, 12, 14,
23, 24, 25, 29-30, 42, 44, 45,
49-50, 52, 55, 57, 60, 62, 63,
70, 71-72, 77, 80, 83, 84, 90,

91-93, 95, 96, 99 n.6, 105, 109,
115, 118, 124, 125, 127, 142,
144, 145, 147 148-149, 151-152,
153, 154, 158, 159, 160, 161,
200, 204, 206, 215, 217, 218,
219, 220, 223-224, 226, 228,
229, 230, 232, 233
Whitechapel 14, 17, 21, 25, 26, 89,
90, 94, 95, 109, 134, 166, 167,
170, 175, 180, 181, 183, 188,
216, 221
women workers, female labour 9, 49,
52, 108, 110, 115, 117-119, 121,
123-124, 127-128, 129, 196
Woolwich 108, 119, 120, 121, 123,
143, 194, 196
Workers Circle 174, 182, 186
Workers' Suffrage Federation,
Workers Socialist Federation 72-
73, 77, 99 n.6, 149-150, 178,
187, 198, 206, 230-231, 237
n.96, n.97
Workers Union 116-118, 120, 121,
142, 147, 154, 156
Workmen's and Soldiers Councils 77,
79, 151, 152

Zangwill, Israel 17, 175, 181